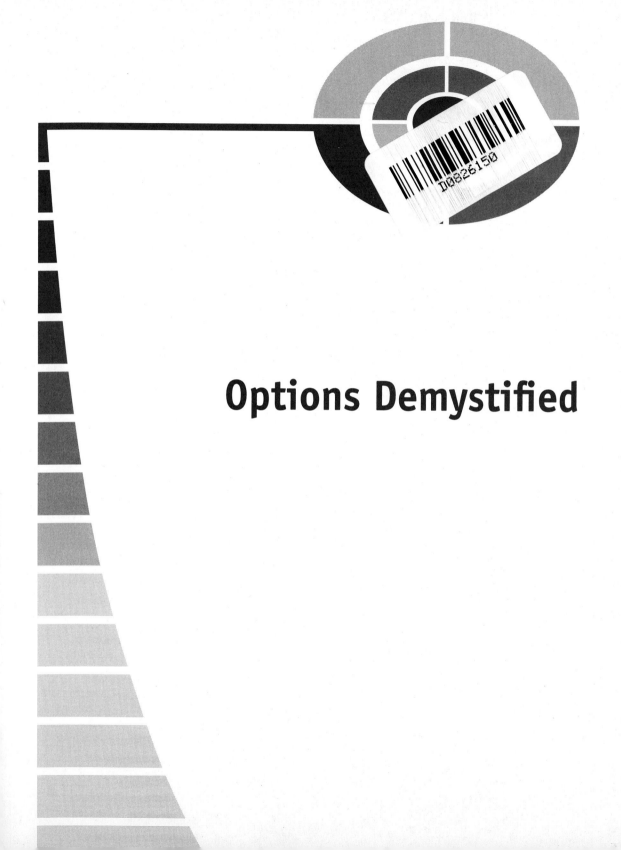

Options Demystified

Demystified Series

Advanced Statistics Demystified
Algebra Demystified
Anatomy Demystified
Astronomy Demystified
Biology Demystified
Business Statistics Demystified
C++ Demystified
Calculus Demystified
Chemistry Demystified
College Algebra Demystified
Databases Demystified
Data Structures Demystified
Differential Equations Demystified
Digital Electronics Demystified
Earth Science Demystified
Electricity Demystified
Electronics Demystified
Environmental Science Demystified
Everyday Math Demystified
Geometry Demystified
Home Networking Demystified
Investing Demystified
Java Demystified
JavaScript Demystified
Macroeconomics Demystified
Math Proofs Demystified
Math Word Problems Demystified
Microbiology Demystified
OOP Demystified
Options Demystified
Personal Computing Demystified
Physics Demystified
Physiology Demystified
Pre-Algebra Demystified
Precalculus Demystified
Probability Demystified
Project Management Demystified
Quantum Mechanics Demystified
Relativity Demystified
Robotics Demystified
Six Sigma Demystified
Statistics Demystified
Trigonometry Demystified

Other Works by Thomas McCafferty

The Market Is Always Right
Understanding Hedged Scale Trading
Winning with Managed Futures
All About Options
All About Futures
All About Commodities
In-House Telemarketing

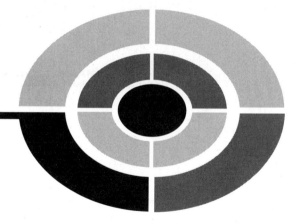

Options Demystified

THOMAS McCAFFERTY

McGRAW-HILL
New York   Chicago   San Francisco   Lisbon   London
Madrid   Mexico City   Milan   New Delhi   San Juan
Seoul   Singapore   Sydney   Toronto

5 6 7 8 9 0 QWF/QWF 0 9 8 7

ISBN 0-07-145415-2

This publication is designed to provide accurate and authoritative information in regard to the subject matter covered. It is sold with the understanding that the publisher is not engaged in rendering legal, accounting, or other professional service. If legal advice or other expert assistance is required, the services of a competent professional person should be sought.

> —*From a declaration of principles jointly adopted by a committee of the American Bar Association and a committee of publishers.*

McGraw-Hill books are available at special quantity discounts to use as premiums and sales promotions, or for use in corporate training programs. For more information, please write to the Director of Special Sales, Professional Publishing, McGraw-Hill, Two Penn Plaza, New York, NY 10121-2298. Or contact your local bookstore.

Library of Congress Cataloging-in-Publication Data

McCafferty, Thomas.
   Options demystified / by Thomas McCafferty.
      p.   cm.
   Includes index.
   ISBN 0-07-145415-2 (pbk. : alk. paper)
   1. Options (Finance)   I. Title.
   HG6024.A3M393 2005

   332.64'53—dc22   2005004242

To Carol, Cynthia, Monica, Colleen, and Sadie

CONTENTS

Contents

Preface

You cannot predict the future or control the present—these are prime directives governing the creation and use of options.

This text takes the mystery out of predicting and profiting from the future price trends of stocks and futures contracts using fundamental and/or technical analysis along with option strategies that manage the associated risk. Savvy market operators have devised methods of attacking the markets aggressively, while protecting themselves from the daily risk of loss. As you will learn, long call option contracts offer bulls unlimited opportunities to gore the markets profitably, with a clearly defined risk parameter; while long put positions sharpen the bears' claws to rip out opportunities that can break the bank, again with predetermined risk-reward ratios. These strategies are only the first swig of knowledge that you are about to swallow from this book. This is one of those books Dr. Johnson was referring to that should be digested.

Whenever you see an offer like this one, suggesting the availability of vast reward with minuscule risk, immediately start looking for the catch. As the age-old proverb warns, "If it is too good to be true, it probably is." The hook of options is that the vast majority of long put and call contracts expire worthless, and the proud owners lose 100 percent of their investment.

If this is true, why in the name of all that is worth investing in are options so popular—over 4.5 million option contracts are traded daily? It is for the same reason that poker is popular. The essence of being a successful poker player is not winning the most hands. It is not like bowling, where the best players have the highest scores. Rich poker players and option traders have lousy batting averages. What they do have is a knack of winning the big hands.

The essence of poker is, bet big, bet heavy when you hold winning hands, and hold to the last card. Fold on hands when the odds are not in your favor. It is the same with option trading. Dump or offset losing options positions to stay in the game until the big winners hit the trading floors.

I often compare option trading to fly-fishing. You cast and cast. Change flies over and over. Move up and down the stream. Ninety-nine out of one hundred casts are futile. Then out of nowhere, when you least expect it, just as you are about to give up—a trophy trout tugs so hard on your line that you lose your balance, making the hours of standing in ice-cold water a lifelong memory.

Options, the Trader's Body Armor

In addition to explaining how the professionals speculate in the markets, this book teaches you how to hedge with options. This strategy provides a variety of methods for using options to mitigate your worse nightmare—watching the value of your favorite securities plunge like Wile E. Coyote when he overruns a cliff. Options help any investor or trader sleep the sleep of the righteous.

Please take note of some of the words and phrases that I use, like *learning about* and *being exposed to*. This book demystifies options, giving you a solid understanding of what options are and how to use them. It is a place to start your study of options if you choose to

- Speculate for profit
- Generate additional income from your existing assets
- Use options to protect your current wealth

It does not attempt to teach you how to trade. There are hundreds of books on that subject already available. As you will learn, you cannot become a trader by reading or attending classes, any more than you can become a scratch golfer or tennis wizard without hitting balls. It takes time on the links or courts to become proficient. Nevertheless, reading and studying in advance is the first step. My objective by the end of this book is to enable you to decide if you want options to become a part of your investment life.

Do not let my use of words like *market/markets* and *strike* or *striking price* confuse you. When I use the word *market,* I am referring to a specific market, such as the stock, futures, or option market. *Markets* means all markets or the concept of the marketplace in general. *Strike price* and *striking price* are interchangeable and mean the same thing—the price at which an owner of an option can exercise his or her position. In your future reading, you will see different authors favoring one version or the other. Do not let it bother you.

About This Book

I favor the Socratic approach to teaching. Therefore, you will encounter many questions within the text. To get the very most out of this book, read each question thoughtfully, close your eyes for a second, and attempt to devise an answer to the question. Make notes in the margin. This helps you define your investing/trading philosophy. Answering these questions generates insights that will help you understand what you want out of the subject matter and how to apply it. The more thought and effort you put into understanding options, the better the learning experience will be for you, making this book much more readable, enjoyable, and valuable.

At the end of each chapter, you will find a quiz, and at the end of the book, there is a final exam. These are open-book tests. If you do not immediately know or understand the answer, look back in the chapter. Read over the material if need be. Never leave a chapter without completing the quiz. It is part and parcel of the learning experience.

A Word to the Wise

Options are an investment. All investments have risk, as does everything else in life. You cannot cross the street or make love without assuming some level of physical or emotional risk.

Options are no different. This book clearly defines the various levels of risk attached to the different strategies described—from the infinite to the definable. Pay particular attention to your emotional reaction to the various risks discussed. There is no attempt to persuade you to buy or sell options, only to introduce the subject to you for consideration.

It is also extremely important that you always understand and accept in advance the risk of any investment you make. In most cases, but not all, government and semigovernment agencies, whose responsibility it is to see that you get fair treatment, regulate the trading of options. Do not depend on them—rely on yourself, because the regulators usually get involved after the damage has been done. Investing is one sport where it pays to be proactive.

Please understand that any particular investment or strategy may not be suited to you from a financial and/or psychological perspective. Therefore, walk briskly away from anything you are not comfortable with or do not fully understand. Do not even look back. Discretion is always the better part of investing. Failure to follow this advice can make you feel like you are skinny-dipping in a piranha-infested portion of the Amazon River.

Acknowledgments

My thanks go out to Stan Yan. He is a talented cartoonist and illustrator, responsible for all the artwork in this book and several of my previous works. Besides his artistic talents, he understands the securities business, having been a professional broker for many years.

As always, I relied on the help and advice of Stephen Isaacs of McGraw-Hill Professional Publishing. We have worked well together for many years.

An acknowledgment would never be complete without thanking my wife, Carol, who cheerfully puts up with my moods as they swing from bullish to bearish, only to immediately post a retracement—depending on how well the work is going.

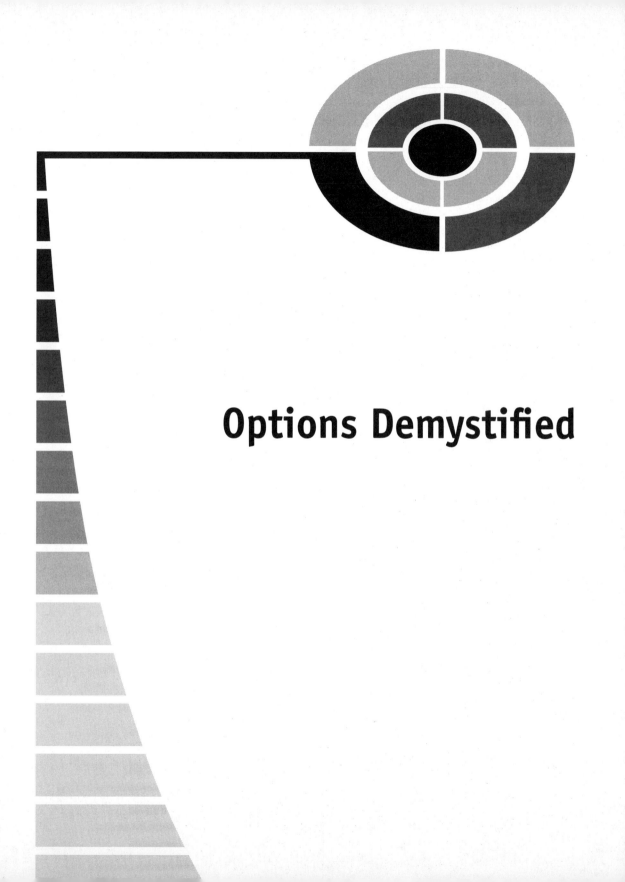

Options Demystified

CHAPTER 1

The Wide, Wide World of Options . . .

An option is simply a conditional contract. It's no different from any other contract you may have entered into, such as that to buy a home, except that many option contracts trade publicly. An option contract simply states the terms and conditions that the buyer and the seller have agreed upon. Options are about acquiring the

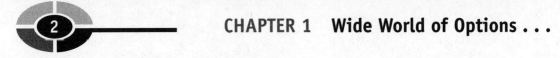

right to do something or buy something, or selling the obligation to do something or deliver something, at a prearranged price on or before a specified date.

An option is a contract on what is known as an *underlying entity*. That entity could be

- Real property, such as real estate, airplanes, or railroad cars

- Financial instruments, such as stocks, bonds, indexes, currencies, or interest rates

- A futures contract on a physical commodity, such as futures options on gold, corn, soybeans, or pork bellies

An option can be placed on virtually anything that can be purchased. You could buy an option on a car, a boat, a plane, a sewing machine, cocoa, coffee, sugar, mortgage rates—the list goes on and on. I once had a client who collected rare watches. There was a very famous watchmaker in Switzerland who was almost 100 years old and who built one watch a year by hand. My client had an option on all the watches he made, with the objective of owning the man's last watch, which was expected to be extremely valuable. Well, the man lived well into his nineties and my client kept buying the watchmaker's annual production at a hefty price. He got impatient, but there was nothing he could do if he wanted the man's last watch. I remember that my client's biggest complaint was being billed by the Union Bank of Switzerland for a clerk to go into the vault each day and wind all the watches he had in a safe deposit box. That expenditure really bugged him as we soared across the United States in his private jet looking for 5,000-contiguous-acre farms for sale.

In everyday life, options can be formal or informal. Often they are not specifically referred to as options, but rather as conditional agreements. For example, you may want a red sports car, but the dealer doesn't have one in stock. You agree to buy one for a prenegotiated price if he can get it within the next 30 days. You put a deposit down. If he cannot produce the car in the allotted time, you get your money back. If he does, you buy the car. You bought a call option on that car.

Options are very common in the real estate market. An example is optioning a piece of vacant land to take it off the market and to lock in the price until zoning and/or financing is finalized. Or an oil wildcatter may option land with the right to drill a series of test wells to verify that the land will be a productive oil field.

With these types of negotiated options, the contract specifies all the conditions of the purchase and takes the underlying asset off the market for a specific amount of time at a price. This is basically true for all the other types of options as well. Take a stock option as another example. If you buy a call option on IBM, you specify the price at which you will buy the stock, the deadline, and the amount you will pay. Let's say IBM is trading at $80 per share, and you think it is going to $90 per share within the next few weeks. [Keep in mind that the stock and futures markets are very volatile and that the prices used in this text may not reflect current market value (CMV).] You decide on May 15 to buy a June $85 call. This is the strike or striking price. Trading in this type of option ceases on the third Friday in June, known as the expiration date. You pay a fixed price per share for the call, the premium. It might be $1 per share for an option on 100 shares. Additionally, the time factor must be taken into account. In this example, the option has approximately 45 days remaining before expiration. If IBM does in fact advance to $90 per share, it is $5 per share over your $85 striking price, or $5 in-the-money. You could sell or offset that option for which you paid $1 per share for $5 or more, since any time remaining on the option adds value. Your profit before transaction costs, meaning commissions and fees, is at least $400. I'll go into greater detail and work through several examples in a later chapter. For now, it is just the overview of the concept that is important, which is that you invested $100 and made $400 in a few weeks' time.

The same type of situation is available in the futures market. Let's say corn is trading at $2.00 per bushel. Your analysis indicates that it is headed to $2.25 per bushel in the next three months. You buy a call option with a striking price of $2.10. If corn hits $2.25 before your option expires, you have 15 cents profit per bushel. Since there are 5,000 bushels in a corn contract, your profit would be $750 before transactions fees and any time value.

These examples demonstrate a key concept of buying long options, which are options that become more valuable when the price of their underlying entity increases. Because they get their value from a relationship with another entity, they are *derivatives*, or financial entities that derive their value from another entity.

Options are not the only financial vehicle classified as a derivative. There are others, like interest-rate swaps, but this book is devoted solely to options.

Even so, there are a ton of options available to anyone who needs or wants one. Besides the ones mentioned so far, you can get options on stock indexes, bonds, interest rates, individual stock sectors, and even total portfolios. Here is a partial list:

- Virtually all the stocks on the major and regional exchanges
  - New York Stock Exchange
  - American Stock Exchange
  - Philadelphia Stock Exchange
  - Midwest Stock Exchange
- Physical commodities and financial futures
  - Chicago Board of Trade
  - Chicago Mercantile Exchange
  - COMEX
  - New York Mercantile Exchanges
- And indexes of every stripe
  - Fortune 500 Index
  - Russell 1000
  - S&P, full-size and minis
  - Aggregate Bond
  - Select Sector SPRD Consumer Staples
  - Select Sector SPRD Energy
  - Select Sector SPRD Financial
  - Select Sector SPRD Industrial
  - Select Sector SPRD Technology
  - Select Sector SPRD Utilities

For a comprehensive list, visit the Options Council's Web site (www.888options. com) and study its pages on option specifications. It is a real eye-opener regarding just how many choices you have if you decide to trade exchange-traded options. As you will see, you can buy or sell an option on anything from one of over 10,000 single stocks to dozens of sectors and indexes to the entire stock market. Or on any major commodity, such as corn, cattle, gold, oil, money, interest rates, bonds, and so on.

Certain types of dealers, like silver firms, offer what are known as dealer options. With these, you buy an option to buy 100 ounces of silver, for example, from the dealer at a fixed price. The dealer agrees to deliver the silver upon your demand at any time during the life of the option. The risk is that the dealer may not have enough silver in its inventory to meet demand if silver makes a substantial move higher and its customers exercise their options. Additionally, dealer options are not federally regulated, as many of the other options covered in this book are, and the buyer often has little legal recourse if the dealer cannot perform. Take the time to carefully research any type of offer of this nature.

You may be wondering why there are so many optionable contracts. Are there really people who are interested in buying or selling options on just about every financial contract under the sun? The answer, of course, is yes, or options would not be a major part of the securities industry, with millions changing hands daily.

Options have the potential to do so much for so many people that they have become one of the most used financial instruments in the world. If a dentist in Peoria, Illinois, sees that the corn crop outside his office window is withering under the hot Midwest sun for lack of moisture, he can speculate on higher corn prices because supplies will be lower. And, he can manage his risk by buying a call option. His risk is only the amount he pays for the call plus a brokerage commission and exchange fees. A call gives him the right, but not the obligation, to take a long position in the corn futures market at the striking price of the option until the option expires. If corn is at a $1.90, he may buy a call with a $2.05 striking price. When corn hits $2.05, he may exercise his option and take a long position in the futures market. If corn goes higher, he makes $50 for every penny the price increases, since the corn contract is for 5,000 bushels.

Or he can hold onto his option and eventually offset it as prices go higher. His option becomes more valuable the higher corn goes because he has the right to exercise it at the $2.05 price. At $3.00, his option is 95 cents per bushel in-the-money with a value of $4,750 (5,000 bushels × $0.95) plus any time value. He must act, of course, before the option expires.

The dentist's downside risk is that corn does not increase in price. If it never goes above $2.05 or if it does and the dentist gets greedy waiting for it to go higher and it crashes lower, he loses the premium and transaction costs. Let's say the premium was a nickel a bushel, or $250, plus $25 in commissions and fees. He has bet $275 that corn is going substantially higher. If it does not, he loses. If it does, he wins. He could also get cold feet and offset the option before it expires and before corn goes up much, say at $2.03. He then would get part of his premium back, but he would have to pay another commission. If he does not act, the option expires worthless. Those are the choices with a long call, which is probably the most popular among part-time or nonprofessional option traders.

That's the world of the individual option speculator. He could be gambling in the stock of IBM, Cisco (CSCO), Amgen, Inc. (AMGN), Comcast (CMCSK), the Dow Jones Industrial Average, the S&P, bonds, or interest rates. The only reason I use the word *gambling* is that when you speculate on which way and how far the price of anything is going, you are guessing. No one knows. The future prices do not exist yet and can only be guessed. Therefore, it is a gamble, no matter how much research backs up trading decisions and strategies.

Now many people in the securities industry may attempt to convince you that investing and trading are not a gamble. But after many decades in the securities industry, I humbly disagree. These industry pundits argue that if you follow their rules and study the market closely, you can invest safely. For example, they will tell you that the stock market has increased at an average of about 10 percent a year since its inception. That sounds really safe, but what about those who invested in the late 1920s and had to wait until after the Second World War to break even, or the folks who invested in the mid 1960s when the Dow Jones Industrial Average fought until the 1980s to break the 1,000 level. If you were in a stock during these years and it stayed flat for 10 years or so, you would be wondering where that average 10 percent gain was that these brokers are always bragging about. Or were you hurt by the crash of the Tech Bubble at the turn of the last century? Or the Enron debacle? What if you retired when Enron stock approached its apex and you cashed out, as opposed to retiring when the stock became worthless? What a difference a year could make in your retirement. Was it luck or good planning on the part of the Enron retirees that caused some to be born a few years earlier than others? Or our current situation, when a terrorist attack can disrupt the orderly flow of the markets—how do you predict that? More importantly, how do you trade it or make money in this type of investment environment?

As an industry professional for decades, it is hard for me to admit how big a part luck and timing play in successful investing. My point is that nothing in the stock market or any other market is a sure thing. The unexpected must always be expected, and this is one of the big reason options were invented. They can be a way of taking a position in a wide variety of markets with a known and fixed risk factor. And as you will learn, there are some limitations and costs involved. You must decide when to opt for safety over aggressiveness and when to choose aggressiveness over safety in your financial activities.

As you have just learned, a call option gave our dentist friend in Peoria the potential to make money if corn prices moved higher—and his risk was fixed. There is also such a thing as a put option, which offers the opportunity to cash in when

prices go down. Let's say an engineer in Silicon Valley sees the trend in the price of Intel stock moving south, breaking an important price level called support. This leads him to think that Intel stock is in for some hard times. He can buy a put on Intel stock, and that put will become more valuable the lower Intel's stock drops.

A put option is just the opposite of a call option. It gives the owner the right, but not the obligation, to take a short position in the underlying entity at the striking price until expiration of the option. Let's say Intel is trading around $22 per share. If the engineer were to buy an Intel put with a $20 strike price, he could exercise that option before it expires and be short Intel at $20. If Intel sinks into the $15 area, the put becomes very valuable, and, if he so desires, the engineer can either offset it at a profit or take delivery of a short position in Intel stock. If it rallies above his strike price of $20, the put becomes less desirable and less valuable. The higher Intel moves, the more out-of the-money this put becomes and the less desirable. At this point, the engineer would have the two other alternatives mentioned in the corn example, which are to offset the option before expiration or to let it expire worthless. He certainly would not take possession of a losing short stock position.

Speculation, or betting on the directional movement of stocks and futures contracts, is one of the most common things the average trader or investor does. But there is a whole lot more, such as hedging, spreading, straddling, and selling options, which I'll get into in upcoming chapters. Here I just wanted you to get a feel for what options are and how they can be used. Later we'll get into the mechanics and the more complex strategies.

As you begin to speculate using options, you realize that the art and magic of success is being able to predict the direction and speed of the price trends of the entities you invest in or trade. Earlier you saw the dentist speculating that the supply of corn would be lower in the months ahead, driving the price of corn higher. This is supply versus demand. The dentist was using fundamental analysis to project future prices. The engineer, on the other hand, was reading charts and using technical analysis to come to the conclusion that Intel's stock was weakening when it penetrated an important price support level. You will be exposed to the basics of both of these approaches to price forecasting shortly.

Even more important, you will learn that a good defense is the best offense. Almost any market, especially in this post-9/11 era, can move violently in your favor or against your positions. Accepting this premise as a proven theorem allows you to become wealthier and sleep more soundly if you decide to venture into the world of options.

Another very important fact you should be aware of is there are two basic types of options. Historically, the older is the OTC (over-the-counter) option. Some historians like to trace OTC options to the Old Testament's Book of Genesis. In Chapter 29, Jacob buys an option to marry Laban's daughter Rachel. The cost is seven years' labor. Unfortunately, Laban reneges on the option, creating the first recorded default on an over-the-counter option. Jacob then marries Rachel's sister, Leah. Since polygamy was acceptable at the time (c. 1700 B.C.) and Jacob was a determined option player, he bought another option on Rachel. This one was successfully exercised, and Jacob and his wives had 12 fine sons, who became the patriarchs of the 12 tribes of Israel.

OTC options got their name because these options were negotiated over-the-counter at brokerage firms. All the conditions and the timing of this type of option are negotiated between buyers and sellers. This characteristic allows these options to be as exotic and complex as the two parties feel necessary. But this causes a real problem if one party wants to offset the option. That party must find another person or entity who is willing to accept all the conditions and the timing. This is possible, as you will read in the chapter on real estate options, but it is not common.

The second basic type of option is the exchange-traded option, which is much more widely used. An example is the calls and puts described earlier in this chapter. The difference between these options and OTC options is that all the conditions of the exchange-traded options, also known as listed options because they are listed on an exchange, are prearranged. The only thing that is not settled is the price, and that is negotiated by open outcry on an exchange floor or by trading rules on an electronic exchange. Therefore, the option trader must decide how many options to buy or sell, whether to be long or short, and what price to bid or ask. All of these questions will be addressed in detail shortly.

Summary

As this point, you know that . . .

- An option is simply a contract between two parties governing all the conditions of a possible transfer of an entity, which can be real property or a financial instrument of some sort.
- Options are one of the oldest and most widely used financial vehicles.
- The number and type of underlying entities that it is possible to option is staggering.
- A call or a put option contract gives the owner the right, but not the obligation, to assume a long or a short position, respectively, in the underlying entity.
- Options can be OTC (over-the-counter) or exchange-traded (listed).
- To successfully use options, you must have a method of forecasting the price trend of the underlying entities

Most importantly, you learned that no matter how sophisticated or advanced the forecasting model is, no one can foretell the future. There is always risk involved in the use of options and any other type of trading or investing, as in most other aspects of our daily lives.

Quiz

1. An option is
    (a) a contract.
    (b) something that can have intrinsic and/or time value.
    (c) either a put or a call.
    (d) all of the above.
    (e) none of the above.

2. Options are a recent invention.
    (a) True
    (b) False

3. All options can be
   (a) freely and easily traded.
   (b) used in both the securities market and the real estate market.
   (c) written only by lawyers.
   (d) traded only on an exchange.

4. The beauty of buying a put or a call is that
   (a) your risk is zero.
   (b) they never expire.
   (c) you can never lose your entire premium.
   (d) your maximum risk is the premium and transaction costs.

5. There are OTC or exchange-traded options available on
   (a) airplanes, boats, and trains.
   (b) gold and silver futures contracts.
   (c) interest rates, bonds, individual stocks, indexes, and stock sectors.
   (d) all of the above.
   (e) none of the above.

6. Option trading is esoteric, and only experienced professionals should try it.
   (a) True
   (b) False

7. Which of the following can be considered risky and even gambling?
   (a) Stock, option, and futures trading
   (b) Life in general
   (c) Investing all your 401(k) in your company's stock
   (d) All of the above
   (e) None of the above

8. Making money in the stock, futures, and options markets requires
   (a) hard work and study.
   (b) good timing and some luck.
   (c) a sufficient amount of capital.
   (d) all of the above.
   (e) none of the above.

9. Which market is the easiest to make money in?
   (a) Stock market
   (b) Futures market
   (c) Option market
   (d) All are difficult to make money in consistently.

10. What are your alternatives when closing out an option position?
    (a) Offset it
    (b) Let it expire
    (c) Exercise it
    (d) All of the above
    (e) None of the above

Answers

1. d; 2. b; 3. b; 4. d; 5. d; 6. b; 7. d; 8. d; 9. d; 10. d.

CHAPTER 2

Everyday Options

Real Estate Options

Employee Options

Let's begin our study of options with real estate and employee incentive options because they do not require an in-depth understanding of the trading mechanisms needed to handle exchange-traded options. Real estate options, for example, do not depend on an understanding of some of the esoteric trading rules and strategies that will be discussed later. The other type of option, the employee option, is offered to employees as a hiring, performance, or longevity incentive.

As Mark Twain said, "Buy land, they're not making it anymore." Tens of thousands of Americans follow his advice each year, and more fortunes have been made in real estate than in just about any other economic endeavor people have attempted. When you control land, your hand is on the throttle of progress. And, one of the best ways to acquire land is through the use of options.

So how can you go about it? What is your game plan, your strategy? What type of real estate are you going to specialize in—new homes, distress homes, large or small commercial properties, industrial sites, farms, raw land? You need a strategy before you need an option. Options execute strategies.

For example, it is common for someone to buy an option on a potential new residence. Let's say your family is moving from Philadelphia to Seattle. One of the members of your family precedes the others to hunt for a new home. A house is found that meets your family's criteria, and the housing scout wants to take it off the market until the other family decision makers can visit Seattle to inspect the property. Is it close enough to schools? Jobs? Shopping? Church? Can the family afford it? Does the neighborhood suit the entire family? Is the nuclear waste dump next door a problem? Time is needed to get the other family members involved with the new property so that they are committed to it before you close the deal by signing a binding contract.

An option is a great tool for taking a prospective residence off the market until the rest of the family can contribute their insights to the decision. For any contract to be legal, all the terms must be agreed to by all parties, the grantor (seller) of the option must be compensated, and an expiration date must be set. A simple option like this could have terms precluding the owner from selling it for a specific period of time, perhaps four weeks, in return for $500, which is the compensation and is known as the option's premium. It would also be common to include the agreed-upon selling price as well; let's use $300,000. In other words, you pay the owner $500 and the owner holds the house off the market for four weeks, even if somebody walks in with a cashier's check for $350,000. On or before the end of that period, you have to act if you want to exercise the option. This means entering into a purchase contract to buy the home at the stated price. Or you can walk away from the home and your $500 and let the contract expire. On the day after the expiration of the option, the owner can sell the home to whomever he or she wishes at whatever price the market will bear.

Real estate options are only one of many types of options you can use to acquire assets, make profits, and manage risk, as you will learn shortly. The key point is that no matter what kind of options you use, they all have the same elements—a premium (the exchange of value/money), a term (time limit), an underlying entity (property, long/short positions in stocks or futures contracts), and a buyer and seller. Negotiated options are generally referred to as OTC (over-the-counter). As mentioned earlier, they got their name because they were initially negotiated over-the-counter at a brokerage office.

The reasons for using options, rather than just buying the underlying entity outright, are very important. In the example just given, the reason was that the house hunter wanted to buy some time to get his family's approval of a particular home before committing $300,000. To do that, he risked losing $500, or 0.2 percent of the purchase price. The option he negotiated would normally include a clause stating that the premium either would or would not be used toward the purchase of the house, the down payment, for example, if the buyer executes the option. On the other hand, if the other members of the buyer's family strongly disagree with the buyer's taste in housing or the location, the family walks away from the deal a little wiser and $500 poorer, but they are not saddled with a home they do not want to live in.

The loss of the premium is a key issue to understand and accept when dealing in any kind of option. If you buy an option and you do not either sell it to someone else before expiration or execute the option to accept ownership of the underlying entity, you lose the premium. Another way of saying this is that you lose 100 percent of your investment. As you will learn in later chapters, some option users think about option premiums the same way they do about insurance premiums—they buy an option to do a certain thing, like protecting an asset against a market downturn, and the expense related to this insurance is just part of doing business. That is why options are described as wasting assets: because they often waste away to nothing. All this will become clearer and have more relevance in the stock option sections, when the time and intrinsic value of options are discussed. Option brokers too often sell their clients on the idea of buying options and neglect to make it absolutely clear that the entire investment can be lost. This is particularly true for some investment-type options that are traded on regulated exchanges or unregulated options sold by companies, previously referred to as dealer options, but it is equally true for real estate options.

Before I go too far, you need to become more familiar with the lingo of options. The *premium* has already been discussed—it is the money one pays to the seller for the option. The *term* is the length of time the option contract is in existence. A term is necessary because it would not make any sense for a seller of property to take it off the market indefinitely. The date the contract terminates is called the *expiration date*. This will become even more important and meaningful when I discuss options traded on exchanges.

The purpose of a real estate option is to get control of a parcel of real estate without actually buying it. One of the beauties of this is that you can take control, in the sense of having the right to buy and resell the property, and the original owner in most cases continues to pay all the ongoing bills—maintenance, taxes, assessments, and so on. All you do is pay the premium and work toward realizing your plan/dream/profit for the property.

In my estimation, the key ingredient for success is tailoring your strategy so that it is in synchronization with the trend of the local real estate market for the type of property you plan to invest in. Real estate markets tend to be localized. Some communities are expanding like plankton in a warm ocean current, while others haven't seen a new building erected in two years. The hotter the market, the more valuable options become. For example, you can get a six-month option on a home that lacks curb appeal and is stagnant in a hot market. You use half the time to polish this rough jewel and the rest to flip it for a substantial profit before the option expires. Entrepreneurs with imagination and guts do this every day.

Your risk is the premium that you must pay the owner of the property and the cost of improvements. This can be substantial and is at the very heart of optioning anything. You must know the business or you will be left holding a worthless option and a fistful of unpaid improvement invoices. Always remember, options are a wasting asset.

Another common real estate strategy is known as a lease-purchase option. You could find yourself on either end of one of these options. One person or entity agrees to lease a piece of real estate to another person or entity, who agrees to pay the lease with the option of buying the real estate on or before the end of the lease-purchase option. This technique is often used with low-end housing and can be very lucrative for either the lessor or the lessee, depending on how well the option agreement is written.

Time⊸⟶

Let me explain. Lessees are generally attracted to lease-purchase options to get houses because they do not have enough money to make a down payment and obtain a conventional loan. The parties offering lease-purchase options do it because they think they can structure the option in such a way that they will make a higher return than if they either rented or sold the property. Plus, there is a larger universe of buyers-leasers-renters than of those who can afford a home, and the idea of living in a home rather than an apartment is appealing in itself. The lessors attract a lessee by offering what appears at first to be a lease payment that is slightly higher than the going rent, but with a portion of each month's rent going into an account. The funds in this account are available for a down payment when the lessee is ready to buy the home. It appears to the lessees that they are paying rent and saving to buy the home at the same time. The terms of the lease state that if the lessees do not buy the home at the end of the lease, they forfeit the amount in the home equity account. The lessors know that only a very small percentage of the families that enter into a lease-purchase option agreement will exercise the option and buy the property. For lessors, the worst-case situation is that they sell a house at their price, which is not so bad—it's a win-win play for the granter of the lease.

Another key element of any real estate lease that lasts longer than a month or two is the buyout price. For example, let's say a lessor enters into a lease-option in a very hot market but underestimates the rate of home price inflation when setting the buyout price. If homes are accelerating at a rate of 10 percent, 15 percent, or even more per year over the three-year lease, the lessees could exercise their option to buy the home, even if they could not afford to own it or even if they could not get a loan to buy it. They could find a buyer willing to pay 20 percent more than the buyout price but a little less than the going market and have a double closing— buying the home from the lessor and immediately reselling it to their buyer. They would make a cool 20 percent profit that the original owner passed up by not including a clause in the lease to accommodate price acceleration.

When writing a lease-option as a lessor, it is important to include a price acceleration clause so that the buyout price of the home increases in value monthly in an amount equivalent to the Consumer Price Index or a local index of similar-type real estate. If you are the lessee, try to negotiate this type of clause out of the contract.

If you think this is only a theoretical problem, let me tell you a true story that happen to me when I was a farm real estate broker in the Midwest. In the mid-1970s, farmland prices were spiraling out of control. Top farmland in Iowa and Illinois climbed to unheard-of prices at that time, over $4,000 per acre. I had a line (in truth a small line, but a line nonetheless) of Europeans in front of my office clamoring to buy American farmland. A dentist in Germany, for example, bought a quarter section, or 160 acres, in Iowa sight unseen. He just wired the money and bought the farm on faith. That is the kind of market it was.

At that time, I had a good piece of farmland in southern Illinois listed. It was just under 900 acres. A large farmer in the area took an option on it for three months and told me that if I came up with another buyer before the option expired, he would happily pay me another real estate commission. One of my European prospects showed some interest. We met with the farmer with the option, and an acceptable offer was tendered. At closing, the farm moved from the hands of the original owner to the local speculator to the European. The original farmer was furious with me. He wanted to know why the speculator got $300 per acre and never really owned the farm or worked the farm. It violated all the values that this hard-working farmer believed in, but farmland prices were out of control at the time. As a side note, nonresident aliens could not buy farmland in Illinois, so the buyer created a corporation that actually bought the farm. The buyer, being Italian, had restrictions about investing outside Italy. To get around that obstacle, the corporation he set up was offshore, and the bank he used was the Union Bank of Switzerland. My point is simply that you must fully understand the federal, state, and local laws when dealing in real estate. Not doing so can be very costly.

My second point is that real estate markets, like all markets, are often totally unpredictable, and you must craft your options carefully to account for the unexpected. You'll see shortly how using brainstorming sessions before structuring your options can add immensely to your success over the years. Now, let's get back to some basics.

Real estate options are OTC options. There are no real estate exchanges that trade options with all the terms and conditions predetermined and price the only thing left to be negotiated. The fact that all the terms and conditions must be negotiated is a mixed blessing. First, it allows you to attempt to tailor the option to fit your specific requirements and time schedule. The mixed part of the blessing is the little bit about negotiating and attempting to tailor the option to fit your thinking while the person on the other end of the conference table is doing the exact same thing. Negotiation means compromise, give and take—not always getting everything you want and having to adjust. Most importantly, if you are not willing to walk away from a deal because you have not gotten the edge, some day you will regret it.

When structuring options that are out of the ordinary or completely new, you should consider using the Ideal System. This is a tool where you write down the terms of the option that would be ideal for you. A good way to do this is to organize a brainstorming session with your employees or colleagues. These associates could be your wife, your grown children, friends, your real estate broker, your lawyer, and even friendly competitors if you are a one-person show, as many are in the real estate business.

The brainstorming session should be scheduled not to exceed a specific period of time, say one hour. In most cases, after you've gotten most participants' initial thoughts or reactions to the proposal, dragging the process out does not prove worthwhile. It helps to have a blackboard or a large sheet of paper available. One person is designated as the session leader. Normally that would be you. Instruct the participants (four or five is a good number) that there is no such thing as a bad idea—the more off the wall, the better. The objective is to get ideas that are outside the box and uncover some concepts you would not have come up with on your own. You prepare in advance a list of topics to be covered. This may include the use of the land or property, ideas on how you can sweeten the deal—at little or no cost to yourself—to make it more attractive to the opposite side, and the financial conditions that are best for you. For example, let's say you are looking to acquire some vacant land. The brainstorming team may come up with the following uses:

1. An ice skating/roller ring
2. A bar and grill or teen club with dancing
3. An apartment building
4. A low-cost housing project
5. Franchise or private warehousing
6. A strip mall
7. An office complex
8. A public swimming pool
9. A ballpark
10. A parking lot

I'm sure you would have thought of some of these ideas yourself but probably not all of them. You will probably end up with a few you had not considered. Additionally, you can see which ones really excite the group, and you can probe the group to find out which use really turns them on. For instances, you can ask the participants to rank the concepts in order of which would be most profitable and/or most desirable. As a bonus, unforeseen consequence, like zoning restrictions you are not aware of, may be revealed.

You can also seek insights regarding the current real estate market. Should you try to immediately flip the property or hold it for appreciation? How strong or weak does your group think things are in your locale? What unfilled needs await creative entrepreneurs, and how can you help fill those needs? How would each of member of the group structure the deal if it was his or hers? And, be sure to ask any other questions you have in mind. All you are trying to do is get a fresh perspective on the deal you are looking at and any insights that may alert you to pitfalls you may be overlooking. My only caveat is to select only people you know well and trust. You do not want any unexpected competition showing up when you go to do the deal.

Once you have captured all the ideas, suggestions, and advice from your focus group and given the deal some serious thought, it is time to organize all you have learned. Take two sheets of plain paper and draw a large "T" on each. The first one is for the pros and cons of the deal, and the second is for the terms of the option you plan to write or have your attorney prepare. On the left side of the first sheet, write all the good things about the proposed deal; on the right, put everything that you do not like about it or that worries you.

Part of the pro side of the first ledger must be your goals. To write options that get you what you need for successful deals, you must clearly define your goals. What are your price goals and the maximum you will pay or the minimum you will take for the property? Under what sort of time frame are you working? How much cushion might you need? List the points you absolutely need for this deal to be a success. Know in advance what terms are deal killers. You must have the

Pros	*Cons*
Location	*High Price*
Neighbor	*Zoning*
Condition	*Competition*

attitude that you can live without the deal in order to get what you really want. The time to work all the kinks out of a deal is before you meet with your adversary face-to-face.

Take the second sheet, and on the left side write the terms you want. Mark the must-have conditions with an asterisk. On the right side, list what you think the person you will be negotiating expects, noting the key conditions that you think are deal breakers for him or her. Try to get inside your opponent's head. What is your opponent after? Is it just the best price? What roadblocks will be put in your path? Write all these down on the opponent's side of the ledger. Then put some thought into what you can live with and what are totally unacceptable conditions. How can you jump the obstacles your opposition tosses in your path?

Buyer	Seller
Low Price	High Price
Long-Term	Short-Term
Zoning	No Conditions
Condition	

Study these two sheets as you develop your negotiating strategy. Once you have clearly conceived what you want, what you think your opponent wants, what you can live with, and what are deal breakers, you are now prepared to list the terms and conditions of the option. Arrange your list of conditions in order of importance. Then take them to your attorney to have them committed to paper. Look to your lawyer to add the legalese and to include clauses that will protect you and make the option enforceable in your legal jurisdiction.

All this may seem to be overkill to you. In some cases, it well may be. But if you get into the habit of thoroughly preparing yourself for every contingency, you will seldom be surprised or taken advantage of. As anyone who has been caught with his or her pants down at a negotiation session knows, it is a lousy feeling. Being better prepared than your opponent gives you a definite edge.

Employee Options

Employers often give or sell options on the stock of their company to their employees. It does not matter if the corporation is privately owned or public. The practice exists in all industries, not just the high-tech companies where it became very popular and got out of hand. At some time in your work life, you will probably be given or offered some options. The option you receive will give you the right to buy stock in the company at a fixed price that is less than the current market value. This means that immediately upon execution of your options, you will have a profit. This is naturally a very positive event, but it is also important that you understand the potential tax liabilities that can occur and have some insight into when to execute your options and sell all or a portion of the stock you receive. These are not the type of options that you can trade on an exchange, like the ones to be discussed in the upcoming chapters.

Under the U.S. tax code, there two types of employee stock options that receive special tax benefits—incentive stock options (ISOs) and employee stock purchase plans (ESPP). Some of the reasons companies give ISOs are to supplement income, recruit key employees, reward performance, and hang onto key performers. For example, during the dot-com boom, it was a common practice to offer big stock option packages to get top software developers to join start-up companies that could not pay top-dollar salaries. These companies sold the idea of joining the company now and getting your reward when the company goes public. In many cases, this made millionaires of twenty-something programmers. Other times, the companies went bust. Major firms, like Microsoft, used options to hold onto their top employees, and so many of them became millionaires that they had to form self-help groups to assist them in dealing with and managing their new-found wealth. Employers often use the second type of option, the ESPP, to build employee loyalty thorough ownership of the company.

All option grants come with conditions governing how and when they can be exercised. Your employer wants to get some benefit from them in the form of work on your part before you get the reward, which is only normal and fair. Other conditions may involve how you can dispose of the options other than by converting them to stock and holding or selling that stock. For example, privately held companies often restrict to whom you can give or will your options. This is done to retain ownership control. For example, if you were to die while working for the company, there may be a stipulation that your options or stock must be sold back to the firm and the proceeds go into your estate. Some performance-based options may seem very lucrative, but you must give serious thought to how achievable the goals are. You could do some very fine work and still not earn the incentive. Always

Microsoft Millionaire Club

get the details of the option plan in writing and read it very carefully—even the footnotes, if there are any. The devil hides in the details, so you may want to run it by your attorney.

Before I go any further, I want to remind you that the following is only an example of the kinds of problems you might encounter. This is not legal or tax advice, which would be impossible to give because of how quickly our tax laws can change. You must go to your tax adviser or attorney for advice that pertains to your specific situation and that is in tune with current laws, rulings, and case law.

The special tax treatment depends on whether the option program is qualified or nonqualified. With both qualified and nonqualified options, the employee can buy the company's stock at a fixed price and resell it at fair market value. The big difference is the tax consequences for the employee and the employer. You need to know this in order to protect yourself, as you will see.

Let's start with a nonqualified plan. An employee receives an option to buy 1,000 shares of stock at $10 per share. After two years with the company, the employee can exercise the option and buy the 1,000 shares for $10 each. At that time, the current market value (CMV) of the stock is $30 per share. The lucky employee now owns 1,000 shares with a CMV of $30 per share, which is $20 per share more than was paid for it, or a $20,000 profit. The difference between the CMV and the fixed option price is called the *spread*. With nonqualified programs, the employee must immediately pay taxes on the spread at ordinary income rates, and the company gets a corresponding tax deduction. What this person should consider is immediately selling enough stock to pay the taxes. If she or he doesn't, there is a risk of reaching tax time with a substantial tax bill, only to learn that the value of the stock has dropped dramatically.

Now let's go through the same example using a qualified program. By the way, the terms *qualified* and *nonqualified* are used in the securities business to refer to programs that are or are not qualified for special tax considerations. For example, a regular IRA is funded with pretax income, and the income it generates qualifies to be tax-deferred until the money is withdrawn. The idea is that at that time, the owner of the IRA will not be working and thus will be paying taxes at a lower rate.

Do you remember reading any stories of someone who received a great option package from his or her employer, never sold any shares of the stock, and was hit with a gargantuan tax bill that he or she could not pay because the stock price had crashed? These are real stories, and some of these people were millionaires one day, only to be bankrupt the next. Here is what can happen. An employee receives a block of options under a nonqualified program. The price of the stock soars. The employee holds the stock and enjoys being a millionaire on paper, only to watch the price of the stock plunge. When he or she goes to file income taxes at the end of the year, a massive amount is owed.

What happened? With qualified options plans, the employee pays no taxes when he or she exercises the option. If the employee holds the shares for two years after the grant and for one year after exercising the option, the employee pays only capital gains tax, which normally has a substantially lower rate than the tax on ordinary income. For highly paid executives, I'm talking about a saving of as much as 20 percent. The risk is holding the stock an extra year, since there is no telling what the stock's price will be at that time.

Some of the people who exercised their options did not realize that the gain or spread between the CMV and the price in the option, called the *grant price,* is subject to the alternative minimum tax (AMT). This tax was passed to prevent high-income people from avoiding paying less than their fair share of taxes. The AMT requires the taxpayer to calculate taxes using the regular rules and then redo them adding back certain deductions, one of which is this spread. During the dot-com era, hot tech stocks gained literally hundreds of dollars per share. If you exercised anywhere near the high, the stock could have lost all of the gain by the time the taxes were due. Not understanding this, some people who felt very wealthy at one time lost everything. Here is how the AMT works:

Alternative Minimum Tax Calculation

1. Standard tax calculation:
   Income
   Less all deductions
   Equals taxable income
   Taxable income × tax rate = tax bill

2. AMT Tax Calculation:
   Standard taxable income
   Less $45,000
   AMT taxable income

   AMT taxable income × 26% = AMT tax bill
   (use 28% if income over $175,000)

   Taxpayer pays the higher of the two.

   What could these folks have done? One thing would have been to sell some of the stock immediately after exercising the options. If they had done that, the profits would have been taxed as ordinary income, as with unqualified programs. But during that period, everyone thought the party was going to last forever. The moral is to spend some time with your tax person so that you understand in advance the tax ramifications and the maximum downside risk of any option program you are offered. Also keep in mind that any statement or reference to the tax code or the implications of the tax code mentioned in this book is subject to change by Congress or our legal system. Always take the time to get current information.

Quiz

1. You can trade real estate options on an exchange.
   (a) True
   (b) False

2. Which of the following are key parts of an option?
   (a) The premium
   (b) The term
   (c) The underlying entity
   (d) The buyer
   (e) The writer

(f) All of the above

(g) All except e

3. The advantage of buying real estate using an option is that
   (a) you freeze the purchase price for a period of time.
   (b) you get a reduced price on the property.
   (c) the option takes the property off the market indefinitely.
   (d) it is a risk-free strategy.

4. You must use a real estate lawyer when preparing an option.
   (a) True
   (b) False

5. The advantage of buying a home on a lease-purchase option is that
   (a) all of the lease payments go toward buying the home.
   (b) it gives you time to accumulate a down payment.
   (c) you can easily make a profit.
   (d) the lessor will almost always extend the lease.

6. One of the most important things to do when preparing a lease for yourself is
   (a) to talk it over with anyone who will listen.
   (b) to do it as quickly as possible so that competitors will not hear about the opportunity.
   (c) to make sure the project is in synch with the local economy.
   (d) to avoid putting anything in writing until the very last minute.

7. All employee options are qualified plans.
   (a) True
   (b) False

8. Employees must be careful regarding the following aspects of options.
   (a) Being trapped in a job in which they are unhappy
   (b) The tax consequences
   (c) The volatility of the price of the underlying stock
   (d) All of the above
   (e) None of the above

9. The AMT
   (a) helps option holders keep more of their gains when exercising an option granted by their employer.
   (b) was designed to reduce taxpayers' burden.

    (c) is easy to understand and should not be taken seriously.
    (d) can make a big difference in one's lifestyle if it is not
        understood.

10.   All employee option programs are solely for the benefit of the employee.
    (a) True
    (b) False

Answers

1. b; 2. f; 3. a; 4. b; 5. b; 6. c; 7. b; 8. d; 9. d; 10. b.

Your First Serious Look at Using Options

Motivation
Speculations
Income
Protection
Vocabulary

It wasn't until April 1973 that options were reintroduced to the trading public after being shut down following the Great Depression. This time it was under the close supervision of the industry regulators. For example, all option advertising is regulated by the NASD (National Association of Security Dealers), which is the securities

TICKLE TAPE   BY STAN YAN

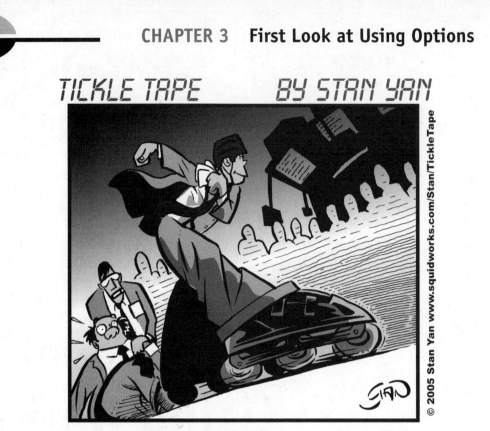

© 2005 Stan Yan www.squidworks.com/Stan/TickleTape

"They advertise that they offer the
fastest floor executions in the business."

industry's self-regulatory organization (SRO in industry lingo), but I see and hear some that, in my opinion, should not be allowed. You should be aware that you cannot depend on any government or quasi-government agency to always protect you from unfair practices if you decide to trade options. Unfortunately, the SROs often get called in only after a situation gets out of control. You must learn to protect yourself, and if that does not work, then look for outside assistance.

The first step is to carefully read the extensive paperwork you sign when you open an account. The account-opening document you sign states that you understand that the risk you are about to accept as an option trader has the potential to do serious damage to your net worth. This will be used against you in any future dispute.

This is done in the spirit of full disclosure. Like so many occasions when lawyers are in control, it is overkill. Page after page of small type tells you how risky option trading is at the same time that the broker has raised your greed level to new heights. Between the multipage boilerplate recitations describing every possible negative outcome that may occur and the broker's urging them to act quickly, is it any wonder that few people take the time to read the fine print thoroughly? Sometimes the disclaimers are printed in a small typeface on the back of the forms. Please take the time, no matter how much it takes, to understand exactly what you are getting into.

Granted, there are complaint policies and procedures in place, but they do not guarantee that you will be protected and not taken advantage of by unscrupulous brokers. My advice is to think carefully and act (meaning trade) rationally.

Now let's get back to the business of demystifying options. Stock options are listed and traded on exchanges. Thus they are referred to as listed options and exchange-traded options, as opposed to over-the-counter options. Since all but one of the provisions (underlying stock, number of shares, call or put) of the option is set in stone, the only area for negotiation is price. How much should an option buyer "bid" for a specific option, and how much should the seller or grantor "ask" for the same option? That is what is known as the *market* for a specific stock option, or the bid and ask price. The best bid (lowest) and best ask (highest) are known as the *inside market*. The difference between the best bid and best ask is the *spread*. I will go a lot deeper into this background material regarding how exchanges work in the next chapter, on the mechanics of trading stock options.

For now, I want to discuss the decisions that the typical stock option trader must make before considering opening a trading account and doing all the preparation needed to fire off the first trade. Some questions the potential option player must answer are:

• Should I even consider trading options?
• What is my goal?
• What strategy shall I employ?
• On what stock should I place an option?
• Should I buy or sell a put or a call?
• How many options should I buy?
• What will be my exit strategy?

First, you may be thinking that you are an investor and not a trader, so none of this applies to you. To clarify the difference between the two, investors seek wealth and traders seek income. The former has a long-term perspective, and the latter a short-term perspective. Even if you feel that you are only interested in investing in stocks, you may encounter market conditions that make it advantageous to use options to protect gains, generate extra income, or enter positions. All these will be discussed later.

Since options have a set term or expiration date, they cannot be considered long-term investments in the classic sense. You cannot hold options for years or even decades, as you can stocks. Stocks, or the corporations behind them, have a theoretically infinite life. Options do not. Even LEAPS, which are long-term options, have a definite expiration date. Therefore, when one talks about options, it is always in the context of trading options, rather than investing in them.

Now, there is trading and there is trading. By this is meant, there are active option traders, and there are others who occasionally use options for specific purposes. You can be a day-trading option player executing dozens of trades per trading session or a conservative option trader who hedges risk with options once or twice a year, depending on market conditions. But both are option traders. Some option traders use very risky trading strategies, like naked shorts, while others are more risk-averse and trade only covered calls, long positions, hedges, spreads, and straddles. All this will become clearer as you work your way through this book.

The first two questions on the list intertwine. Before you play the options game, you should have a reason, and that reason often dictates the strategy. Let me give you some instances.

One of your friends or associates at work trades options and is constantly bragging about his or her success. He or she tells you that a lot of money can be made and the risk is inconsequential. This person convinces you that trading options is a simple and safe way to make a lot of money. Greed is your motivation.

Greed is a very common driver in the securities industries, maybe the primary one. If it were not for greed, the industry would have died out in this country shortly after the Buttonwood Agreement in 1792 that founded the New York Stock Exchange. Twenty-four prominent stockbrokers met, supposedly under a buttonwood tree, on Wall Street and created the world's premier exchange.

Please don't be put off by the fact that you might be motivated to get into the options game by greed. Virtually every human being possesses some degree of greed in her or his psyche, along with a smattering of the other six deadly sins. It is only when greed, or inordinate greed, takes over one's life that it is a problem. This is especially true of traders and investors of all stripes. Greed clouds reason and allows traders to take risks that they are not prepared to take or able to withstand. This is something everyone who gets involved with any investment in general and options in particular must guard against.

Now, let's say your fellow employee sparks an interest in trading options. For average folks, this is a very common motivation. They act on a tip, perhaps from the person who originally got them interested. "Hey, Jared, you should buy some calls on Johnson & Johnson. It's coming out with a really hot product that will sweep the market!" Or, you might get an unsolicited call from a broker hawking a stock you never heard of that has a new service that is going to provide Internet access in every 7-Eleven in the country. Or a commercial on CNBC shows how a high school student has a helicopter to take him to school or a truck driver owns a private island—all of which came from option trading.

You are now interested, but is option trading for you? Your first step is giving some serious thought to the risk-reward ratio. If you invest $1, what can you

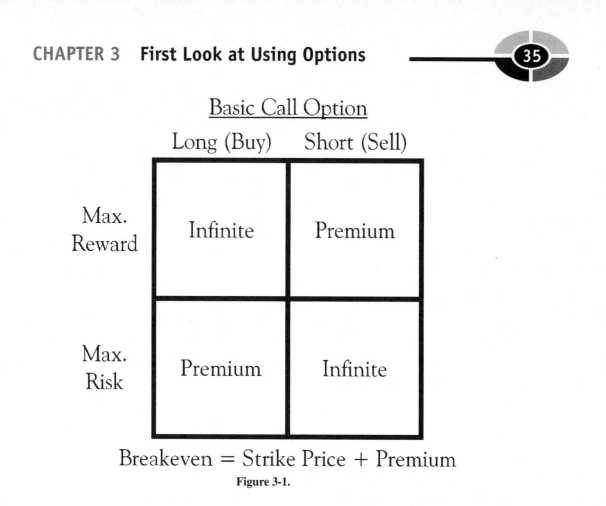

Figure 3-1.

expect as a return? Look at Figure 3-1, "Basic Call Option," which indicates that you have two basic choices—you can buy an option, or you can sell an option. The first thing to notice is that the rewards available to sellers are very limited. On a call or a put, the seller's maximum gain is the premium (or the amount the option sells for, its price), and the maximum risk is theoretically infinite. In real life, stocks rarely increase in value to infinity, but the seller of a call is nonetheless legally responsible to deliver to the buyer of a call a long position in the stock at the striking price of the option on demand, no matter how high the actual trading price has risen. Although a stock price may not approach infinity, a move of 25 or 30 points beyond the striking price happens regularly, especially on the Nasdaq. A hundred shares times 25 points is $2,500. If the original call sold for 50 cents a share, or $50, the risk-reward ration for the seller is 50:1. Wow!

With puts, the maximum risk for the seller is from the striking price to zero. (Study Figure 3-2, "Basic Put Option.") Again, stocks seldom decline to zero, but it happens more often than stocks skyrocketing to infinity. If a stock drops $25 per share instead of rallying, the seller must deliver a short position to the buyer of the put at some point along the 25-point decline. It would be the price at which the buyer exercises the option. The maximum profit potential for the seller is the same as for a call, which is the premium. But premiums, as you will see when you begin checking out prices in the paper or online, tend to be lower for puts than for calls. The world of traders is one of bullishness, and calls are normally in higher demand than puts; thus calls are usually priced higher.

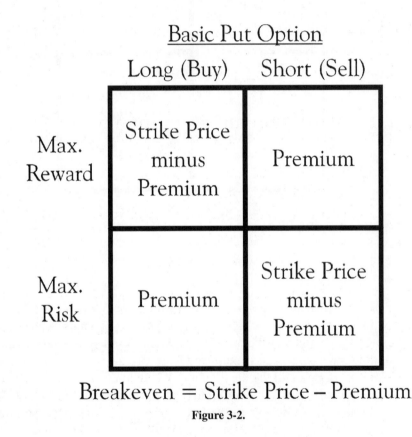

Basic Put Option

	Long (Buy)	Short (Sell)
Max. Reward	Strike Price minus Premium	Premium
Max. Risk	Premium	Strike Price minus Premium

Breakeven = Strike Price − Premium

Figure 3-2.

The buyer of this call or put would have made $2,500 on a $50 bet. That's should be enough information for you to become a buyer, rather than a seller, of options. And, for most people, this is the right decision. What few option traders ask is: With the risk-reward ratio so out of whack for the seller, why would anyone sell options? The answer is simply that most sellers tend to be top professional traders. They have developed some of the most sophisticated software to price options and forecast price trends. Additionally, they are constantly monitoring their positions, and if any of them appear to be in trouble, they close them out or cover them. Covering means that they buy the stock, the underlying entity, of the option they sold or have it in their inventory so that they can deliver the stock, a long position, to the person who is long a call if exercised upon. When this happens, their loss is from the price they originally paid for the stock to the market price at the time the option is exercised. And, they could possibly have bought the stock years ago at a much lower price and had it in inventory. Finally, as members of the exchange, they pay very small transaction costs, which means that changing, offsetting, hedging, or adjusting positions is not as costly or troublesome as it is for the individual trader. The professional sellers also have tremendous advantages in information gathering, analysis, equipment, and experience compared to the dentist in Peoria or the engineer in California. Additionally, they diversify their risk, so that if they lose on the chip stocks, they win in the oil sector.

This all means that for the part-time option trader, selling options is a very high-risk, low-reward trade. Don't get me wrong; buying is also risky. Why? For two reasons. The first is that a very high percentage of options expire worthless. The buyer may only lose $50 or $500, but that is 100 percent of the investment. Any time you can take a 100 percent hit, no matter how much is at stake, you are in a risky business.

For some, the motivation is just fun. Taking a flyer on the idea that Dell's new marketing scheme will move its stock 10 points can be a rush. Or others may be motivated by their second sight—they think they see something that the market missed. It could be a new trend, like an upcoming bull market in a particular sector. It might be some news that will crush the market. Or, they just get talked into something by a convincing, excitable broker or friend. If one can afford to indulge oneself this way, there is nothing intrinsically wrong with it. Who knows . . . maybe the tip or epiphany is right on target, and you will pocket a bundle. It happens, but not often.

Why do you think the vast majority of options expire worthless? The answer is related to the professional sellers being able to price the options correctly, as mentioned earlier. Sellers build a pricing edge into their ask price with the expectation the options will expire worthless. It is just common sense. If you were to price an option with the risk of losing a substantial amount of money, wouldn't you add a little extra to compensate you for the risk you are taking? If professional traders didn't do this, they would be constantly delivering long or short positions to buyers and taking big losses. This would lead to bankruptcy for their firms. Pricing options is a very complex subject to be covered in a later chapter. What I need to do now is continue elaborating on the six questions posed at the beginning of this chapter.

So far, I have talked about speculating for the sole purpose of making money. Again, there is nothing wrong with this as long as it doesn't get out of hand. Also, unless you are going to commit to becoming a full-time professional, you will be better off buying calls and puts than selling them—at least in your first year or so of trading.

What else can you do with options besides speculate? You can generate income by selling covered calls. This strategy has risk, but substantially less because you already own the underlying entity. That means that if the market runs away from you, you deliver the stock you already own. This strategy will be dissected in the next chapter.

A third use of options is called *hedging*. As the name implies, you get yourself positioned on both sides of the market—long and short. On average, you are comfortable. The objective with hedging is to prevent loss and maintain the status quo. If you own a stock portfolio that you wish to hold onto through a market correction, you could buy puts that reflect the size and composition of your portfolio. When and if the market plummets, your puts gain value while your portfolio loses. Correctly structured, the gain on the puts offsets the loss in the portfolio. I will go into this subject more later.

On AVERAGE, you are comfortable.

Another common strategy involves the use of puts and calls in combination. These can be spreads or straddles. The purpose, as you will learn soon, is to manage risk and profit from overall market movement. You will also find how you can take long-term positions in options, known as LEAPS (an acronym for Long-term Equity Anticipation Securities). These are great when you are convinced that a company or a trend is absolutely going to drive prices higher or lower, but you do not have a clue as to timing.

Most stock option traders have experience with stocks before they begin to trade options. They probably have bought a mutual fund or two, made investment selections for their IRA or 401(k), or bought individual stocks as a long-term investment. Many have stock-trading accounts with one or more brokerage firms. My advice to newbies to options is to begin trading options on stocks you are familiar with. You will have a feel for how big a price swing (volatility) these stocks make over a given period of time. You will also probably have some channels of information on the financial prospects for stocks you already own.

If this is not the case, choose a few stocks—no more than four or five—and begin tracking them. Start doing technical and fundamental analysis, subjects yet to come, on your selections. Then paper trade for at least three months. Paper trading is simulated trading where you pick trades, select an entry price that is currently available, such as the bid price in the paper or an online price quotation source, and then pick a time to close the trade using the ask price. In advance of making each paper trade, list your reasons for selecting the stock and for deciding to buy a call or a put, and specify at what price you will offset the options at a profit or at what price you will cut your losses. All this will become crystal clear when I discuss specific trading strategies and plans. The purpose of paper trading is the same as that of practicing for a sport or rehearsing a play. You can just do a better job if you walk through the steps before actually doing something new and difficult. There are some excellent software programs that teach option trading using a simulator.

The move to option trading from stock trading is an easy one, but it is important to understand the differences. The most obvious difference is that stock ownership represents actual ownership in the company that issues the stock, while an option is only a conditional contract to buy or sell a certain number of shares. Second, stocks are permanent and options are transient, as discussed earlier. Another difference is that there is always someone ready, willing, and able to buy stocks when you want to sell. These people are called specialists or market makers and will be discussed when I talk about how the exchanges work. This does not mean that you will like the price they offer you, but nonetheless you will be able to sell any time you want. Options, particularly those that are out- or deep-out-of-the-money, are not always liquid. That means that you may not always find a buyer when you wish to sell, which is another reason a great many options expire worthless. In other words, you can usually salvage something out of a stock that has gone sour, but this is not always true with options.

There is also the risk factor mentioned earlier. If you are a buyer of options, all you have at risk is the premium and the transaction costs. Stockholders risk losing the entire amount they pay for a stock. In both cases, the loss can be 100 percent, but the premium is always a small percentage of the entire cost of buying a stock. This means that options are much more highly leveraged than stocks, which accounts for the large percentage of profit that can be obtained from an option that skyrockets into the stratosphere. For example, if you paid $500 ($5 per share) for a call option with a striking price of $50 on Amazon and it leaps 50 points higher, you have just made $50 on each of the 100 shares of that option, or 10 times ($5 × 10) your premium. That is a winning ratio of 10:1. If you owned the stock, you would also be very happy, but your win ratio would be lower. Your initial purchase on a 50 percent margin when Amazon was at $50 per share would have cost you $2,500. If you sold when it hit $100 per share, your gross would have been $10,000 and your win ratio 4:1. In one case, you multiplied your investment by 10 times and in the other by 4.

That is what leveraging an investment does. The odds against making a 10:1 gain are much greater than those against making a 4:1 gain. This also helps explain why so many options expire worthless: because they are greater long shots. Leverage is a very serious subject because in some cases, which will be discussed in the chapter on options on futures contracts, is can result in devastating losses. It is a two-edged sword.

For the seller of options, something different happens. The seller creates a security that did not previously exist. He now has the obligation to provide the underlying entity, in most cases 100 shares of stock, to the buyer on demand. To do that, the seller would have to take it out of his inventory or buy it on the exchange at the CMV (current market value). He is, of course, betting that the option he creates out of thin air will evaporate into the same thing. He has no obligation to buy that option back once he has sold it, and there are no market makers in options who are required to maintain two-sided markets, as there are in the stock market, which you will learn about when I get to the exchanges. Therefore, there are many owners of out-of-the-money options who are hoping to sell them before they expire valueless, but there are few or no buyers. Again, these options expire worthless.

Earlier I discussed buying calls when your analysis indicates that prices are heading higher. You can just as easily buy puts with the same risk as buying calls if your research indicates a bear market in the making. Where calls give you the right to a long position, puts give you the right to a short position. Puts mirror calls and have the same characteristics. It is imperative you have this distinction between puts and calls very clear in your mind before you begin trading.

So far, I have addressed the questions posed in the beginning of this chapter about what motivates traders (greed, income, protection), and I have touched on strategies and economic motivations. What I neglected was all the psychological reasons for trading. Many people trade to show off. Others are in the market to prove that they are smarter or braver than anyone else is. Just being competitive and aggressive is enough to lead some people to take up trading. On the other hand, I have seen several traders attempt to use the market to overcome insecurity, while many others believe that if they trade successfully, others will love or admire them. A few even trade for the same reason some soldiers find killing fascinating— the adrenalin rush. It can be intoxicating and addictive.

The psychological reasons are as varied as the human mind. The best and most successful traders I have ever met trade just for the love of trading. Win, lose, or draw—there is nothing they would rather be doing.

Question 6, about how many option contracts to buy, is easy to answer in one sense and difficult in another. First, how serious an option trader are you going to be? How much past experience and knowledge of the underlying entity do you have? Which strategy do you plan to use? The answers are totally different for someone who has been trading stocks for years, closely follows the market, and has a decent-size portfolio than for a person who is being exposed to options for the first time. The older hand has a feel for the market and how capricious it can be, or may be using options in an attempt to tame its volatility with hedges. A newbie has a more awesome task ahead. The novice option trader must develop a reasonable trading plan, which, as you will learn, includes educating him- or herself about the trading patterns of the underlying entity and the nuances of option pricing, money management, the mechanics of trading, security statements, projecting prices—the list goes on and on.

My experience has been that those who are new to the options game have been lured into it by promises of easy money with little or no work. As I am sure you have guessed already, this usually ends up as a quick trip to the money Laundromat.

Another part of this question is, how much can you afford to lose without the loss seriously affecting your current standard of living? Wow! Did he say, "Affecting my current standard of living?" Yes, and those are tough and important words. Can option trading result in the loss of your home? Your car? Your spouse? Can it force you to go back to work after an early retirement? These are the extremes, but option trading can be just as addictive and dangerous as gambling for the wrong personality type.

For example, when I was a broker, our branch had a client who was a real estate broker handling large commercial deals. His commissions were in the hundreds of thousands of dollars whenever he closed a deal. Right after closing, he would promptly send us a check for $50,000 or more. Then he would trade until he lost it all and literally begged us to keep his account open until he closed another deal. We—myself and the brokers I worked with—repeatedly encouraged him to seek some professional counseling, but he refused. We eventually closed his account because we felt we were contributing to his addiction. The sad thing is, I am sure he had no trouble opening another account with another brokerage firm.

If you have or ever had a gambling addiction, my advice is to avoid option trading. It is just too similar. This type of trader puts down bets (the premium) on tips from option brokers and hopes to hit it big. That is not the way to do it.

The serious option trader works hard at developing a system to predict the price trends of the underlying entity, has a reliable method of calculating the fair value of the options to spot the over- or undervalued ones, and acts only when there is a favorable risk-reward ratio. Just as there is a big difference between the gambler who recklessly throws his money on the table and the analytical card counter who bets only when the odds are substantially in his or her favor, there is a big difference between the serious practitioner of options and the reckless trader who acts solely on emotion.

The last question you need to answer before starting to trade is: What is your exit strategy? When will you know that it is time to offset, exercise, or abandon a position? Not answering or carefully considering this question before opening a position is, in my opinion, the biggest reason traders lose money. It is the most critical decision, yet it is seldom planned in advance.

Always keep in mind that you will never know for certain what the underlying entity is going to do, but you do know it will go either up, down, or sideways. The real questions are how much and how fast. Those of you who have traded liquid securities, like stocks or futures, may be thinking about putting a stop-loss order to prevent downside risk. A stop order is simply an offsetting order that is placed properly to close out a position before a major loss occurs. But stop-loss orders do not work well in illiquid markets, like out-of-the-money options. Very few people are interested in buying them and offsetting your losing position. What does happen occasionally is that a professional trader will see a stop order that is not designated as such in the market and manipulate the market to take out both your positions for the spread between them, taking a small profit. Pros who are members of the exchange can do this because their transaction costs are pennies per contract. Your positions are gone. You lose the opportunity for a profitable trade and the commissions. My point is that you cannot use stop-loss orders in an illiquid market. So this approach to exiting trades on the downside doesn't always work in the options markets.

Your best protection on the downside is usually what is called a mental stop-loss order. In other words, you decide that once your option position loses 50 percent of its value, you will offset it. To do this, you must monitor your positions regularly.

Many option traders can't, and this becomes another reason that a large percentage of options expire worthless.

What about the upside? How much profit is enough? This is an even tougher question, and one in which our friend Rev. Greed comes looking for poor souls to convert to his religion.

The first thing to do before opening a position is to decide what you are going to do with that position if and when it is in-the-money. At that point, the position has real value, called *intrinsic value*. For example, you own a June 40 Exxon Mobil (XOM) call, and it is trading at $45 a share, or $5 in-the-money or $5 of intrinsic value. This means that if you exercise your option, 100 shares of XOM will be transferred into your stock account at $40 per share, giving you an immediate $5 per share or $500 gain. Once you have this position in your account, what are your plans? Hold for the long term? Hold for a specific price, say 55 or 60? You now have an actual position in a very liquid stock, so you can now safely put a stop on it—even a trailing stop that would move higher as the stock moves higher.

Or are you going to offset the position or hold it for more profit? If so, how are you going to protect the $500 profit you have? A stop-loss order? A mental stop? Are you going to begin monitoring the position more closely, possibly in real time?

You have a lot of choices. If you do not spend some serious time thinking about them before you open the position, you will most likely end up like too many option traders who acquire a winner and hang onto it until it becomes a loser or expires worthless. I have seen this happen more often then I care to think about. Greed wins more than his fair share of bouts with otherwise very sensible people. I'll get back into this when I discuss developing a trading plan.

Quiz

1. The price of an option is called the
   (a) spot price.
   (b) premium.
   (c) striking price.
   (d) market price.

2. What are the four elements of an option?
   (a) _____
   (b) _____
   (c) _____
   (d) _____

3. When do options expire for the public trader?
   (a) Flag Day
   (b) The last day of trading
   (c) After 90 days
   (d) When exercised

4. The CMV for the underlying entity is at 40. A 50 call is
   (a) in-the-money.
   (b) totally valueless.
   (c) at-the-money.
   (d) out-of-the-money.

5. A 105 December IBM put when IBM stock is at 95 is
   (a) at-the-money.
   (b) about to be forfeited.
   (c) unable to be exercised.
   (d) in-the-money.

6. It is easier to get into an option than to get out because
   (a) there is too much liquidity.
   (b) there is too little liquidity.
   (c) amateur traders buy too many options.
   (d) the professional trading firms only sell options.

7. Options prices respond to
   (a) the overall trend of the market.
   (b) the price and volatility of the underlying entity.
   (c) brokerage firm predictions and recommendations.
   (d) the buying and selling activity of part-time traders.
   (e) all of the above.
   (f) none of the above.

8. The most lucrative part of the options business, year-in and year-out, is
   (a) buying out-of-the-money calls.
   (b) playing option tips.
   (c) regulation of the industry.
   (d) selling options.

9. The theoretical reward potential for the owner of a call is
   (a) the striking price plus the premium.
   (b) the market price minus the striking price.
   (c) zero minus the premium.
   (d) infinity minus the premium and transaction costs.

10. The maximum risk for a seller of puts is
     (a) margin calls.
     (b) the striking price minus the premium.
     (c) a runaway bull market.
     (d) a buyer who defaults on the premium.

Answers

1. b; 2. Premium, Term, Underlying entity, Buyer/seller; 3. b; 4. d; 5. d; 6. b; 7. e; 8. d; 9. d; 10. b.

CHAPTER 4

The Playing Fields

Exchanges

Volatility

Your first step, as a fledgling option trader, is getting a feel for the price movement or volatility of the underlying entity. In the case of stock options, one must first take into consideration the exchange on which the stock trades. If the overall exchange is in a volatile state, this seriously influences the volatility of the stock and, in turn, the volatility of the options on that stock. It is a chain reaction. The opposite is equally true—calm markets calm down volatile stocks. This is not an absolute rule. An individual stock can be very volatile in the calmest of markets. The reason may be something specific to that stock, like another firm launching a hostile takeover or a negative earnings report. If something like this happens, the stock is an excellent candidate for a short-term option trade.

Volatility can strike like a herd of buffalo spooked by lightning, stampeding traders in every direction. Alternatively, it can start slowly and build on itself, like a rising tide, until the entire market swells higher or lower, threatening to capsize everything in sight.

It is also the single most important element of the many analytic tools predicting the fair market value of options or any of the key indices you study to get a fix on market trends. Therefore, it behooves you to take a quick look at the two basic types of stock exchanges so that you have an understanding of their impact on the volatility of whatever entity you trade.

The oldest type of exchange is floor-based. This simply means that these exchanges have a physical trading floor on which the buyers and sellers meet via their representative brokerage firms. Prices are set by open outcry (literally the calling out of bid and ask offers) of the members on the floor of the exchange. Think of it as an auction. Examples of these exchanges are:

- American Stock Exchange (AMEX)
- Chicago Board of Options Exchange (CBOE)
- Midwest Stock Exchange (MWSE)
- New York Stock Exchange (NYSE)
- Pacific Stock Exchange (PSE)
- Philadelphia Stock Exchange (PHLX)

Floor-based Exchange   Screen-based Exchange

The second basic type is the electronic or screen-based, as in computer monitor, exchanges. The most prominent is Nasdaq, which is also referred to as the OTC market. Nasdaq is referred to as OTC not because options on its stocks are negotiated individually as they once were, but because the method used to arrive at bid and ask prices is negotiation. The first four initials of this acronym stand for National Association of Securities Dealers, which is the self-regulatory body (SRO) for the OTC market, and the last two letters stand for automatic quotation system. Initially NASDAQ (all capitals then) tracked the prices of stocks in the over-the-counter market. Security dealers negotiated among themselves by phone (thus the over-the-counter label), and then posted the price on the electronic price quote system. This system eventually added the capability to post bids and asks and provide order execution—it became, de facto, an electronic exchange, and its name changed from all capital letters to upper- and lowercase, i.e., Nasdaq.

Therefore, there are listed and OTC exchanges and listed and OTC stocks. Historically, corporations thought it more prestigious to have their stock traded on a listed exchange than in the OTC market, since they were older exchanges with higher financial requirements. The New York Stock Exchange is the most prominent listed or floor-based exchange in the world. Brokerage firms and brokers generally feel the same way, and, since both require registration with one or the other, those listed on the NYSE feel it is more impressive than being a Nasdaq member. When you see a sign for a brokerage firm, it will state whether the firm is a member of the NYSE or Nasdaq. This also tells you who the SRO of that firm and its brokers is. In the former case, it is the NYSE, and in the latter, the NASD. This can be important if you ever have a problem with your broker, as will be discussed later.

Besides the listed and OTC exchanges, there are ECNs (electronic communications networks). ECNs allow traders to buy and sell stocks among themselves, bypassing the exchanges. This does not mean that you do not have to trade through a brokerage house. You still must have a brokerage account to handle the accounting and to access the clearinghouse. I will get to these details shortly. ECNs have become especially popular for trading certain high-volume stocks, and they add volatility and liquidity to the overall market. You may have heard of the ECNs named InstiNet, Island, or Archipelago. They are particularly useful to very active stock traders, like day traders, who must get orders filled in a nanosecond when possible. ECNs became very fashionable during the day-trading craze at the end of the last century. Options do not trade on ECNs, but they do trade electronically.

The merger of the electronic trading technology of the ECNs with the exchanges increased volatility on the listed exchanges. All the exchanges have been forced to upgrade their electronic trading capabilities to meet the challenge presented by these networks. For example, Archipelago merged with the Pacific Stock Exchange and Nasdaq made substantial upgrades. Even the NYSE currently accommodates some electronic orders and is looking at providing a completely electronic trading platform. Most importantly from the perspective of options, an electronic exchange that trades options is now operational.

The importance to an option trader of which type of exchange the underlying stock trades on goes back to volatility and which type of exchange has a propensity to be more or less volatile. Always keep in mind that high volatility, or wide swings in prices and lots of price movement, gives your options more opportunity of moving into the money and generating profits. Low volatility assists you when your goal is extra income from your stock portfolio, as you learn to trade covered calls. It is for these reasons that you need to understand as much as possible about volatility from all points of the compass. Always remember, volatility does not indicate the direction, higher or lower, in which an underlying entity is heading.

Historically, the floor-based exchanges are less volatile than the over-the-counter exchanges. The NYSE is the best example to use because it handles three-fourths of all shares traded on floor-based exchanges and most regional exchanges use the same or a similar model. The reason for the lower rate of volatility is structural. At the NYSE, virtually all trades go through the hands of a senior trader known as a specialist. I qualified this statement with the word *virtually* because some small trades are now handled electronically.

The role of the specialist is extremely powerful and has an inordinate influence on the price of the stock entrusted to his or her care and protection. Is being a specialist a good job? I do not think you will ever meet a specialist on the NYSE who is not a multimillionaire. The position is virtually inheritable, passing from father to son for generations. Many great fortunes trace their start to the specialist system; some fortunes have been lost as well as a result of greed. The role of the specialist has come under much fire of late from securities industry critics because of abuses.

The classic function of the specialist is to act as the buyer or seller of last resort if a customer cannot get a fill from the floor brokers. One of his other important tasks is to stem volatility. He (I use the masculine pronoun because most specialist are male) acts as the price policeman as he works to maintain an orderly market—one in which prices move smoothly and all participants receive fair treatment. To do this, he owns a good-sized inventory of the stock he specializes in— one stock per specialist on the NYSE. This is a key point that will become more important shortly. The purpose of holding this inventory is to sell into the market when it is rising too fast and to buy into the market when it falls too steeply. This is how he manages volatility and maintains an orderly market.

To accomplish this, the specialist has a booth on the floor of the exchange. Anyone who wishes to buy or sell that particular stock joins the crowd around his booth. This terminology goes back to the original days of trading beneath the buttonwood tree in old New York. If you, at home in Pittsburgh, Pennsylvania, or Canton, Ohio, place a trade for a NYSE-listed stock with your local broker, the broker's firm fires it to the firm's trading desk at the NYSE. Your order immediately goes to the company's floor broker in the crowd of other floor brokers around the booth at which the stock you wish to buy or sell trades. The floor broker cries out your order to the specialist, who enters it in his order book. If your order is a market order, it is immediately filled at the current bid or ask price by one of the floor brokers. If your floor broker needs a better price on a limit order, the specialist records the price and size in his book to be filled when the price reaches the limit (or stop) price. The reason for the "open outcry" of orders goes back to the earliest days of the NYSE, when an open outcry order could be heard by every member of the Exchange. The specialist's book is a ledger with limit or stop orders for buys on one side and for sells on the other, along with the number of shares for each trade. Originally, it was an actual book, but now the process is computerized.

Since the specialist's book is available only to him and his assistant(s), they are the only ones with knowledge of how many orders are open, meaning not yet filled. Knowing the number of buy or sell orders, the share quantities, and the desired prices gives the specialist an invaluable insight into the near-term price trend. If there are thousands of shares on the buy side and only hundreds on the sell side, the outlook is bullish. On the other hand, if almost the orders are sell orders, the bear is about to enter the pit. Being aware of the price levels that will trigger most of these orders alerts the specialists when to expect major moves or changes in the price trend. If you had that knowledge, you would be sitting in the catbird seat, and your trading account would be in seven figures.

The specialist needs to know every order and its size to be able to "manage" the market for that stock. He needs to know when to sell into the market to increase supply and quell demand and when to buy to reduce supply. Markets of all sorts are supply-demand organisms.

This is fine until you realize that the specialist can trade for his own account and for outside institutions and some large customers. Think of it as a poker game. You are sitting around a table with six other players. You are analyzing your cards and deciding how much to bet—is your hand strong or weak? You look over at the dealer, and you suddenly realize that he is the specialist of this card game and knows every card every player is holding and how much each plans to bet. He has the ability to bet only when he has the winning hand. Is it any wonder that specialists are wealthy and do everything in their power to keep the job in the family?

The point is that keeping his market orderly is the easiest way for the specialist to make money for himself and his clients. Chaotic, out-of-control price activity results in losses for the specialist. He wants and usually has the power to quell the unexpected disruptions that hit the trading floor from time to time. For example, if news that could drive prices unexpectedly higher or lower reaches him before the market opens, he has the power to delay the opening until he can handle it in an orderly fashion. Alternatively, he can close trading early or call a pause in midstream to quell a violent move that is disrupting the orderly flow. Halting trading is a powerful tool used to maintain order. What if the dealer at a poker game had the power to halt betting until he is dealt a more favorable hand?

Now these powers are not used flagrantly, but they are available to the specialists. However, they do not eliminate volatility by any stretch of the imagination. The NYSE, along with all the other exchanges, has become more volatile over the last few decades. There have been more days with 50- or 100-point moves in the major indexes, like the DJIA (Dow Jones Industrial Average), in the last 20 years than in the previous 200. I expect the specialist system to break down or lose power in this age of electronic trading. The system may be totally eliminated. There are just too many professional and amateur traders who feel wronged by it. Nevertheless, there are some other mechanisms built into the floor-based exchanges that are not available on the OTC or screen-based exchanges.

First of all, both have what are known as curbs or curb rules, allowing the exchanges to call a halt to trading when conditions become too volatile. These rules vary by exchange and are adjusted from time to time. Basically, curbs go into effect if a market, the NYSE or the Nasdaq, is moving up or down too fast with no sign of slowing; when that happens, a halt in trading is called. No one trades for a half hour. When trading resumes, if it is still out of control, a second halt, this time for an hour, is enforced. If this does not work, trading can end for the rest of the trading session. After the 9/11 terrorist attack in New York City, the markets closed for several days.

You may be wondering how a short pause could make any difference. The answer is that markets thrive on rumors, and in a half hour or an hour, a rumor can be proven false. Or the traders might realize that whatever happened was not as important as they had initially suspected. Remember, the serious traders have large sums of money at stake and only seconds to respond to unexpected events. The first thing they do is jump to the safest position within reach. After time for thought and reflection, traders often go back to normal trading and even reestablish positions they have just closed. Unforeseen events can be just as disruptive, like major weather-related catastrophes. Some news is digested quickly, while more damaging information may take days or weeks for assimilation.

The announcement of major government reports can jar markets. The stock market is an anticipatory animal. It is always attempting to trade stock prices two, three, or six months into the future. If the expectation is incorrect, depending on how important the subject is and how much money is at stake, the market will have varying degrees of disruption. Read all this as increases in volatility.

Let's move to the mechanics of the OTC market, specifically the Nasdaq. There are no omnipotent specialists here. It is *mano a mano* or, more accurately, dog eat dog. The Nasdaq uses a market-maker system. To qualify as a market marker, a brokerage firm must be ready, willing, and able to make a two-sided market in

Specialist   Market Makers

certain stocks of its choice. Making a market means being ready to buy or sell the stock whenever the Nasdaq is open. Being ready to buy or sell simply means having a bid (offer to buy) or an ask (offer to sell) price in the market at all times. Either of these prices or both could be substantially away from the current market price.

Besides being a market-maker system, Nasdaq is a multiple-market-maker system compared with the one stock-one specialist NYSE system. For a stock to be listed on Nasdaq, it must have at least five market makers who are prepared to make a market in its stock, plus it must meet certain financial and reporting requirements. The fact that there are multiple market makers and that they are not located in a single location, like an exchange floor, adds to chaos (read volatility here). Additionally, the market makers have no idea what the other market makers—and there can be a whole lot more than five market makers for an active, popular stock—hold in terms of orders for their customers and for their firm's account. These firms are broker-dealers, meaning that they broker trades for customers and deal in stocks for their own account. None of them possesses anywhere near the information that a specialists has.

Think back to the poker game analogy for a moment. The specialist, as dealer, knew what every player held in his or her hand. On the Nasdaq, it is a game where none of the players has any inkling as to what cards (orders) are held by which other player. In the true spirit of the game of poker, they play cutthroat. Every market maker knows only what is in its own hand, meaning its orders to buy and sell.

You might be wondering, if the market-making broker-dealers are on both sides of the market, how do they control what they buy and sell? Price is the answer. Take a moment to study the simulated computer screen in Figure 4-1. The columns on the left as you face it have all the bids, or offers to buy stock. The first column has the symbol of the market maker, followed by the number of shares and how much it is willing to buy the stock for. On line 1 you see that GSCO (Goldman Sachs & Co.) bids 24.50 for 1,000 shares. On the right side, you see that MLCO (Merrill Lynch & Co.) is offering to sell the stock in question for $24.51 per share and wants to sell

```
WXYZ    24.51 +.21       100
              High 24.52    52 wk High 27.48
Bid    24.50 Low   24.36    52 wk Low   18.07   VOLUME
Ask    24.51 Prv Cls 24.43 Open 24.41          300,789
```

SYMBOL	VOL	BID	SYMBOL	VOL	ASK
GSCO	1000	24.50	MLCO	100	24.51
INET	5000	24.50	BEST	100	24.52
ARCA	900	24.49	INCA	500	24.52
NITE	2000	24.48	ARCA	100	24.52
SBSH	500	24.46	CIBC	100	24.53
HRZG	600	24.46	SBSH	500	24.56
DLJP	200	24.40	HRZG	100	24.60
BEST	100	24.39	DLJP	200	24.65

Figure 4-1.

100 shares. The difference between the two prices is a penny and is the spread. The wider the spread, the more volatility there is in the market, which is another clue to judging the rate of volatility. A narrow spread means less volatility.

The best bid and ask is called the inside market. In the bid column are all the firms that want to buy the stock. If you want to buy something ahead of others, you offer the highest price. Therefore, the highest price offered is on top, and the prices descend the lower you go. On the right side are all the sellers showing their asking prices. This column is arranged in just the opposite way: The lowest price is at the top. If you wanted to buy something at the best price, it would be the lowest price. Remember, stock shares are fungible, or all exactly alike, and can be freely interchanged. A stock certificate for 100 shares of Dell Computer is just as valuable or worthless as any other certificate for 100 shares of Dell. A fungible commodity is required in order to make a market and to facilitate the speedy transfer of ownership, as in overnight, from one party to another without having to do any verification.

The large box at the top of this screen sums up the situation for WXYZ stock. Here you find the current market price and change from the open, the amount of the last trade (100), the inside bid and ask, high, low, previous close, opening price, and the volume up to this moment for the current trading session.

What if you were a market maker and had to be on both sides of the market, but you only wanted to buy? You would raise the price at which you are willing to buy to a level higher than or matching the highest bid, or, as they say in the industry, you would be on the inside bid or you would be at the bid. You would then lower your ask price to put it at the bottom of the ask list. This puts you in a position to buy stock and to have a whole lot of other broker-dealers ahead of you to sell. If prices go down and you still do not want to sell, you just keep lowering your asking or offering price. Once you have bought all the stock you wanted, you lower your bid, allowing other buyers to move ahead of you in line.

As you learn to read the bid and ask price tickers, you can see who really wants to get its hands on a lot of stock and who wants to dump it. This is done by watching how fast prices change and how high or low volume moves. These two factors are also clues to the rate of volatility. Some day traders who have mastered this skill and never went any further in their trading education have made good livings from day-trading stocks—but the option trader has a long way to go.

The Nasdaq is a negotiated market, as opposed to the open outcry market of the floor-based exchanges, and thus carries an over-the-counter designation. The negotiation occurs as the brokers constantly adjust their bid and ask prices to reflect what they or their customers are willing to pay or take for a stock. This market does not have a price cop, like the floor-based exchanges. Every market maker is on its own and is constantly competing with all the other brokerage firms and even some orders from individual traders via ECNs. Some ECNs, for example Archipelago, send orders to the Nasdaq system if they cannot fill the order from their or other ECNs' book of orders.

Since all the orders appear on the Nasdaq trading screen and all the brokerage firms and traders have access to the Nasdaq screen, all the orders are transparent—but you do not know what is behind each order. A broker-dealer may want to buy 10,000 shares of Dell, but does not want its competitors to know that it needs that much because they will drive the price higher (known as market impact cost). To avoid this, the B-D (broker-dealer) shows an order for 2,000. When that order is filled, another order for 1,500 shares is released. The B-D keeps feeding orders until all 10,000 shares needed for a customer are accumulated. While it is doing this, a sharp day trader spots this broker-dealer's repeated orders. She jumps in and buys a thousand shares, riding the stock higher. The minute she spots the broker-dealer leaving the market, she sells her thousand shares for a half-dollar profit, or $500. This may not seem like much, but the day trader's objective is to make $1,000 a day, and with 250 trading days a year, this means a gross of $250,000. The day trader's strategy is call "following the Ax." To throw off the day traders who push prices higher, the primary buying broker-dealer, the Ax, jumps to the sell side of the market from time to time as a feint. This is all part of the poker game as played on Nasdaq, which adds to its high volatility.

Individual traders, working out of their home or office, can have access to the Nasdaq screen. It is available to them from their brokerage firm or via trading software programs for a monthly fee. Since anyone who wants access to this price information can get it, Nasdaq is much more transparent than the floor-based exchanges. With the floor-based exchanges, all one gets is a stream of quotes with volume. You do not know what unfilled orders are in the specialist's book. No one but the brokers who make up the crowd around a trading booth on an exchange floor can see who, meaning which firm, is aggressively buying or selling a particular stock. All the public sees is the ticker tape below the screen on CNBC or some other source. Transparency can be very important for getting a feel for volatility on a specific stock, but this helps only very short-term traders.

Transparency can also result in confusion. On the Nasdaq system, thousands and thousands of people see who is placing orders for which stocks, the size of the orders, and the pricing. All these people in cyberspace are guessing and scheming how to outfox one another. This can lead to confusion and bizarre market moves. The participants cannot see one another and read their body language the way floor traders do. Remote traders guess what is happening. If market-making/breaking news hits, they must react and react fast. No one is there to halt trading until they figure out what is going on and its impact on prices. On the Nasdaq, it goes boom! Prices jump or plunge $10, $20, or more per share in minutes—only to recover if the news proves false.

Back in Gotham City, one person, the specialist, has all that information at one time and has the power to stop the brokers from destroying themselves over nothing. Does that mean that the NYSE is a safer market than Nasdaq? Maybe, sometimes—but nothing humans have created works perfectly all the time. Just as Nasdaq market makers can overreact, the specialists can panic. A specialist can just as easily cut off a super opportunity in the bud as save the market from self-destructing. It is in these periods of major risk that options shine.

From this brief description of the two basic types of exchanges, it is clear that the one with the reputation for volatility is Nasdaq. The market makers are constantly bidding or negotiating with one another to buy and sell stock for their customers and their company's inventory without a hall monitor. You know there will be some food fights come lunchtime.

Volatility in both types of exchanges can come from other sources as well. For example, many of the brokerage firms have in-house trading operations, which means that they are competing with their customers for various stocks. Another occasional source of volatility is the large institutional traders, like mutual funds, retirement funds, hedge funds, banks, and so on, that buy and sell millions of shares at a time. These are usually institution-to-institution transactions over the special ECNs, called InstiNet. When the report of these transactions hits the tape, it often spikes volatility. Always keep in mind that volatility refers to price movement and has nothing to do with direction. A spike in volatility spawns bullish or bearish price moves.

A favorite institutional trick, which sets volatility off, is program trading. Generally defined as the simultaneous buying or selling of at least 15 stocks with a value exceeding $1,000,000, it is usually done as a form of arbitrage between cash stocks and futures contracts on the same stocks—the S&P 500 cash index, for example, versus the S&P 500 futures contract. From time to time, prices get out of line. Cash is cheaper than futures, or futures are cheaper than cash. All the institutions do is sell the more expensive one and buy the cheaper. The difference is profit. The institutions have trades like these programmed into their trading computers for execution at the touch of a button.

These trades can be spotted in advance by monitoring cash and futures. When you become familiar with the concept of the fair value of the futures contract on the S&P 500, you can set a computer trading program that warns you when program trading is about to be triggered. Knowing that a spike in volatility is coming, savvy traders take advantage of the opportunity. Some short-term option traders are among this group of elite practitioners. My point is that you will see many blips in the rate of volatility that you may not be able to explain, but do not let that bother you. None of us understands all the strange things that make prices move the way they do because price movement is a reaction to the human mind, which is not always the most logical apparatus.

What about the exchanges where options trade? Are they floor-based or OTC? The answer is that they are both, and some are hybrids. Options trade on the following exchanges:

- American Stock Exchange (AMEX)
- Chicago Board of Options Exchange (CBOE)
- International Securities Exchange, Inc. (ISE)
- Pacific Stock Exchange (PCX)
- Philadelphia Stock Exchange (PHLX)

With the exception of the ISE, all of these are floor-based exchanges utilizing a specialist system and floor brokers. The specialists at these exchanges, unlike those at the NYSE, handle options on more than one stock. The NYSE is the only American exchange with the one specialist, one stock structure. This is because its volume can support it.

The CBOE has an after-hours electronic system allowing traders to execute after regular trading hours. The PCX merged with an electronic stock exchange called ArcaEx, and the AMEX has been the leader in the creation of many new and creative trading vehicles, such as indexes and spreads.

The new kid on the block is the ISE, which is a new type of option exchange launched on May 26, 2000. Its objective is to utilize the latest in technology to satisfy the needs of both market makers and specialists across all other exchanges. It is completely electronic, and it attempts to fill orders within seconds or even faster. The ISE trades 679 listed stock options that represent approximately 90 percent of the options industry volume.

It uses a unique structure. The 679 options are divided into 10 bins. Each bin is overseen by a primary market maker (PMM). In addition to the PMM, there are up to 16 competitive market marketers (CMM), whose function is to supply liquidity to each bin. The PMMs are operated, for the most part, by very large trading firms with international reach and significant capital. Rather than posting just the specialist bid and ask on the issues it trades, the ISE displays on its trading screens the most competitive bids and offers in its entire system. All the market makers on both levels continuously post revised prices.

The ISE has two claims to fame. The first is the speed of its operation, meaning almost instantaneous fills. The second is the anonymity of the counter-party to a trade. The buyer and seller receive confirmation of all fills, but they do not learn who is on the other side of the transaction. Anonymity is usually of little importance to individual traders, but it can be important to institutions. For example, a major retirement fund does not want the world to know it is buying a large amount of puts to protect its portfolio for fear that its action may trigger a bear move.

As an individual trader, you will not be able to route your order to a specific exchange in most cases. You will e-mail or call your order to your broker, and his or her firm's order desk will route the order. The exception is some of the latest trading software, known as direct access software, which allows the individual trader to become his or her own order desk. Individual traders use software similar to that on professional order desks. They type in the symbol of the option they wish to trade, check the buy or sell button, and type in the quantity and type of order. Then they send it directly to the exchange on which the security trades. Some of these systems allow traders to select which exchange to route the order to if the security trades on more than one exchange, which happens for some listed stocks that trade on the NYSE and a regional exchange. This is also true of some options. They even offer the opportunity to select the best price, if the prices are different, and to "arb," as in arbitrage, between two markets.

Another question: Where do the options come from? Who is responsible for creating them? The Options Clearing Corporation (OCC), owned by the floor-based exchanges that trade options, is empowered to standardize option contracts, guarantee their performance, and issue the options. Let's look at each of these functions separately.

Standardizing option contracts goes back to a word mentioned earlier, fungible. All contracts in a given class must be interchangeable or trading would be impossible. The term *class* means all the put and call contracts on the same underlying entity. All these contracts must have same number of shares. You would not want to buy a contact containing $37\frac{1}{2}$ shares of Texaco and then try to find someone else with a contract for $37\frac{1}{2}$ shares when you want to offset it. It is just easier for all stock option contracts to be for 100 shares. Besides class, there is another term you should be familiar with, and that is *series*. This means all options on the same underlying entity with the same strike price and expiration date. For example, all options on Oracle Corporation would be in the same class, while all June 40 calls and puts on Oracle would be in the same series.

Next is guaranteeing performance—this is a big one. When you buy or sell a security, be it options, stocks, indexes, or futures contracts, you do not buy it from the seller. Nor do you sell an underlying entity to the buyer. You go through a third party, which is the clearing firm. The clearing firm buys the contract from you and resells it to the new owner, or you buy a contract from the clearing firm that purchased it from someone else. By using a middle entity, there is never a problem for the buyer or seller regarding the transfer of ownership of a security. At the end of each trading session, the clearing firms balance all the activity. This system prevents any delay in transferring ownership.

If there is a problem with too many sellers or buyers or if a transaction does not match up, the brokerage firm that handled the trade must stand behind it. Naturally, the firm often then goes back to the broker for satisfaction. The customer is not a part of these situations, and all transactions flow smoothly as far as he or she knows.

Developing or creating new option contracts is usually a joint venture. Exchanges often respond to their members' requests for new products. Let's say a new stock grows in popularity. Trading volume is soaring. Several large brokerage firms go to their exchange and ask for an option on it. The exchange makes presentations to the Securities and Exchange Commission and gets its approval. It goes to the OCC to create the new option's specifications—to devise the standards and be prepared to clear, guarantee, and issue the new option. The option committees on the exchanges plug it into their system.

The last step is introducing the new option to the marketplace. Professional firms that specialize in selling or making markets in this type of option start their computers running simulation programs. As soon as the first buyer places an order, they sell it, and a brand-new option contract is up and trading. Options are contracts, and contracts exist only when a buyer and a seller agree on all the terms. The last and only undecided contract term with options is price.

Now, let's take a closer look at volatility because it is such a powerful influence on options. All options gain or lose pricing strength as a result of the volatility of price, which is a reflection of the ever-changing economics or supply-demand situation of the underlying entity (stock, futures, options, gold, interest rates, coffee, real estate, airplanes, ships, or anything else).

Quiz

1. How would you characterize the relationship between the volatility of an underlying entity and the market on which it trades?
   (a) None
   (b) Sporadic
   (c) Slavish
   (d) Generally they move in concert

2. The NYSE can be described as
   (a) a negotiated market.
   (b) high rolling.
   (c) an auction.
   (d) transparent.

3. What type of exchange would you consider most volatile?
   (a) Outdoor
   (b) Floor-based

(c) Regional

(d) OTC

4. The duties and responsibilities of a specialist include
   (a) regulating trading in a particular stock.
   (b) selling into runaway rallies.
   (c) buying during bear-market moves.
   (d) halting trading when appropriate.
   (e) none of the above.
   (f) all of the above.

5. NASD is an acronym for . . .
   (a) National American Socialist Democrats.
   (b) National Association of Social Drinkers.
   (c) National Association of Security Dealers.
   (d) National Association of Scuba Divers.

6. What is the purpose of the curb rules?
   (a) Halting trading to calm trading down
   (b) Keeping traders from being hit by passing cars
   (c) Punishing the bears when they drive the markets down
   (d) Making sure traders stay in the trading pits

7. A broker-dealer conducts the following types of business:
   (a) brokers trades for customers.
   (b) buys and sells for and from its own account.
   (c) helps maintain the financial integrity of the markets.
   (d) all of the above.
   (e) none of the above.

8. Which can market makers not do in the normal course of business?
   (a) Trade for their own account
   (b) Outbid other market makers
   (c) Leave the market they make a market in
   (d) Avoid buying or selling the stock they make a market in
       by staying away from the inside market

9. Which of the following options is not in the same class?
   (a) IBM June 90 call
   (b) Cisco June 90 put
   (c) IBM December 85 put
   (d) IBM April 125 call

10. Which of the following has the potential to increase volatility?
    (a) A very poor jobs report
    (b) A major terrorist attack against the United States
    (c) Program trading
    (d) Revelation of an Enron-type scandal
    (e) Lack of transparency
    (f) None of the above
    (g) All of the above

Answers

1. d; 2. c; 3. d; 4. f; 5. c; 6. a; 7. d; 8. c; 9. b; 10. g.

Hitting Moving Targets

Volatility

Probability

Profitability

By now, you should understand that the intensity of the price movement (volatility) of the underlying entity and its environment (exchange, stock, or sector) are the primary engines driving option prices. Let's use a simple example of someone buying a call. To be specific, the call is a June IBM 90. Our trader pays $1 per share, or $100, for it when IBM is trading at $80 a share. Since the stock is over $35 a share, the increment between options is $5. If the price or the stock were below $35, the options would be spread by $2.50. This gives us the following calls available (see Figure 5-1):

- June IBM 95 call—$15 out-of-the-money
- June IBM 90 call—$10 out-of-the-money

- June IBM 85 call—$5 out-of-the-money
- June IBM 80 call—IBM is trading at 80, so this option is at-the-money
- June IBM 75 call—$5 in-the-money
- June IBM 70 call—$10 in-the-money

IBM Calls

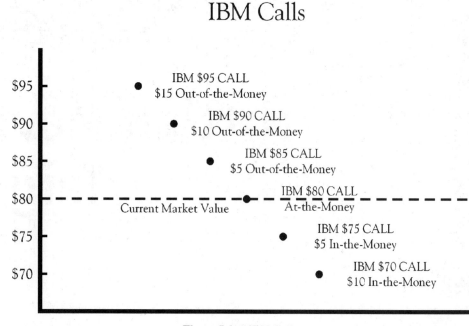

Figure 5-1. IBM Calls.

With IBM at 80, the 90 call is two increments, or $10, out-of-the-money or $10 above the going market. The transaction costs (commission and fees) are $15 per side, or $15 for buying the option and $15 for eventually selling it. The holder of the call has a total of $130 invested in the option if he offsets or exercises it. If he lets it expire worthless, the loss is $115, only one commission. To break even, IBM must reach $91.30, which is $90 per share and $1.30 to pay for the $100 premium and two $15 commissions. The second commission is required to realize the gain and actually break even. In this example, I have intentionally ignored any time value the option may have from the time of the trade to expiration. In addition, an option two striking prices out-of-the-money would be a poor bet and considered on some exchanges as being deep-out-of-the money. Both of these concepts will become clearer when the mechanics of option trading are explained in more detail shortly. Nevertheless, these numbers work fine as an example.

Before this trader bought this option, one of the major concerns was the odds that IBM would make an $11.30 move before expiration, just to break even. That is about a 12½ percent increase. I don't know about you, but I'm often happy if some of my stocks make that much in a full year, let alone over the life of an option, which is normally less than nine months. Not only that, but the 12½ percent move only gets the trader to break even. There is still no profit in it for him. Granted, the investment of $130 is relatively small, but the trader could still lose 100 percent of his investment if the price target is missed.

Once IBM reaches $90.00, the option is at-the-money. As it moves higher, it moves into the money. This means that it has intrinsic or real value. If the owner of a 90 call exercises it, he would have 100 shares of IBM deposited in his account. Along with the ownership comes the associated risk—the stock price could go down as easily as up. If the trader offsets the call when IBM is at $91.30, he breaks even. For each additional dollar IBM gains before the option expires, the owner gains another $100 of intrinsic value. At $96.30, the owner of a $90 call makes a 500 percent profit if he offsets it at that price. That is the reward side of the risk-reward equation.

The incentive for buying calls is the unlimited upside potential and limited downside risk. When buying puts, the maximum profit potential equals the difference between the striking price and zero; the risk, as always when buying options, is limited to the premium plus transaction costs. But what are the odds of achieving the maximum profit or any profit at all? This is where the study of volatility and probability come together for the option trader. Volatility provides an insight into how much price movement is possible, while probability is an indicator of the chances of the move occurring. First, you need some price movement (volatility). Second, you need to know how likely that price movement will be. Third, you need to know in which direction the move will be. Fourth, all this must occur before your option expires. Once you have a fix on these four variables, you are ready to trade options.

Serious thought must be given to what causes the price of the underlying entity to move higher or lower and how you detect and measure the extent and velocity of the change. That is what option traders call the delta. *Delta* is a term used to quantify the impact of price changes in the underlying entity on a corresponding movement in the option's price. It is also referred to as the *hedge ratio*, which will be discussed when we get to hedging strategies. For example, if a stock increases $1 and the price of the option increases 50 cents, the delta is 50 or 50 percent. If the option is at- or in-the-money, the delta is 100 percent because the option's intrinsic value increases penny for penny as the stock climbs higher. The delta never exceeds 100 percent, or the option would be more valuable than the underlying entity.

What causes stock prices to move? The most basic answer for stocks is earnings. The more a company earns, the more valuable it is to investors and speculators. I will discuss this and all the other key factors, like the economy, corporate infrastructure, and so on, when I get into fundamental analysis. With commodities, you will learn that supply and demand rule prices. This is because many of the key futures contracts are on physical commodities, such as corn, sugar, gold, and oil, and the supply changes from year to year as production varies.

When it comes to supply for stocks, options, and financial futures, it is a somewhat different story. The supply of options or financial futures is unlimited. These, being simply contracts, are "created" when a seller agrees to sell one to a buyer. As long as there are sellers, there is supply. And there will always be sellers because they have pricing power. Corporations issue stock, and, in theory, the supply is unlimited. However, the issuing company knows that if it issues an unlimited supply of shares, the stock's value will plunge. An increase in the number of shares reduces the percentage of the company that each share represents, known as *dilution*. Since the owners and senior executives are often major shareholders, this is not done. There are two instances when supply and demand can come into play. First, this can happen when greedy corporate management issues too many shares to the public because it overestimates the demand for the stock. Second, it can happen when there is a supply and demand tug-of-war constantly going on between buyers and sellers for undiluted shares. Let's take a quick look at these two situations.

The basic rules governing price change are quite simple. It is all a matter of supply or demand:

1. As demand increases, prices increase.
2. As supply increases, prices decrease.
3. As demand decreases, prices decrease.
4. As supply decreases, prices increase.
5. Price remains unchanged when supply and demand are in equilibrium

To interpret these rules in the real world, uncovering the essential information and quantifying the data needed to apply them is neither straightforward nor simple.

One would think that when it comes to stock, supply would be a piece of cake. Just look at the float. The float is the total number of shares of a stock that are publicly trading. This is also referred to as the outstanding shares. A firm can authorize more shares than it issues and hold them in its treasury for future release. It has the power to authorize and issue new shares. Public notice is required when any action of this nature occurs. Any of these actions would increase supply and reduce price in most situations. Keep in mind that it is common for the senior executives to be major owners of their company's stock and to have options to buy more. This makes them very sensitive to fooling around too much with its price, except to push it as high as Elliot Spizer will let them.

It was not too long ago that you could rely on the float being consistent unless there were unusual situations, as when a company announced a secondary offering.

When companies needed stock to provide for options granted to employees, they bought it in the open market. Companies made an effort to avoid diluting ownership. For example, if you own 1,000 shares of the stock of a company and there were 100,000 shares outstanding, you own 1 percent of that company. But if the company authorized and issued 50,000 additional shares in any way other than proportionally to existing shareholders, your portion of the ownership decreased to 0.6 percent. That is dilution; it is legal, but it is somewhat unfair to shareholders.

During the dot-com boom at the end of the last century, many companies hired and retained employees by using fantastic stock option programs. When the employees exercised these options, the company issued new shares, adding to the float and diluting ownership. When stock prices were being blown off the charts, no one seemed to care. The same thing happened with the compensation packages of many greedy executives during the heyday of the tech explosion. How many millionaires worked on the top floor of the Enron building?

You just need to be aware that companies have more than one type of stock. Besides the issued stock in the market, they can have stock in their treasury to give to employees. This would increase supply or the float. The board of directors may have authorized thousands or hundreds of thousands of shares that have not been issued to the public. This is a potential dilution problem. Some companies issue legend stock to top executives, who must hold it for a period of time before they can sell in on the open market. It is called *legend* because it bears a legend printed in red ink stating that it cannot be sold and must first go through the company's transfer agent. This type of stock is usually part of the executive's compensation package or a golden parachute. It might be issued to employees at no cost or at a price substantially below the market price.

The quantity of stock that comes onto the market usually does not affect pricing severely. And the Securities and Exchange Commission (SEC) requires companies and principals of companies to issue notice in advance of releasing or issuing new stock certificates. Also, major shareholders, like holders of 10 percent or more of a company's stock, or company insiders, like senior officers who are privy to key financial and sales data, must notify the SEC before selling or buying their company's stock. All of this information is available on the Internet, and several financial Web sites track it.

You should be aware of one other supply abnormality. It occurs when a company goes public but sells only a small portion of the authorized stock at its initial public offering (IPO). The owners and key employees retain the remainder. These key individuals are locked out of selling shares for a period of time after the IPO is launched, usually about 180 days. At the end of this lockout period, they are free to sell their stock. During the heyday of the tech explosion, many greedy owners dumped thousands of shares as soon as they could. At times, this onslaught of shares doubled the number of shares in the float, causing the price to plummet.

Savvy option traders bought puts to take advantage of this phenomenon. A special-interest Web site tracked the lockout periods, and a subsequent study pegged the average price retracement at 35 percent. You might have noticed this phenomenon when Google went public.

Other than the lockout incidents, increases or decreases in the supply of a stock rarely have a serious impact on price. The exception can be companies that buy back their own stock. These corporations are demonstrating a vote of confidence in their company. An announcement that Microsoft is buying back several million shares of its stock normally gives the company's stock price a shot in the arm. But this has more to do with the confidence factor than the supply-demand equation.

The most meaningful supply-side factor in stock trading is the number of willing sellers of any given stock at any given price point. In general, the lower the price of a stock goes, the more sellers come out of the woodwork and the more shares are offered for sale. Thus the Wall Street saying, "A bear market falls by its own weight." This, of course, drives prices even lower. The reason for this is that most people who trade or invest in the stock market are bullish. They buy stock with the anticipation that it will increase in value. If a particular stock or index does not do this, they dump it.

Conversely, most market participants are not comfortable shorting the market, and some major market participants, like mutual funds, by law cannot short. Shorting is the practice of selling stock first at one price and buying it back at another, hopefully at a lower price. To do this, you must borrow the stock from your broker and sell it. Later you buy it back in the marketplace at a lower price and return it to your broker. For example, suppose a stock is trading at $30 per share and you think it is going to $20. You borrow some stock from your broker (paying interest on the total cost of the shares), then sell it at $30. When the stock declines to $20, you buy it and return it to your broker. Your profit is $10 per share. Going short is just the opposite of going long, but it has never been as popular with the public. The risk is that you sell it at $30 and it goes to $50, instead of $20. That requires the short seller to buy the stock in the open market at $50 in order to return the borrowed stock to the brokerage firm. The loss is $20 per share plus interest and transaction fees. In options, if you are bearish, you buy a put, which is much easier and has lower risk.

The sellers are the ones who provide the supply of stock to buyers. There are certain price points, called support and resistance levels, at which the buyers and sellers meet to exchange stock. If you have ever reviewed price charts of stock, you have noticed that prices are always going up or down—seldom are the price trends flat. When a trend is flat, it denotes a period of equilibrium, meaning that there are an equal number of buyers and sellers. If you look at the bottom of most price charts, you will see a section that records the volume of shares traded at each point in time. With the volume of many stocks exceeding 10 or 20 million shares traded per day, it is not surprising that the price line is rarely flat.

The demand side deserves attention when projecting future price trends. Our IBM option trader must answer the question: What change in demand will occur before the June 90 calls expire to drive IBM's stock price far enough over $90 per share to make it worth risking $130 on the call? Now, the money involved is not serious, but that person could be buying 10, 20, or 100 calls or more. Regardless, it is the concept that is key.

There are hundreds and hundreds of possible events that could trigger a $15 move in IBM. It could be a new product announcement, the awarding of a giant government contract, a technology breakthrough, or a merger or acquisition. These are all fundamental factors that are in the province of fundamental analysis. Equally possible are technical signals, used in technical analysis: major resistance broken, the completion of a reverse head-and-shoulders formation, or a trend line broken after a major saucer formation was completed. In the chapter on forecasting, all these will be explained. The point here is simply that a move of 10 percent, 15 percent, or 20 percent or more is major for a blue chip stock, and the buyer of a call who is two clicks out-of-the-money must have some solid reason to expect a major move to occur before making the investment in the option. The danger is buying an option just because it looks inexpensive.

The first step might be to evaluate IBM's volatility. How is the stock performing? Is the trend up, down, or sideways? How steep is the trend? What is the range of volatility of IBM's options? In other words, does it look like there is enough juice to give the stock a kick of $15 to $20 per share or more before expiration?

Now back to the real tug-of-war between supply and demand occurring on the floors of the listed exchanges and the computer monitors of the OTC exchanges. Each stock usually has three or four key players. The first and most stable are the major institutions. Insurance companies, retirement plans, banks, mutual funds, and the like can own millions of shares of any given stock. When you have that much of a stock in your inventory, it is difficult to sell a substantial portion without hurting yourself by nudging prices lower. When several hundred thousand or a million shares hit any market, it disrupts the supply-and-demand equation, driving volatility higher. In the case of a buy, the market leaps higher because of the demand. In the case of a sale, down it goes, wallowing in excess supply. This, of course, is the opposite of what the buyer or seller wants. If you are buying, you want the lowest price; if you are selling, the highest. Therefore these big institutions take extraordinary steps to cover their tracks. They may negotiate a private sale directly with another institution over InstiNet, the ECN mentioned earlier. The actual trade could take place at midnight and hit the tape sometime the next day. By then the deal is history, and traders are trading the next day's news. Folks take notice, particularly of the price, which is not necessarily near the market price, but it does not have the impact that it would if the parties tried to do it during normal trading hours. The day's volatility is affected modestly, if at all.

When an institution has to buy or dump large amounts of stock through an exchange during trading hours, the impact on volatility can be severe. Again, the institutions try to camouflage their intentions as best they can. If they need to sell 1 million shares of QUALCOMM (QCOM), for example, they might farm out orders to 10 broker-dealers, so that each is selling only a hundred thousand. Additionally, they would give each a dollar discretion, meaning that the broker-dealers could sell the stock within one dollar of the targeted selling price. If the institution wants $40 per share, the average price each broker sells his consignment for must average $39 per share. A time limit, call it three days, would also be set.

You can tell that QCOM is an OTC stock because its symbol has more than three letters. If a stock symbol has three or fewer letters, it is a listed stock. The 10 brokers would be competing among themselves to dump the stock. Since daily volume on QCOM stock is around 10 to 15 million shares, there would be some impact on volatility, but it would probably be mild. This is a really key fact about volatility—it measures activity and rate of changes in price, but it tells you nothing, absolutely nothing, about direction. Volatility can increase or decrease as the stock's price moves up or down.

Another key player is the broker-dealer community. They have a stake in high volatility, although they rarely admit it. As long as prices are going up, their retail customers buy. When stocks crash, these same customers sell. Since commissions are paid on both sides, life is sweet for the broker-dealers when volatility is popping like corn in a hot pan. Additionally, they have large, well-paid staffs to do research and hype their favorite stocks, all too often ones that they have an underwriting relationship with.

Underwriting is the process of doing all the work required to take a stock public, which can be a time-consuming but very lucrative process. It includes

- Advising corporations as to the best method to raise long-term capital
- Raising capital through the sale of stock
- Buying securities from the issuing corporation and then reselling them to retail and institutional customers
- Distributing large blocks of stock to other broker-dealers to sell to the public

Broker-dealers doing this kind of business are referred to as *investment bankers*. This market, the IPO market, is extremely profitable and often generates a great amount of volatility. Although new stocks are not optionable, their introduction often adds to the overall volatility of the market. Additionally, the internal trading floors sponsored by broker-dealers add even more to the rate of volatility.

And you, as a retail brokerage customer, have the potential to really affect volatility. At one time in the late 1990s, retail day traders were doing more volume on a daily basis than institutions. Nor should you underestimate all the volume generated by Mr. Joe Average. He is a long-, short-, and intermediate-term buyer and seller in his personal accounts. He participates through IRAs, 401(k)s, and variable annuities. The volume is tremendous and is a truly important part of the forces generating volatility.

Think for a minute about how all these players clash in the stock market. All the active players are aggressively pushing and shoving to get the best price for what they are selling or buying. It reminds me of the bargain basement sale my mother dragged me to at Macy's Department Store in New York City. At a counter full of pillows, sheets, lamps, and socks, hundreds of women converged like vultures on a dead camel in the Sahara Desert. Obviously, I never got over it. Push, shove, trip, punch—whatever it took, these ladies did it to get that perfect pair of socks at the lowest price.

This is where volatility comes from, the imbalances in the supply-demand equation:

- Limited supply = too much demand—the sky's the limit!
- Too much supply = not enough demand—anything can go to zero!

Up and down. Down and up. Boom to bust. Cold to hot. Good to bad. Yin and yang. The daily price range grows larger each day, gaps between prices occur until at some point the energy and the money exceed the limits of orderly trading—then there is a loud boom! It could be on the upside . . . or it could be on the downside.

Traders are driven by fear and greed. You take a 10-lot option position and it rockets into the money. You want more, more, more! You up your 10 lots to a century. You're now sitting on 100 winning positions, and you can hardly talk. In less time than it takes to visit the loo, all your shiny, hot winners are leaking water like the Andrea Doria. Fear encircles you like a shroud. You are sweating like a marathon runner passing mile marker 15 on a hot, humid day. You just want to puke. You must make a decision, but you cannot think straight. Bam! You slam the door on what you thought was your future and offset all 100 of your options at a fraction of what you paid for them. Welcome to the world of trading. The winners gloat; the losers lick their wounds. Then, before you have a chance to catch your breath, it starts all over again.

Your task, if you choose to pursue it, is to make sense of all this commotion and learn to anticipate major increases in volatility and predict the direction in which the market for the underlying stock (and thus its options) is headed next. Then buy some calls if you are bullish or some puts if you are bearish. In the beginning, as you are gaining experience, I recommend that you first explore only the buying side of the options game, not the selling side, because the buyer has a known and

Volatility

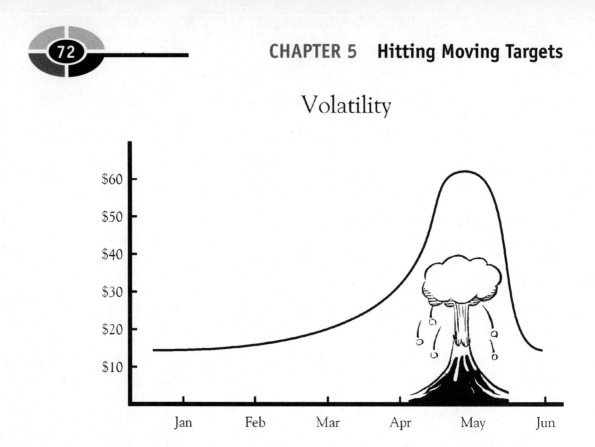

fixed risk factor, that is, the premium and transaction costs. The market can be much crueler to the sellers, whose risk can be, at least theoretically, infinite. The only exception might be selling covered calls for income, which is ahead in the trading strategies section.

Next on the agenda are different types of volatility and their measurement. There is historical volatility and there is implied volatility. *Historical volatility* is simply volatility measured over a specific period of time using actual price data. This can be any period of time: a portion of a trading session, 5 trading days, 10 days, 20 days, 50 days, or 100 days. Roughly 200 trading days represents a year. One could even calculate the volatility over the life of the stock or option in question.

It is often important to compare one period with another. Analysts or traders ask themselves whether the volatility of the current period (trading session, day, week, month, quarter, year, life of contract or entity) is more or less than the volatility of the previous period. Is volatility growing or diminishing? The specific interval the analyst is interested in depends on the trader's style. A day trader cares only about the immediate time frame. How did the stock perform yesterday? So far this week? At the open? (Options traded on listed exchanges have a staggered start.) How is it reacting now compared to the overall market and its sector?

An investor who is looking for a price point to hedge her portfolio may be thinking about buying puts that are one or two striking prices off the current market.

She may study longer periods of time. If she thinks that a price retracement will occur in the next quarter, she would be looking at historical volatility for the last 50 days and comparing it to the last two weeks. Is volatility trending higher? If volatility is still low, she might select puts that are two striking prices out-of-the-money because the risk of a steep drop is less, it gives the stock some room to move, and the puts are cheaper. Her motivation is protection just in case a sudden and deep retrenchment occurs. If the rate of volatility is increasing and the price trend is still up, she might select puts that are just below the market, thinking that a reversal is possible and wanting to be fully protected. In the former case, she may use just enough options to protect her portfolio; in the latter situation, she may throw on a few extra with the thought that when the world gives you lemons, open a fruit stand.

Implied volatility is quite different. It is a guess or an estimate, as opposed to historical fact. It is a prediction of what the volatility of an option or an option strategy you are considering will be in the future. The future could be later in the current trading session or a year from now.

Since it is a guesstimate, what does that tell you? Implied volatility is not a reliable predictor of future volatility. Guess what? Few, except for maybe Nostradamus, make a name for themselves by prophesying. Nevertheless, traders and everyone else try it almost every day just the same. Don't we all speculate on which school to attend, whether to change jobs, who to marry, how to bring up our children, what to invest in our 401(k), and which house or car to buy? We are forever attempting to forecast the future and make decisions based on our shaky guesses. Why should options trading be any different?

Option traders are always expecting historical and implied volatility to converge— like the price of the S&P 500 futures contract at expiration with the S&P 500 cash contract, which must converge, since the futures contract settles in cash. Therefore, when the futures contract expires, it becomes cash. Not so with volatility. Implied volatility is a poor predictor of future historical volatility. It is used because it is all there is and because volatility is the moving force behind pricing.

It is a general rule for option traders that when implied volatility decreases, option sellers feel confident and become aggressive and option buyers run for cover. A second rule is that when volatility increases, option sellers raise their prices and buyers become very aggressive. Rule of thumb 3 states that a cheap option is one with low volatility; an expensive one has high volatility. The term professionals use to quantify the impact of volatility changes on the price of an option is *vega*. There are many Greek letters used in option trading, and you will hear option traders refer to them as "the Greeks."(See Glossary for definitions.)

The method for calculating historical volatility brings the laws of probability into option price modeling. For example, calculating standard deviations from the mean of the actual closing prices of an entity (stock, futures contract, or option) over a specific period of time provides a picture of how widely dispersed closing

prices were or how volatile they were. The first standard deviation from the mean includes 68.3 percent of all the closing prices for the period measured. The second brings the total to 95.4 percent, and the third brings it to 99.7 percent. Normally only the first standard deviation is used because it covers almost 70 percent of the data points.

It is common to create pictorial representations of the data, the famous bell curve. The midpoint of the bell curve is the average or midpoint of the data. The wider or flatter the bell curve becomes to encompass 70 percent of the data indicates how volatile the entity being measured is. Narrower curves mean lower volatility. Let me remind you once again, volatility does not have anything to do with price direction or whether you are gaining or losing money. High volatility means that the price is jumping around wildly, while low volatility equates to an orderly price discovery process.

Once standard deviation has been calculated, it is converted to a percentage and often charted. It is common to talk about volatility, particularly implied volatility, using ranges and approximate values: "Its volatility is roaming around 30 to 50." If you are buying an option expecting the underlying stock to make a large move before expiration, you had better pick one whose volatility is trending higher or have a good reason for the move to occur. Better yet, you should have both factors in your favor because you must forecast both the future volatility and the direction of the underlying entity. Forecasting means making statistically valid estimates of what can be expected. Hopefully, what this will do is put the odds in your favor, giving you an edge, but nothing is guaranteed.

Let me make it perfectly clear: you can calculate the volatility of any price series you want. It does not have to be the closing prices. You can look at all the prices during a day to get a volatility rating for that specific trading session. Closing prices are used in the normal charts you will have access to because they are very important prices. Traders and analysts will calculate the volatility over the period that they are trading, that is, the long or the short term. It is common to create moving averages of weekly volatility, for example, to determine whether volatility is trending higher or lower.

If historical volatility is calculated using actual data, what data would you use to predict implied or future volatility? Naturally, you cannot do a standard deviation from the mean of data that do not exist yet. To get implied volatility, you work backwards, using a formula that calculates what is known as the fair market value of an option. There are several formulas, most based on or a variation of the Black-Scholes formula, which won Professor Scholes the Nobel Prize in 1997. This formula uses five variables:

1. The amount of time to expiration
2. The price of the underlying security

3. The striking or exercise price
4. The carrying charges, such as dividends, interest, and so on
5. Volatility

To get implied volatility from this formula, you simply plug in the first four variables, which you would know for an option under consideration. The formula calculates the fifth, volatility. You can also play what-if games. What if the price of the underlying entity increases or decreases by 10 points? You can change the strike prices to find out which options are over- or underpriced. I always make at least one run using what my analysis predicts. If I am right that the stock I am looking at is going to increase $10 per share in the four weeks left to expiration, what will the price of the option be then? Then I ask, "Is the risk-reward equation satisfactory based on the premium asked by the seller?"

Before you panic about having to learn a ton of mathematics, you have free access to volatility data, both historical and implied, on the Internet and calculators or software programs to run the Black-Scholes models. A word of caution: any sort of formula or calculator you choose to use in the securities business will be helpful only as a guide to what may happen to a security in the future. Markets are the composite of everyone in the world who is trading or holding positions at any one time. The decisions to buy, hold, or sell securities can be rational or irrational. Trade decisions are made for tax reasons, divorces, deaths, estate planning, and other reasons unrelated to profit or gain. Some are rational; others irrational. This simply means that no formula, no computer program, no calculator—no nothing—can predict exactly what is going on in the minds of the tens of thousands of individuals, institutions, and professionals, the informed and the uninformed, who are making those trading decisions.

What you are doing when you calculate volatility or fair market value is taking a snapshot of a fast-moving entity, like a close-up shot of a NASCAR driver streaking by, at one moment in its price discovery history. It does not tell you how the race will end. When you do this, three things can go awry. First, even if you use the third standard deviation, there is a 1 in 369 chance that the next data point will be outside the parameter, or in the fourth standard deviation. These are known as "black swans" or "fat tails," meaning very rare events. But they do happen and I'll describe one later.

Second, you could anticipate a positive move and a negative one occurs. With such things as the War on Terror, the enormous debt load of the United States, the world oil dependency, or the growing economic strength of China and other Third World countries, nothing is certain, and the unexpected must be taken for granted.

Third, you could be using incorrect volatility values. Volatility values change whenever a new data point occurs. The change may be virtually immeasurable if the new data point falls near the mean, but it occurs nonetheless. It is for this reason you must think of price modeling as only a guide and continue to shoot these stills as the process moves toward expiration. Underline the word *process*. For price discovery is indeed an ongoing process.

As mentioned previously, the amount of data used to calculate volatility varies. For example, a week or a month or a year's worth of data can be input into the equation. Also, any particular price, such as the open, high, low, or close, can be used. The standard approach is to use the closing or settlement price, which is the daily price at which the clearinghouses settle all accounts between clearing members for each contract and contract month. The settlement price and the closing price are not always absolutely identical. In other words, there is some discretion required when selecting the closing price. Thousands of trades may be executing at various prices at the moment the bell ending a session rings. On trading floors, the brokers making trades at the bell may not be physically next to each other, and the last trades executed may be at slightly different prices. The best representative price becomes the closing price.

It is also possible that two traders, one using the settlement prices and the other using the opening price, could calculate different volatility factors for the same contract over the same period. The same is true for two analysts where one uses the settlement price for the last 5 days and the other uses 200 days. Obviously, these volatility values will not match.

You must also be aware of the fact that intraday price movements or daily price ranges can be greater than one standard deviation price change on any given day. Your calculation of one standard deviation for a certain contract gives the mean as 50 cents. Your calculations of volatility could be right on the money, yet some of the daily prices could range beyond the mean. There is a lot of good horse sense and Kentucky wind in this work—the pros like to call it experience.

As you will learn, the more you attempt to forecast price trends and pick options, the more intuition plays in the process. If it were possible to create a formula that worked perfectly, the markets would no longer function and someone would be as rich as Croesus!

Quiz

1. General Motors stock is trading at 50. Which option(s) is (are) in- or at-the-money?
   (a) GM January 45 put
   (b) GM February 45 call
   (c) GM April 45 call
   (d) GM June 45 put

2. What is intrinsic value?
   (a) The difference between the premium and the CMV
   (b) The amount by which an option is in-the-money
   (c) The spread between the striking price and the CMV
   (d) The value, if any, at expiration
   (e) All of the above
   (f) None of the above

3. What price would the underlying stock have to reach to be at breakeven if a
   70 June call cost 2 points and the transaction costs were another point?
   (a) 67½
   (b) 73
   (c) 65
   (d) 67

4. The maximum profit from a call is
   (a) strike price plus CMV.
   (b) strike price minus premium plus transaction costs.
   (c) infinity minus premium and transaction costs.
   (d) the difference between CMV and the premium plus
       transaction costs.

5. Traders use the Black-Scholes model to find which of the following?
   (a) Intrinsic value
   (b) Implied volatility
   (c) The theoretical value of an option at some time in the future
   (d) Which options are over- or underpriced

6. Historical volatility provides a clue as to how explosive the price of a stock
   may be in the future.
   (a) True
   (b) False

7. Pricing models provide which of the following?
   (a) A blueprint for a trade
   (b) The best trading strategy
   (c) An estimate of where an option's price will be at some
       time in the future
   (d) Trade entry and exit points

8. The value of price models is that they
   (a) help the analyst define the pricing problem.
   (b) foretell the future for the analyst.

(c) are 100 percent foolproof.

(d) are of no use in projecting future price trends.

9. Most option-pricing models use which of the following variables?
   (a) The amount of time to expiration
   (b) The price of the underlying security
   (c) The striking or exercise price
   (d) The carrying charges, such as dividends, interest, and so on
   (e) Volatility
   (f) The breakeven price

10. The maximum profit for the buyer of a put is
    (a) the premium.
    (b) the CMV minus the premium and transaction costs.
    (c) the strike price minus the premium and transaction costs.
    (d) infinity minus the premium and transaction costs.

Answers

1. b and c; 2. b and d; 3. b; 4. c; 5. b, c, and d; 6. a; 7. c; 8. a; 9. a through e; 10. c.

CHAPTER 6

Getting Down to the Business of Trading

Brokers
Buying
Selling

The trading of listed options is federally regulated, a subject that is discussed in more detail in the next chapter. This means that you must open your stock or futures accounts through licensed brokerage firms. Do you go to the mountain, or do let it come to you? One of the potential dangers is waiting for a broker to come to you rather than initiating the meeting yourself. I say this because there are far too many aggressive options brokers who are more than willing to sell you options that sound super but have as much chance of getting into the money as Congress does of balancing the federal budget. You are ahead of the game if you are the aggressor—researching firms, interviewing brokers, and finding a good brokerage firm that suits your needs and that you have confidence in.

Do you go with a full-service brokerage firm, like Merrill Lynch, or a discount broker, like Scottrade? In the Financial World Village of the Internet, you can open an online account without any direct contact with a broker. Is this good or bad? The answer is very personal and depends on (1) whether you need or want direct contact with a broker to advise and educate you, (2) the honesty and quality of the broker, and (3) what exactly you need from a brokerage firm besides basic clearing and accounting. Do you want trade recommendations and research?

There is as big a difference in the amount of service you get from a brokerage firm as there is in the amount you pay in commissions. Full-service firms provide research, trading ideas, and shared experience. Discount brokers give you access to the research, but you have to know what you are looking for and how to analyze it. With discounters you usually have substantially lower costs and more direct control over your trading. To accept more control, you must be more educated in the theory and mechanics of trading.

If you are currently trading or investing with a firm, does your broker have any experience trading options? Will your broker honestly admit a lack of options experience and risk losing you as a client or sharing commissions with another broker? Will your firm assign another broker to handle your option trades? If your current broker is knowledgeable about options, this is a big plus, especially if you like the firm and have confidence in the broker. But if your broker lacks an understanding of options and tries to talk you out of option trading, you should consider opening a second account somewhere else. Part of the basic training of brokers includes options, so brokers can talk as if they know a lot about options without having trading experience. The customer may not be able to tell if the broker is really qualified to trade options until it is too late, meaning that money has been lost. If you have any questions or doubts, call the office and ask to speak with the manager. The manager should give you some straight answers, but take notes or tape the conversations. If you have any problems later on, or if you think the manager has been less than forthright, you will be able to bring a complaint against the firm and may be able to get compensation if you suffer losses.

If you feel you have to open a new account at another brokerage firm, perhaps one that specializes in option trading, there may be some advantages. For example, opening another account makes is easier to keep your stock trading separate from your option trading, since reading and understanding brokerage statements is never easy. It is very important to set specific goals and be able to measure them, which might be simpler with a separate option account. However, using a second firm could be a problem if you plan to sell covered calls on stocks in your current account. Additionally, you would not be able to use free cash and excess margin in your old account to trade options in your new options account. If selling covered calls is your only or your primary strategy, stay with the firm where the stocks are. If you plan to stay with your current firm, there is nothing stopping you from setting up a second account with that firm to keep your trading separate. If you plan to trade options on futures, you must open a separate futures account. Some firms—Penson Financial Services, for example—allow clients to link stock and futures accounts. This gives you the freedom to move funds to where they are needed, making for a more efficient use of capital.

Judging the honesty and integrity of a broker is not easy. Brokers have very tough conflicts of interest to juggle. Most full-service brokers make their income solely from the commissions they earn from selling trades. If they tried to rely only on filling orders that blew in over the transom from their accounts, they would starve. To make a living, a broker must solicit accounts, trades, and other financial services. Full-service firms spend millions of dollars each year to generate research to convince customers to buy certain products, such as specific options that they recommend. If brokers do not sell these products, they are history. It is not uncommon for brokerage firms to prevent brokers from doing anything themselves, like research and analysis. At the first firm I worked at, brokers were not even allowed price quotation equipment because it interfered with the selling process. The reason for being for most brokers is opening accounts and selling trades. That is the primary profit center for brokerage firms dealing with the public, but it does not mean that they cannot have useful research and a reliable trading record. You must get around the conflict of objectives and evaluate the firm based on your needs. Your goal is to find the best trades; the brokers' objective is to repeat and sell what they were told at the morning's sales meeting. "Caveat emptor!"

Meanwhile, back at the discount brokerage firm, the brokers may be on salary, but they normally get some commission and year-end bonuses based on sales volume. If the firm's customers do not buy any trades from the firm, it goes under. The discounters buy, generate, or provide plenty of research for their customers, but they usually do not make trading recommendations. Either way, directly or indirectly, brokerage firms, whether full-service or discount, depend on customers buying products, just like any other business. This simply means that both face the same conflict of interest to varying degrees.

The bottom line is that you cannot trade any security without a brokerage firm because it is the link to the clearinghouse. The clearinghouse processes all the trades executed by all the players—retail customers, institutional clients, hedge funds, professional traders, and so on. Everyone who is trading has an account with a brokerage firm. The firm contracts with a clearinghouse to match every buy or sell trade with the other side of the trade. Overnight millions and millions of trades are matched up, funds are transferred, ownership changes hands, and the accounting is ready by sunup. The results are at your brokerage firm for you to inspect via computer link in the morning. You can switch on your computer and see exactly where your account stands. This includes all trades executed, your current portfolio, profit or loss, trade history, excess capital, buying power, and whether you owe your brokerage firm additional funds. This happens every night, rain or shine, and you should always have an accurate accounting of your funds and assets each morning. On rare occasions, there will be problems or there will be something about your account that you do not understand. If this happens, call your account representative before doing anything else, especially trading. In other words, you must check your account regularly; especially the day after any activity takes place. Several of the better online firms provide excellent back office software. For example, you can run profit-loss studies over any period, retrieve statements, check transaction records, download trading activity to a spreadsheet for analysis, do cash flow analysis, retrieve 1099s or other tax documents, and do just about any accounting required to track your progress and pay your taxes.

Chain of Responsibility

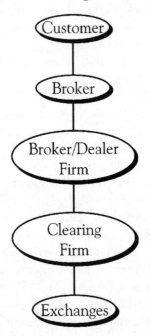

The way I look at the need for a full-service or discount/online brokerage firm is strictly personal. If you feel that you need a full-service brokerage house, you should probably pass on option trading. I think you must make a commitment to take the time to do all the homework yourself in order to be a trader of any kind. Estate planning, long-term asset allocation, discretionary money management, and so on—these are the province of a full-service firm. If all you want to do with options is to hedge your portfolio against downside risk or execute a covered call strategy, work with your broker to get it done. Actively trading options, in my opinion, is something you should do yourself.

On to some basics—a stock option gives you a hold on a stock certificate for 100 shares. Stock certificates are fungible, meaning that they all are identical and freely transferable, as are the options on them. This is a requirement if any exchange is to function. If the contracts or certificates were not exactly the same, it would be impossible for the clearinghouses to match up millions and millions of trades each night.

The expiration dates of stock options are set up automatically and published by the Options Clearing Corporation. The expiration dates for options have three cycles:

1. January, April, July, and October cycle
2. February, May, August, and November cycle
3. March, June, September, and December cycle
4. Plus the two months nearest the month closest to expiration

For regular options, the longest term never exceeds nine months. This means that the normal cycle is usually three to four months because there is usually little trading in the distant (to expiration) months, as opposed to the nearby months. Trading activity, and thus volatility, increases as the expiration date approaches. The last day of trading for all exchange-traded options is the end of the trading day on the third Friday of the month of expiration. The actual date of expiration is noon on the Saturday after the last trading day. There are also exchange-traded stock options with expiration dates extending out for years. These are called LEAPS and are treated separately in this text.

Stock prices ebb and flow like the ocean's tides, as do the prices of the options associated with them. The price of an option is the only element of the contract left to negotiation. To illustrate, I will use a stock with the symbol WIX that is trading at 25, or $25 per share (see Figure 6-1). The high reaches 40 and the low 18, a $22 trading range. Since WIX trades below $35 per share, the striking price intervals are 2½ points. Stocks over $35 have striking prices at 5-point intervals. All the basic specifications for exchange-traded options are set by the Options Clearing Corporation, and the actual options (months and prices) that are available to trade at any one time are selected by the options committee of the exchange on which the options are traded based on the demand of the exchange's members, which reflects the public's trading activity. I will use the following striking prices for WIX: 22½, 20, and 17½ on the downside and 27½, 30, and 32½ on the upside.

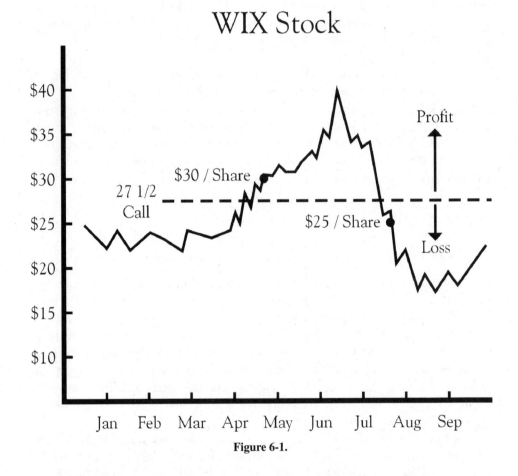

Figure 6-1.

The striking price is the price at which the underlying entity transfers to the holder of the option if the option is exercised. Therefore, if the price of WIX increases to 30, the holder of a June 27½ call option could exercise that option and buy the stock, which is now worth $30, for $27.50. If WIX continued to rise and this person continues to hold the shares, the trader makes additional profits. If WIX drops to 25, the trader is down 2½ dollars per share. The owner of a long-call option assumes a stock long position upon exercising an option. If a long put is exercised, the option holder takes a short position. Upon exercising an option, the trader is required to meet the margin requirements for the position established based on the stock's price and the number of options exercised.

Another alternative for the option trader is to sell an offsetting option and pocket the $250 gross profit. The premium and two commissions (one for buying the original option and one for offsetting it) plus exchange fees (usually inconsequential) are deducted from this amount. Some traders prefer this approach because it requires much less capital. For example, the cost or premium may be $50 (fifty cents per share) plus two commissions at $25 each (total cost $100), for a net profit of $150 on the $100 investment over a relatively short period of time. Note that each time I discuss selling existing long options, I use the word *offsetting*. This is important because selling, shorting, granting, or writing options is an entirely different concept. Offsetting means selling an option that is the same as the one you bought or buying back an option that is the same as the one you sold. To offset the June WIX 27½ call, you sell a June WIX 27½ call. The calls are identical except that the price increases or decreases as the price of the underlying stock moves higher or lower.

An expensive mistake some newbie traders make is offsetting a call by buying a put, thinking that they are the opposite of one another. The sad trader ends up with two positions in his or her account instead of being flat. When you place an order to close an existing option position, check the box marked offsetting if you are trading online, or if you use a broker, begin the order by stating that you are offsetting an existing position. Thus, there is no confusion. If you just say you want to sell one June WIX 27½ call, the brokerage firm may interpret this as meaning that you wish to write the option. As you will soon see, there is a big difference.

To summarize, a call gives you the right—but not the obligation—to take a long position in an underlying entity at the striking price prior to the expiration date. A put gives you the right—but not the obligation—to assume a short position in an underlying entity at the striking price prior to the expiration.

- Long call = the right to buy a long position
- Long put = the right to buy a short position
- Short call = the obligation to sell/deliver a long position
- Short put = the obligation to sell/deliver a short position

Getting back to the example: What do you do when your option becomes near at-the-money? WIX is at 24, and you are holding a 25 WIX June call, only $1 out-of-the-money. If you do nothing, the option expires worthless and you lose your premium. If you offset, you might not break even on this trade because the option is out-of-the-money, there is only some time value left, and there is another commission due if you offset it. The first thing to do is check the price of the option, to be sure. You paid 50 cents. Has the price moved higher for any reasons? Any value it has, other than intrinsic value, is time value. Has the market given up on it because volatility has subsided, forcing the market lower? How much time is remaining? If it is May 15, you have approximately six weeks left to expiration. What is the trend of WIX, the stock sector that WIX is part of, the overall market, and volatility? Is the trend of the market strong, or is it fading? When you bought a call, you were bullish about the prospects for WIX. Is your outlook the same now? Are you mildly, moderately, or wildly bullish on the prospects for WIX? Has anything changed in the market to make you want to bail out and hope to break even or just salvage a portion of the premium paid for the option?

The most important factor is any change in the volatility of the underlying entity and the option itself. Check the Volatility Index (VIX). This index represents the implied volatility of a basket of widely traded options on the S&P 500 Index. Option traders use it to help them determine the direction of the market. A low VIX (a range of 20 to 25) indicates that traders have become somewhat uninterested in the market and generally is the precursor to a selloff. The value of the VIX increases as the market goes south and decreases when it is heading north. In other words, it moves inversely to the market. On some charts, you will see it printed in reverse for this reason. It moves inversely to the market because the higher the risk in an underlying entity, the higher the implied volatility of that stock's options. The higher the implied volatility, the higher the price of the option goes. This is particularly true for puts. As you should know from our previous discussion of volatility, implied volatility has more to do with risk than with the size or direction of the upcoming price move. So if you own an option that is at-the-money and the VIX is on the rise, you know to hold onto that option.

One other consideration if you reach the expiration date and your option is still not in-the-money—do you want to roll it over? If you have a June option, you can offset it for its current market value and buy an August option of the same class. You would do this if you felt very strongly that your analysis was still correct, but you just ran out of time.

Your alternatives are

1. Holding the option to expiration
2. Exercising it to assume a position in the underlying entity
3. Offsetting it to claim the current market value, which may or may not result in a profit
4. Rolling it over into an option in a more distant month

Now I want to describe the people who sell, write, or grant options. These are the folks who sell the options.

While the buyer of an option has the right but not the obligation to exercise the option (put or call) in question, the seller must stand ready to deliver the underlying entity from the moment he or she sells it until noon on the third Saturday of the month of expiration, not the closing bell on the preceding Friday. On that Saturday, all the accounts are settled among the brokerage firms, and these firms often, because their clearing rate is so low, deal in options that are barely in-the-money.

To make life even more interesting for the seller, on most exchanges options to be exercised are assigned randomly, rather than on a first-in, first-out regimen. You could be assigned shortly after writing an option or even on the Monday after an option that you wrote expired, if someone exercised the preceding Saturday. It is rare, but it can happen. Assignment means that when someone exercises an option, someone (a firm or individual) must fulfill or deliver the position. If the assignment is on a call, a long position is delivered; if it is on a put, a short position is delivered.

The best way to understand the difference between buying and selling options is to think about the risk parameters. (You may want to refer back to Figure 3-2, "Basic Put Option.") As you already know, the buyer's risk is limited to the premium and transaction costs. The seller, on the other hand, is facing much more risk. On a put, how far can the underlying entity plunge? The answer, of course, is to zero. If the seller writes a put with a striking price of 20 and the underlying entity becomes worthless, you can bet the farm that all the put options will be exercised. The maximum loss on this example would be $2,000 (100 shares $\times$ $20) per option written plus transaction costs less the premium paid to the seller. The formula is: striking price − exercise price + premium received − transaction costs per contract $\times$ number of options $\times$ 100.

What about a call? Using the same striking price of $20, the underlying security could go to infinity. (See Figure 3-1, "Basic Call Option.") The extremes of zero and infinity are theoretical limits. Nevertheless, a stock moving $10, $15, or even $25 in a single day happens frequently and would result in losses to the seller of $1,000, $1,500, or $2,500 per option sold. The futures markets have, as you will learn in a later chapter, daily trading limits on how much certain commodities can move up or down in a single trading session. When these limits are reached, trading halts. For example, the limit on hogs is $800 per contract, and I have seen them make six limit moves on consecutive trading days, which would be a loss of $4,800 per contract for a seller of the options. When trading stops, the option writer does not have the right to exercise the option and cannot deliver the position to the buyer. This right is the buyer's—no transactions occur during a halt in trading. It is worth noting that professional option sellers deal in thousand of option contracts at a time.

Most sellers diversify to help manage their risk, but my point is: who has the greater risk? More importantly, who has the greater profit potential? The buyer's reward for a call is from the striking price to infinity, and the buyer of a put has the potential from the striking price to zero. The risk in both cases is limited to the premium. The seller's risk has already been described, and his or her reward never exceeds the premium. The one who takes the greatest risk gets the least reward.

Sounds a little backward to me, what about you? The irony, as I mentioned in an earlier chapter, is that the sellers normally make the most money in the options business.

To deal with all this risk, traders have but one line of attack—especially anyone new to trading—and that is to sustain only small losses. Think about it. There are

The Essence of Money Management

Big Profit

Small Profit

Breakeven

Small Loss

Big Loss

only five outcomes to any investment or trade. You can make a large or a small profit, break even, or take a large or a small loss. The essence of money management is to avoid being blown out of the market, so that you can play another day. Your objective is to get yourself in the right place at the right time to become a net winner big time. The flip side is that the deeper you dig a hole, the harder it is to climb out. I call it the Sisyphus syndrome. See Table 6-1.

The professional option trader avoids the knockout blow. You can live and survive with the other four outcomes, but when you get too far behind, the pressure becomes extreme. And scared money never wins because it puts too much pressure on the trader. There is no wiggle room left. All of a sudden, every trade must be a winner in order to survive, and the odds of that happening get slimmer and slimmer the deeper and deeper you go. Losing is as much a part of option trading as winning, but poor management of it is often the most important component retarding success. Keep Sisyphus in mind. When he tried to climb the hill, the ancient Greek gods knocked him down just as he was about to reach the top. That was his eternal punishment—do not let it be yours.

The concept of keeping losses under control has always been a part of option trading, but it has often been misused and abused. By that I mean that when you buy an option, you know what your downside risk is; it is the amount of the premium and transaction costs. As long as you do not exercise the option, you will never have any margin calls, and your loss is fixed. Options must be bought in a margin account, but they are not marginable. In your trading account, long options are a cash item. You must pay the entire premium by the day after your order is executed. This is known in the securities industry as T + 1. T stands for Treasury Department, which sets margin limits and rules.

The reason I said that the idea of buying an option because one knows the maximum risk was not one of the best parts of the option business is that unscrupulous option brokers have twisted this concept to sell worthless options—options that have only a very remote chance of ever getting in-the-money. The broker raises the customer's greed level by exaggerating the profit potential of the trade and then hammers away at the fixed risk. "The new product this company is coming out with is bound to run its stock price up $20 or more a share. That's a profit of $2,000 on each option. The premium is only $1.50 per share. I can get you 100 contracts at that price, making you a serious player in this stock. For $15,000, you'll make $200,000 or more! Remember, that's all you invest—no margin calls, no additional contributions." What the broker neglects to tell the prospect is that a $20 move is very rare for the stock in question and that if this broker knows about the new product, the rally he or she is talking about is built into the price by the time you hear about it.

Worse yet, if the customer tries to get away by telling the broker that she has only $5,000 to invest, the broker sells her a deep out-of-the-money option priced at

Table 6-1. The Sisyphus Syndrome.

% to Break Even vs.	% Loss
5¼	5
25	20
43	30
67	40
100	50
233	70
900	90
You're out!	100

50 cents per share. If the first option was away from the money, the second is even farther away. The odds of either of these options making the customer money are remote. Nevertheless, there have always been buyers for them when the commissions paid to brokers have been high enough to get them to go over the line when selling these options. There are telephone and mailing lists of people who repeatedly fall for these schemes, and these lists are shared and traded among unscrupulous brokers. Don't ever get on one of these lists.

Another little thing you need to know is as you enter the options market is the difference between American- and European-style options. American-style options are exercisable any time prior to the expiration date. European-style options permit the trader to exercise them only at the expiration date, not before. Some European-style options are sold on U.S. exchanges, so just be alert.

Quiz

1. What should you look for in a broker/brokerage firm?
    (a) An attractive receptionist
    (b) A swank office

(c) Persuasive sales literature

(d) Research, recommendations, a strong back office, reliable accounting, great online resources, honest and intelligent brokers

2. Should you hire a full-service, discount, or online brokerage firm?
    (a) Full-service
    (b) Discount
    (c) Online
    (d) Direct access
    (e) The decision rests on your needs and skill level

3. Stock options expire
    (a) when trading dries up.
    (b) at noon on the Saturday after the third Friday of the month of expiration.
    (c) on the third Friday of the month of expiration.
    (d) at a date set by the Options Clearing Corporation.

4. Options become more valuable when
    (a) the volatility of the underlying entity increases.
    (b) they get close to expiration.
    (c) they are highlighted on CNBC.
    (d) demand slows.

5. Most options expire worthless.
    (a) True
    (b) False

6. Winning in the options game often means
    (a) taking tips from brokers who call.
    (b) buying only calls.
    (c) surviving long enough to hit the mother lode.
    (d) reading this book twice.

7. A smart option trader never exercises an option.
    (a) False
    (b) True

8. Sometimes the hardest part of option trading is
    (a) being able to offset a position.
    (b) finding good trades.
    (c) opening an account.
    (d) spending your profits.

9. Which two groups make the most money from options?
   (a) Individual traders
   (b) Farmers trading options on farm commodities
   (c) Brokers selling options to individuals
   (d) Sellers of options

10. What is the difference between American- and European-style options?
    (a) European-style options are priced in Eurodollars.
    (b) American-style options do not include options on foreign currencies.
    (c) European-style options can be exercised only at expiration.
    (d) American-style options can be exercised only at expiration

Answers

1. d; 2. e; 3. b; 4. a; 5. a; 6. c; 7. a; 8. a; 9. c and d; 10. c.

CHAPTER 7

Who You Do Business With

Regulators

Brokerage Firms

Arbitrators

Back Offices

In the last chapter, I discussed working with brokerage firms and opening trading accounts. Now I want to give you a little background on how it all works so that you know how you, as an individual option trader, fit into the grand scheme of the securities industry. This way, you will know your rights as an options player.

Following the Crash of 1929, the federal government assumed regulation of the securities business. There was a general feeling that speculators were partially responsible for causing the crash and that the uncontrollable craze for trading had overwhelmed the country, resulting in excess leveraging. Options came under heavy fire, and it was not until April 1973 that an individual trader could once again buy a listed option.

The first piece of legislation enacted was the Securities Act of 1933. It was a sweeping piece of legislation that took control of all securities and required issuers of securities to provide sufficient information so that investors would know exactly what they were buying. Additionally, all the key facts regarding new stock issues were to be reviewed by government officials, printed in a prospectus, and registered with the government. It also outlawed fraud committed in connection with any underwriting activities, mentioned previously in the discussion of investment banking and the art of taking private companies public, or IPOs (initial public offerings). The IPO market is the primary market, and the secondary market is the stocks already trading on the exchanges.

Another perceived evil of the time was the intermingling of commercial banking with the stock brokerage business, especially during the underwriting process. Therefore, a law entitled the Glass-Steagall Act of 1933, often referred to as the Glass Act or the Banking Act, was passed. It forbade banks from conducting underwriting business and investment banking and brokerage firms from opening deposit accounts and making commercial loans. In recent years, this piece of legislation has been rescinded.

Since the Securities Act of 1933 required that the government oversee the securities business, it dawned on our elected officials a year later that an organization should probably be created to do just that. The Securities Exchange Act of 1934 created the Securities and Exchange Commission, the famous and infamous SEC. The most important stipulation of this act was that the SEC would also regulate the secondary trading of securities.

The Securities Act of 1933 was followed by the Maloney Act. It provides for self-regulatory organizations (SROs) to assist in policing the industry. The ultimate regulatory agency for securities is, of course, the SEC. The Commodities Futures Trading Commission (CFTC) was formed later to be the SEC's counterpart for commodity and futures trading. The New York Stock Exchange became the SRO for brokerage firms and their employees registered with it; the National Association of Securities Dealers (NASD) supervises all other broker-dealers and their agents (brokers and other employees) who are not registered with the NYSE. Futures traders and firms register with the National Futures Association (NFA). To conduct securities business, firms and individuals must register with one of these bodies.

How does all this legislation affect you and your little option-trading account? Keep in mind that besides these initial laws, there have been thousands and thousands of additional laws, regulations, legal precedents, and amendments enacted over the last several decades. The initial impact on you is the account paperwork that you must complete before you can make your first trade, as discussed earlier. That paperwork requires that you supply your brokerage firm with the certain information. The broker you deal with is, under penalties ranging from fines to being barred from the industry, required to "know" his or her customers—not, of course, in the biblical sense, but to know their goals and their financial fitness for the type of trading and investment strategies they plan to utilize.

Regulatory Chain

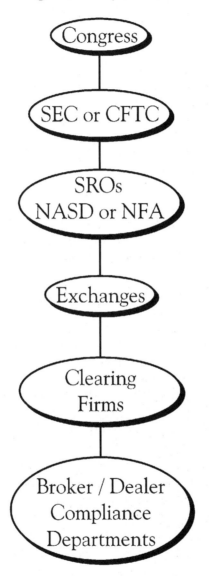

Therefore, you will be asked to complete a statement of your investment objectives—are they long- or short-term, are they speculative or are you seeking preservation of capital or income? The broker has the responsibility of matching your investing or trading activities to your objectives. This restricts the type of option trading you are allowed to do. For example, if you state on the account forms that you seek conservative investment strategies, selling naked options is out, since that is a high-risk strategy. You would be approved for writing covered calls to generate income from existing assets. This strategy is suitable for a conservative investment objective. Before opening an account, give careful consideration to exactly what you want to do. If you do not, you may not be approved for the type of trading you wish to do. On the other hand, if you bluff your way through and get approved for a strategy that is beyond your trading capabilities, you might regret it. Option strategies are rated as follows from least to most risky:

1. Buying long calls and puts or writing covered calls
2. Combination trades, such as simple spreads, straddles, and so on
3. Multiple-option trades, like butterfly spreads, condors, straddles, and complicated spreads
4. Naked long or short option positions

The higher the risk factor, the greater your net worth has to be. Brokerage firms know the financial problems that result when someone gets in over his or her head and cannot bail him- or herself out. If that happens, it becomes the firm's problem, and firms want to avoid that at all costs.

It is for this reason that the brokerage firm needs to know a lot about your financial situation. Do you plan and can you afford to speculate heavily? *Heavily* is a relative term. With one firm, it might be 10-lot option trades; with another, 100. If you indicate that you trade in high volume, you must make an initial deposit to justify your intention of being a serious player. The firm has a stake in your buying power because it stands behind all your buying and selling. If you default on a margin call, the firm must pay its clearinghouse, which in turn pays your commitment to whoever is on the other side of your trades. This is a critical part of the securities business. It protects the integrity of your trades and the contra side of your trades. If you offset 10 options, you expect to get the money deposited in your account by the next day. You do not expect an IOU or an e-mail saying that the buyer of your contracts failed to pay, so the options are back in your account. You want all transactions executed seamlessly. All the industry players in the chain (brokerage firms, clearinghouses, exchanges, and so on) step in to protect the integrity of the market whenever it is threatened. Now, if you are the one who defaults, your firm will make good for you and then come after you for payment. The person on the other side of your trade will not be aware of any problems. Isn't this the way you would want it if someone defaulted on one of your trades?

What happens if the defaults are so big that it bankrupts your brokerage firm? Where would you be then? This is when the securities industry's Seventh Cavalry, known as the SIPC, appears on the horizon and rides in just in time to save the day.

Pyramid of Risk

Highest

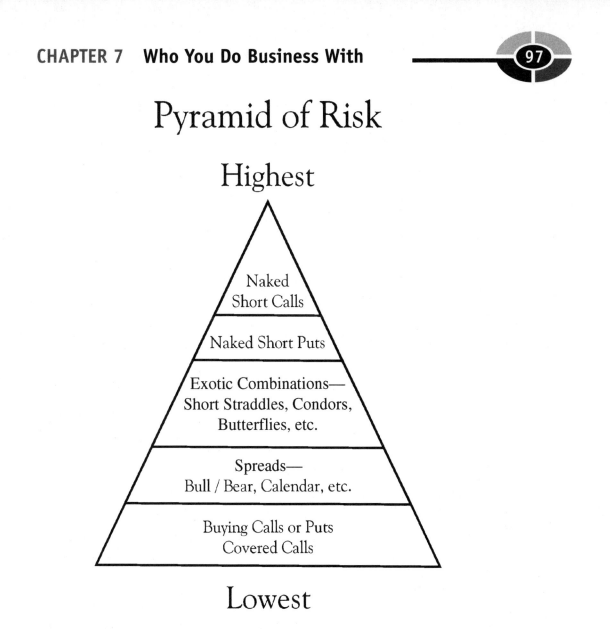

Naked
Short Calls

Naked Short Puts

Exotic Combinations—
Short Straddles, Condors,
Butterflies, etc.

Spreads—
Bull / Bear, Calendar, etc.

Buying Calls or Puts
Covered Calls

Lowest

The Securities Investor Protection Corporation's function is to step in as quickly as possible when member firms, which all regular trading brokerage firms are required to be, get into financial trouble. The SIPC assumes management of the firms, gets all the trading straightened out, and refunds money to customers. It gets its funding from annual assessments on members and has the authority to borrow additional money from the U.S. Treasury.

All brokerage firms are required to file monthly financial reports to their SRO and must maintain funding sufficient to handle the type and size of business they conduct. Whenever a firm drops near or below the minimum capital requirements, its SRO notifies the SIPC and the SEC or CFTC. From this point on, the firm is closely monitored, which may even include daily posting of its net capitalization.

If your firm is taken over by the SIPC, your account will be covered up to $500,000, with cash claims not to exceed $100,000. On top of that, most brokerage firms or their clearing firm carry additional insurance, often up to $10 or $20 million per account. The really good news is that no retail customer has lost money in the securities industry as a result of the bankruptcy of a brokerage firm.

Besides information about your income, net worth, and profession, the brokerage firm is required to know if you are old enough to legally open an account in the state in which you are living, which could be 18 or 21, and when you must begin taking payments from your IRA, assuming that you have one now or will have one in the future. Therefore, they ask for your date of birth. Additionally, the firm is required by industry regulations to know if you are married and have dependents. This may come into play if you die or get divorced while trading with the firm.

Then the firm needs to know something about your previous trading history. Basically, it is important for it to know how experienced you are in order to determine which option strategies you will be permitted to use. Once it knows what you wish to do with options and how much experience you have, the firm tells you which strategies you are approved to trade with that firm. If you are not satisfied, you can protest to the senior registered options principal (SROP) or the compliance registered options principal (CROP), which are the two options supervisors at every brokerage house. You may be able to convince one of these people to allow you to trade the way you wish, or they may refuse. It is not uncommon for a brokerage firm to ask you to trade for a few months, and then it will review your situation and upgrade it if the firm is confident that you know what you are doing. You must accept the firm's judgment; after all, it is the firm's money as well as yours that is at risk. You always have the choice of trying another firm.

In the course of opening an option account, you will receive a small booklet ("Characteristics and Risks of Standardized Options") that describes options and their risks. You need to read this material thoroughly and sign a statement that you have read it and understood it. If you do not return a signed statement to that effect within 15 days, the firm can trade your account to liquidation. That simply means that it can sell everything in your account and put your account on hold until it gets the signed document. This is a SRO regulation, not something that firms do arbitrarily. The information in the booklet is for your protection. It tells you how options work and all the risks you face in trading them. Read it and take its message to heart.

One other thing you will be asked to do is select the type of account you plan on opening. Will it be an individual, joint, corporate, or some other type of account? If you select one that includes other individuals, these other people must also supply detailed information about their finances and trading experience. Then all parties sign the documents and promise to keep the firm informed of any pertinent changes that take place in your circumstances. If you are opening an account for an under-aged son or daughter, called a custodial account because someone other than the beneficial owner has custody, there are some questions as to whether options can be traded in such an account. The reason is that any asset in a custodial account must be in the name of the beneficial owner, your son or daughter, for example, and options are only registered in street name because they are not permanent assets, since they expire. Street name means the name of the firm with which you have an account. Be careful with joint accounts because all owners can trade, not just you. With corporate accounts, be sure to designate who is authorized to trade.

Street name is used particularly in trading accounts where the stocks will be held only for short periods of time. Holding a stock certificate in your own name, rather than in street name, requires that your name be registered as the owner in the books of the transfer agent for that stock. When that is done, the certificates are sent to you for safekeeping. This process takes time; also, there are no certificates for option contracts. As you learned earlier, buying and selling options is part of trading rather than investing. Neither options nor futures have certificates, and both expire.

There is some sunshine behind all these regulatory clouds. First, all the required information about your financial status and securities trading experience is necessary for the brokerage firm, particularly your broker, his or her supervisor, and the firm's compliance officer, to determine if you are qualified to do the type of trading you want to do. Again, the firm is financially responsible to its clearing firm and the exchanges if you get in over your head and cannot pay for the securities you buy.

Equally, if the firm lets you execute certain types of trades that are beyond your experience and you lose money, it could have a compliance problem. For example, suppose you state on your account application that you have little or no experience trading options, yet you request that you be permitted to sell naked options. You then write five naked calls with a $15 strike price. You go on vacation for a week, and you return to find that the stock is at $40. Your voice mail, mail, and e-mail boxes are stuffed with demands for additional margin. You had opened the account with $2,000, and now you have been exercised upon and you have a $10,500 debit ($25 gain in the price of the stock × 100 shares per option × 5 options less your original deposit of $2,000).

You don't have the money. You are living on maxed-out credit cards. A civil liberties lawyer gets hold of you and asks if you were warned how risky the naked call strategy is, and of course you say no. The lawyer files a complaint against the brokerage firm. It goes to arbitration, and you win. The arbitration panel rules against the brokerage firm because you should not have been permitted to trade such a risky strategy. The firm is out the $10,500 plus a few thousand to pay for the arbitration hearing.

One caveat: You had a responsibility to always let your firm know how it could get hold of you in a trading emergency. You did not give it a way of alerting you when the trade went sour, and this would be part of its defense. As a rule regarding trading accounts, take all your open positions flat before you go on vacation or someplace where you are out of touch. You and your broker will sleep much better, and you will find your vacation more enjoyable.

Something that is often overlooked in these arbitration or compliance hearings is that the client was repeatedly told about the risk. The client receives a booklet on the characteristics of option trading that describes the risk in very vivid terms, and the client must sign a statement indicating that he or she read and understood it. There are additional warnings on the various account documents that the client signed. In other words, there is no excuse for the client not realizing the financial risk he or she faces.

Why didn't the brokerage prevail in this arbitration after providing so many warnings to the client? This is a key question as far as understanding what protection all the thousands and thousands of pages of regulations in the NASD and the NFA compliance manuals provide. The firm lost because it did not enforce the NASD regulations. It never should have approved a novice trader for such a high-risk strategy. Nor was the client financially qualified for that type of trading.

In my mind, the client was also at fault. He traded recklessly. This person had no business trading naked options and did not take the time to understand what he was getting into. He was lazy and careless. The trader probably acted on the urging of a friend or business acquaintance who sold him on the idea of the trade by raising his greed level and convincing him that the trade was a sure thing. The firm opened the account because it was greedy for commissions or its compliance department was careless or nonexistent.

What would have happened if the client had been qualified? Let's say she had been trading options for five years and had a hefty net worth. In this case, the situation probably would not have gotten so far out of hand. First, experienced traders never get out of touch with their brokers when they have open positions. As soon as the call owner exercises an option, the option writer receives a margin call demanding money to buy five long positions. If the writer does not send the funds after repeated attempts, the brokerage firm trades the account to liquidation, selling asset in the account. Then it buys the positions in the writer's name and delivers them to the buyer. When you sign account papers, you give your brokerage firm the right to do this. So read the paperwork closely. If the assets in the account are not sufficient to satisfy a margin call, the firm demands the rest. If the margin call is not honored, how to proceed is at the discretion of the brokerage

Who backs up trades?

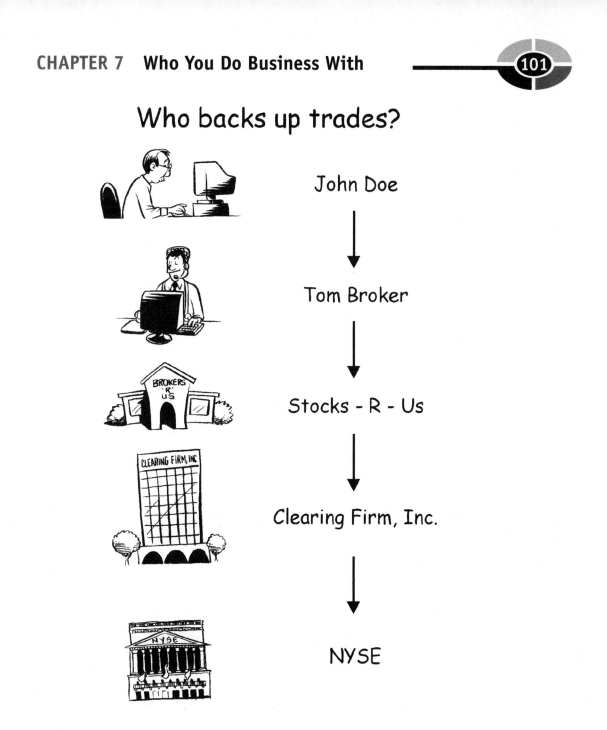

John Doe

Tom Broker

Stocks - R - Us

Clearing Firm, Inc.

NYSE

firm. Does it sue? Does it turn the problem over to a lawyer or collection agency? Does it do nothing? It is the firm's decision. The least firms do is to file the client's name in a special database that tracks deadbeats and clients who sue their broker. Many firms check this database before opening an account, which means that this trader will have a hard time opening another account with a reputable firm in the future.

What if both parties were at fault to one degree or another and the complaint went to arbitration? For instance, the firm opened an account for a person who looked to be unqualified on the account papers. That person defaulted on a trade, losing a substantial amount of money. In the process of preparing for arbitration, the brokerage firm discovers that the trader was indeed qualified, having over ten years' experience, including three years trading naked calls.

How would the arbitration panel rule on this type of case? The three-person panel, by the way, is composed of securities industry professionals, including retired brokerage executives and attorneys practicing or retired from security law. These are professionals who are familiar with securities law and compliance regulations. Since both parties are at fault—the firm should not have opened the account based on the facts on the account papers, and the trader falsified the information given to the firm and was in actuality qualified to trade naked options—the arbitration could hold either party liable or could split the blame.

Arbitration panels can be somewhat arbitrary in their decisions. Even the rules governing the proceedings are much more flexible than those governing a trial. Both parties are permitted legal representation, but it is not required. The rules covering evidence are somewhat casual compared to those in a formal trial. Generally, the industry professionals who sit in judgment tend to be tough on those in the industry who appear before them. Retail customers have a good chance of winning if—and this is a big if—they are innocent. But simply losing money is not a reason to ask for recourse—it is a rule of life when one trades options.

There are some compliance violations that a retail customer can be virtually sure of winning. For example, unauthorized trading, if the client can clearly prove it, is one that the client wins hands down. This is where the broker trades the client's account without his or her permission in order to run up commissions.

Another violation along that line is churning. Here the broker trades the account excessively with the client's permission. In these cases, it is common for the client to have given the broker discretion to trade the account. Discretion means that the client signs a limited power of attorney giving the broker the authority to trade on his or her behalf. The broker abuses this authority by trading his brains out in order to get commissions. The problem is usually determining how much trading is too much trading because the broker often provides some type of written plan to the client describing a very aggressive strategy, such as day-trading options on or at the days just before expiration, when the liquidity and volatility are highest. It is then up to a panel, usually along with a troop of expert witnesses, to decide how much trading is too much and when active trading is churning. This sounds simple, but it is not always when you get two attorneys in a room together. You should also be aware that when you sign most account papers, they include a "predispute arbitration agreement" binding you to arbitration if you have a beef with your broker.

What if you disagree with the arbitration panel's ruling or if your complaint is more serious than what normally goes to arbitration? What other venues are open? You can always sue. Most good lawyers can get around the binding arbitration agreement. It is federal, and so they sue in the state court system. Both the NASD for stock option complaints and the NFA for options on futures complaints have more structured and formal venues for settling major complaints. The first thing to do is to study the Web sites of the applicable SRO, which includes detailed explanations of its complaint procedure. Written material is also available, such as "A Guide to Arbitration of Customer Complaints" from the NASD.

The NFA, for example, offers three levels of complaint resolution. The voluntary is used for claims under $10,000, the summary for complaints for over $10,000, and the formal for major complaints. Each level is more formal than the previous one, until the formal procedure resembles a full-blown trial. If the complaint is still not satisfied, the complainant can appeal to the CFTC or an appropriate court of law.

The case you will most likely lose is one in which you were fully aware of what you were doing, but you lost money. Losing is part of the normal business of trading or investing. You must accept that before you enter the arena. On the other hand, there are a lot of rules and regulations to protect you from unscrupulous brokers and brokerage firms.

You may be wondering why a margin agreement is needed in the first place. All you plan to do is buy a few calls or puts in your stock account. You know that there is no margining of long option positions because they are a wasting asset that eventually expires worthless if it is not offset or exercised. Therefore, long option positions are basically cash transactions. The reason for a margin account is that the owner of an option has the right to exercise the option. When and if he or she does so, a position is delivered to the account. At that moment, there may not be enough cash in the account to pay for the stock. Therefore, the stock goes into a margin account and a margin call is issued. Because you are opening a margin trading account, you will be required to deposit a minimum of $2,000.

Trading on margin can be a little tricky, especially when it comes to options, so let me give you a quick primer. As you know, there are two basic types of accounts—cash and margin. Not all securities can be bought in a cash account, and not all securities can be margined. As you just learned, options cannot be bought in a cash account, and the following securities cannot be margined:

- Common and preferred stock not designated by the Federal Reserve Board (FRB).
- Rights, as in the right to buy a new issue of stock in proportion to the percent of ownership the investor already has, thus avoiding his or her ownership being diluted. These can be bought and sold, but obviously not on margin.
- Insurance contracts.
- IPOs for the first 30 days.

Some securities are exempt from Regulation T, the regulation giving control of margins to the Federal Reserve Board at the Treasury Department. The exempt securities are

- U.S. Treasury bills, notes, and bonds
- Government agency securities
- Municipal securities
- Corporate straight debt (nonconvertible to stock) securities

The fact that they are exempt from Reg. T does not mean that these securities cannot be margined. It means that they can be sold on margin, but that the Reg. T requirement, presently 50 percent, is not binding. Any arrangement that is acceptable to the seller is permissible. If the seller is a member of the NASD or NYSE, the arrangement must not exceed what is called maintenance margin, which is less than 50 percent.

So far, you know that in order to trade options, you must open a margin account, but that long calls and puts are not marginable. Therefore, what can be margined? Here are the basic rules:

1. Stocks are marginable up to 50 percent. This occurs in your account if you exercise a long option. The 50 percent rule can be changed at the whim of the Fed.
2. Long options are not marginable.
3. Short options:
   a. The margin on covered short options is zero. Here you are writing an option on a stock that you already own, so you are 100 percent hedged.
   b. The margin on an uncovered or naked equity option equals 20 percent of the current market value (CMV) plus the premium and plus or minus the amount the option is in- or out-of-the-money.
   c. The margin on an uncovered nonequity option equals 15 percent of the CMV plus premium plus or minus the amount the option is in- or out-of-the-money.

d. An alternative for options that are well into the money is 10 percent of the CMV plus the premium.

The purpose of requiring margin money on a trade is the same as that of asking someone for a security bond when entering into any other type of contract. It qualifies the buyer and commits him or her to the agreement. It also gives the broker some cushion if the deal goes sour.

I have used the term *margin* several times. A more correct term is *initial margin*. That is the 50 percent one must come up with to buy a certain amount of stock. What happens if the stock loses value? More margin money is requested by the brokerage firm, but the balance in the account does not have to be brought back up to 50 percent in order to hold the stock. The margin amount need only be brought up to an amount known as the *maintenance margin* or the amount needed to maintain the account, which is 25 percent in the case of long stock positions. I mention this only because you may experience it if you ever exercise an option.

Margin works two ways. If you own $10,000 worth of stock outright in a margin account, you would have 50 percent, or $5,000, available to trade with. This means that you could buy an additional $10,000 of stock, raising your portfolio to $20,000.

You might be thinking: why would anyone do that? The answer is leverage. It is the key to doubling your money as fast as possible—or losing it twice as fast. In the example just given, you have $10,000 in stock in your account. If the stock goes 10 percent higher, you have $11,000 in the account. If it goes down 10 percent, only $9,000 is left.

If you decide to leverage or margin the $10,000 to buy an additional $10,000 of stock, you will control $20,000 of stock. If the stock rises 10 percent, the CMV of the account will be $22,000. The cash or liquidating value will be $12,000. That comes from selling the stock for $22,000 and paying your brokerage firm the $10,000 you borrowed from it as margin. You will have made $2,000, or 20 percent, on your $10,000.

If the market dips 10 percent, the liquidation value will be $18,000. The cash value of the margined account will be $8,000, since you will still have to pay $10,000 in margin money back to your broker. You will have lost $2,000, or 20 percent of your original $10,000 investment. In both cases, some additional money or interest would be due the brokerage firm for the loan, commissions, and exchange fees.

This concept of leveraging becomes extremely important, as you will see when I get to futures, because there the leverage ratio is 20:1 or more, compared to just 2:1 for stocks. With options, you get even more leverage than with stocks and, some would say, without the risk. Let's say you buy a call option on a stock selling for $50 per share. The stock has a market value of $5,000 ($50×100 shares). The cost of that option could be as little as a dollar a share, or $100. What is the leverage ratio? 50:1! Wow! Fifty-to-one leveraging and only $100 at risk, along with no fear or worry of margin calls even if this stock drops to zero.

This may sound like an investment dream come true, but how far out-of-the-money is the striking price and how big a move is needed to break even? Never forget that the majority of options expire worthless for good reason. To get to breakeven, a stock like this would have to make a substantial gain before the option expires. Even if the option has months to expiration, it will still have to be a big move. It is for this reason that the leverage ratio is 50:1, meaning that it is a long shot. Moreover, the person who sold it to you is no dummy. When was the last time you bet on a horse when the odds were 50-to-1 and won? Long shots do win, folks buy out-of-the-money options regularly, and pigs may learn to fly.

The important thing to remember is that whenever someone offers you a lot of leverage, you can count on two things. First, there must be a lot of risk involved. Second, there probably is only a remote chance of the investment's being a success. For everyone buying hot investments, there is a seller who may know something the buyer does not. And that something usually involves fundamental or technical analysis, which is our next subject.

Quiz

1. Opening a stock or futures trading account requires providing the following information:
   (a) Date of birth
   (b) Net worth and income
   (c) Trading experience and trading preferences
   (d) Legal address and other contact information
   (e) All of the above
   (f) None of the above

2. Regulation of the securities industry began
   (a) with the opening of the first exchange.
   (b) once there was a major problem with a customer.
   (c) following the Crash of 1929.
   (d) right after the Second World War.

3. Brokerage customers are not responsible for
   (a) their losses.
   (b) knowing how and what to trade.
   (c) the risk they are assuming.

(d) providing their broker with all the facts needed to open an account.

(e) all of the above.

(f) none of the above.

4. A clearinghouse performs which of the following activities?
   (a) It matches up all buys and sells.
   (b) It collects debts owed brokerage firms.
   (c) It helps maintain the integrity of the markets.
   (d) It is the lender of last resort for retail clients.

5. Clients can
   (a) ask for arbitration if they feel they have been unfairly treated by their broker.
   (b) sue their broker.
   (c) trade any way they please because in the final analysis, it is their money that is at risk.
   (d) refuse to provide information to their brokerage firm.
   (e) fire their broker at any time.

6. The Mahoney Act
   (a) closed the bars during trading hours in Chicago.
   (b) created the SRO system.
   (c) outlawed securities fraud.
   (d) created a government-owned insurance company.

7. Leverage makes trading more
   (a) risky.
   (b) profitable.
   (c) volatile.
   (d) exciting.
   (e) all of the above.
   (f) none of the above.

8. Which investment provides the most leverage?
   (a) Stocks
   (b) Futures
   (c) Options
   (d) Leasing

9. Margin is
   (a) a down payment on the purchase of stock.
   (b) a performance bond.

(c) currently 50 percent on stocks.

(d) either initial or maintenance.

10. Which of the following are regulators?
   (a) New York Stock Exchange
   (b) NASD
   (c) NFA
   (d) SEC
   (e) CFTC
   (f) All of the above
   (g) None of the above

Answers

1. e; 2. c; 3. f; 4. a and c; 5. a, b, and e; 6. b; 7. e; 8. c; 9. b, c, and d; 10. f.

CHAPTER

8

Fortune Telling 101

Fundamental Analysis

Technical Analysis

You might be wondering about the title of this chapter. I used it not to denigrate the art and science of analyzing and projecting upcoming economic cycles, trends, or the prospective prices of various securities. Instead, I chose it to alert you to the most important and probably only truth there is when it comes to picking winning trades, and that is no one can do it successfully and consistently without suffering losses. Not me. Not you. Not any analyst you pay attention to on television, on cable, over the Internet, in the *Wall Street Journal*, at the top brokerage firms—not anybody!

The reason is that at many times unexpected information—beyond the ability of any analyst to detect in advance—hits the trading pits. It is like driving in Iowa in the early summer with everything under control. As you reach the peak of a gradual incline, you are confronted by a tornado. You panic—your fight or flight response kicks in—and you do the first thing that comes into your mind, no matter how stupid. The same thing happens to traders. They have a market outlook in their heads, a trading plan, a sound strategy, and a visualization of exactly how the trade should unfold. Then a jobs report hits the floor with a number half of what is in the market. The exchange floor looks like a Chinese fire drill as every trader tries to get out of his or her positions at the very same time and at the very same price. If it were not for human nature, just about every trader would be as comfortable as George Soros.

Before the mysteries of securities analysis are revealed, give some thought to your philosophy of life. How do you look at and react to the world around you? How do you manage your career, your personal relationships, and your family? Are you religious? Do you believe in an afterlife? Do you have a plan for your life? How much control do you have or think you have over the major events of your life? Take a moment to answer these questions.

Your answers influence how you will use, interpret, accept, and apply various analytic tools. More importantly, they influence how successful an option trader you are going to be. There are two distinct schools of thought regarding how the price discovery process works. One group, mostly composed of academics, believe it is impossible for anyone to get an edge on the market. They believe that the market is random in nature and efficient.

If markets are completely random and there are no patterns to find, then analysis is bogus. This argument is articulated by Burton G. Malkiel in *A Random Walk Down Wall Street*. He argues for randomness and declares that a broad portfolio of stocks selected by chance will perform as well as a portfolio carefully chosen by the industry's top analysts. He presents a strong case for buying index funds and leaving the rest up to fate.

Then there is the efficient market hypothesis espoused by Eugene Fama. This simply states that at any given time all the information on an individual stock is in the market and is reflected in the price of that stock at that specific time. Therefore, since it is impossible for an individual trader or investor to have all that information at that specific time, no trader or investor can possibly have a trading edge on the market, and thus no trader or investor can consistently beat the market. Think about all the possible news, political events, economic announcements, social upheavals, and totally irrational acts, like terrorist attacks, that have drastic and unforeseen impacts on the market. Worse yet, there are thousands of more mundane occurrences, like government reports on employment, income, consumer confidence, and so on, tugging and pushing the markets every day. To boot, this information is often misunderstood and/or misinterpreted. Too much of it can be manipulated by political factions attempting to influence the public's perception of the country's economic condition.

These two professors and many other very intelligent people have come to the conclusion that attempting to beat the market is futile. If you accept these arguments and your philosophy of life tends toward determinism, please do not attempt to make money trading options. You will shortly be exposed to the two basic analytic disciplines—fundamental and technical analysis. Both assume that you can get an edge on the market and that you have some control over how much you can take out of the market. People who invest or trade actively believe in self-determination to some degree. Granted there is a plethora of events that sweep down on the markets, like the barbarians on Rome, disrupting well-planned trades—wars, major depressions, diseases, natural catastrophes, and so on.

Then there are others times when we seem to have more control over our lives. Plans for a career, marrying, choosing to be religious or not, spending leisure time—things like these. Additionally, I believe you can have some control over your investments and your trading. Not complete. Not absolute, but some. There are many well-known investors, like Warren Buffett, who rely on fundamental analysis. There is also a Traders Hall of Fame filled with individuals who beat the market on a regular basis using technical analysis. Accounts of many of these great traders are available in the "Market Wizard" series of books by Jack Schwager.

My point is that fundamental analysis makes you a value investor or trader by making sense of the key financial data, giving you a trading edge. Technical analysis reveals patterns that human beings make repeatedly as they trade. Both disciplines help traders read human nature, which is unforgivably repetitious. What makes analysis so interesting and challenging—which also accounts for the losses that investors and traders sustain—is the variety of ways in which humans do the same thing differently over and over and over again. To become an option trader, you must accept that you have some control over your environment and that human behavior, and thus price trends, is repetitious. You must then develop or adapt a trading system that divulges the future, at least occasionally. The first step is to learn the pros and cons of fundamental and technical analysis to assist you in your search.

The trading enigma even becomes a puzzle when you give some serious thought to what drives the prices of stocks and commodities up and down. It is earnings for stocks, supply versus demand for commodities—or at least the perception of the strength or weakness of these forces. Any company stock that increases its earnings each quarter, year in and year out, in good and bad economic conditions, will see its stock price rise just as steadily. Any commodity futures contract with an underlying commodity that is always in short supply or always enjoys high demand will set new highs. But there is rarely any entity that always performs perfectly for any substantial period of time, and that's what makes this business so stimulating (or challenging). Additionally, there are many successful traders and investors who are doing something right using either technical analysis or fundamental analysis, and even some who use a combination of the two. There are plenty of winners out there, but most do it quietly less they attract too much unwanted attention. Plus, it is bad luck for a trader to brag.

Let me diverge for a second before I cause too much confusion between the use of the words *commodities* and *futures contracts*. Commodities are physical entities of commerce, that is, corn, oil, gold, silver, coffee, sugar, pork bellies, shrimp, and so on. They are real, physical things that you eat, drink, heat your home with, or stick under your mattress for a rainy day. They are the entities underlying the original futures contracts. When new contracts on things like T-bills, the S&P, insurance rates, interest rates, indexes, bonds, and so on, were added, the terms *financial futures* and just plain *futures contracts* came into vogue. Futures contracts is a more inclusive term than commodities because it represents both financial futures and physical commodities. So when you see the words *commodities* or *futures contracts*, they refer to the futures markets as opposed to the stock markets. I will get much deeper into this in the chapter on trading options on futures.

Therefore, what do you know for sure about all the markets, and what is your challenge? The first thing is, prices go up and down most of the time and sideways occasionally. Next, the more profit a corporation makes, the higher the price of its stock goes; the scarcer a commodity becomes, the dearer it is. To make money buying or selling options, you have to have a way of predicting the velocity and direction of price moves in order to exploit them. If you have done any research on the subject, you know that there are an incredible number of systems, strategies, pundits, books, trading schools, software programs, newsletters, Web sites, newspapers, radio shows, cable commentators, e-mail services, brokerage firms, brokers, friends, associates, coworkers, and other ready sources of information and trading tips. All of them seem to be willing to show anyone who is ready to pay or to listen how to make a fortune in the markets with little effort or risk.

Well—what do you say to all these people? How about balderdash? My answer is, if they can do it, why aren't they? The people that I know who are making money in the market keep it to themselves. If you knew what horse was absolutely going to win in the fifth race at Pimlico, would you put it on your Web site? Would you want thousands of other people to take the same bet and reduce your odds? Obviously the answer is no.

Successful traders are usually the same way. Giving someone a tip on a trade you are going to do is bad luck. Most traders are very superstitious about sharing specific trades. If someone else knows about, it does not work. They feel bad when someone loses money on one of their tips, which often happens, so they avoid offering them. But most important, trading is a very personal enterprise. No two traders trade in exactly the same way, nor do they both see the exact same thing when reading price charts or interpreting data. A very competent option trader could share an idea with you. You could both enter the trade at the same time, and one of you could make a nice profit and the other take a dreadful loss.

There are two and one-half schools of thought on the best way to predict price trends. There is fundamental analysis, and there is technical analysis. Additionally, many investors and traders combine both into a hybrid analytic approach. Let's look at each type of analysis separately and then the crossbred version.

Fundamental Analysis

Fundamental analysis consist of rationally attempting to figure out what events are going to influence the future of something, like a corporation's earnings, and, by extension, what the corporation's stock and options prices will be two months from now. Everyone does a lot of fundamental analysis on a day-to-day basis. Do you ponder and analyze how your career is progressing? Should you be looking for another job? What is the future of your employer? Are its products strong? Is its balance sheet impressive? Do you think the management is first-rate? Should you change jobs, industries, or professions? Which one has the brightest future? Which schools are best for your children? Which one suits their talents and personalities? Where do you find the most Ph.D.s, the best facilities, the strongest finances, or the toughest football team? Which one will best prepare them for the future you project for them? To learn the answers to all these questions requires a lot of reading, research, networking, and interviews with people who can be trusted—all this falls into the category of fundamental analysis.

Trading using fundamental analysis really is not any different. Traders read stories about companies of interest; study financial reports; network with analysts, traders, brokers, and industry participants. Some mutual funds take great pride in the fact that they visit the firms they invest in and interview management. The objective is to find out everything possible about the target company, down to which brokerage firms make a market in the stock. If you have an account with a full-service brokerage firm, you may have access to detailed research reports that include cash-flow projections for the next 10 years and detailed discussions of the industry comparing all the major players. These firms gather all the key financial data and put it in one place along with projections of the stock's price for the next decade. Here are Warren Buffett's fundamental criteria for investing in a company:

- *Easy-to-understand businesses*. He prefers to own a Dairy Queen rather than a Cisco.

- *Low debt levels*. Debt drains a company's energy.
- *Profitability and return on equity*. The company must be making money.

- *Managerial expertise.* The folks in charge must know what they are doing.

- *Intrinsic value, margin of safety, and valuation.* Strong companies can weather storms.

- *Economic moats.* The company needs an advantage that keeps competitors at arm's length.

- *Free cash flow and owner's earnings.* The company must have enough funding to be able to run the business without outside interference.

His secret is that he buys stock as if he were going to buy the whole company, run it, and have to live off the profits. It all sounds so simple—why are not all of us on the *Fortune* magazine list of wealthiest Americans?

If you think investing and trading is a snap, you are wrong. The carefully prepared and detailed reports you get are only the best guesses that the research departments can come up with at a given time and place. At best, they give the option trader who uses fundamental analysis a good idea of what the pros consider to be the key factors.

The historical part of these reports is often the most useful. As you study them, keep in mind the first law of investing: past performance is not indicative of future results. Nevertheless, once you determine that a company's earnings are on the rise and its obstacles are manageable, you can anticipate that the trend will march upward. This, in turn, pushes the price per share of the stock higher. The better a company performs, the more people want to own it. Demand for the stock drives the stock's price higher. The opposite is equally true: the stock of a poor-performing company is not desirable. Stockholders sell it, increasing the supply on the market. Prices decline. It is your job as option traders to distinguish between the rising stars and the falling comets—to buy call options on those that are on the way up and put options on the ones that are heading to oblivion.

Because fundamental analysis is so simple a concept and comes in handy in every phase of our lives, it has been a part of human behavior. It was certainly in use in the late eighteenth century when the first stock exchange opened in Philadelphia in 1790, a year before the New York Stock Exchange. At first of course, only professionals and the most serious stock operators, an old-time term for traders, used it. As time went by and the financial press flourished, the average investor began to get the information needed to do his or her own fundamental analysis.

In this chapter, I limit my discussion of fundamental analysis to the stock market and cover it differently in the chapter on futures. The reason is that the factors influencing futures contracts are vastly different from those affecting stocks.

As has been said, earnings per share is normally the driver, but what drives earning per share? Think for a minute about what factors make one company more efficient or one product more desirable than its competitors. Sometimes the difference is real and measurable; other times it is imaginary and elusive.

The fundamental factors that cause price movement have to do with anything that can lead to substantial increases in income in general and profitability in particular. Also keep in mind that rumors are as valuable to the trader as facts. A good trader buys the rumor and sells the fact, meaning that when a positive rumor hits the floor, prices spike, causing traders to buy. When the facts explaining the rumor come out, the pros sell into the public buying, meaning that they take profits. Rumors usually are an exaggeration of the facts. The pros act on the rumors, while the public misses the opportunity by waiting for confirmation. The experienced option trader who sees the price of the call she is holding spike on a rumor sells along with the pros when the facts are revealed. She knows the option can be replaced tomorrow at a lower price, if she is holding it for a specific reason that has not materialized yet.

Rumors by their very nature are surprises, which is the one thing the securities industry despises the most. Yes, brokers, specialists, market makers, and other participants all hate surprises. Professional traders love them. Many people think the security industry is made up of risk takers, but that is completely wrong. The industry does everything in its power to control the markets and reduce risk. When it can, people in the industry make the most money. There is an old saying in the industry, "When gold is discovered, sell picks and shovels." In other words, when the markets are in chaos, you can make a good living from the commissions the public and institutional clients pay.

Having a good feel for the overall economy is critically important. All ships rise or fall with the tide, so knowing whether the economy is bullish, bearish, or uncertain is always the first step in preparing to trade. The economy moves in cycles, from expansions to contractions and back again. You must know what phase it is in so that you can become more aggressive with calls in a bull economy and with puts in a bear economy. It is imperative that you follow these basic financial fundamentals that affect just about all stocks. Here are some to track:

1. Earnings per share, or EPS, that is lower or higher than the whisper number, which is the number that Wall Street really expects and that is whispered among floor brokers, rather than the number released to the public (now heard regularly on CNBC)
2. Price-to-earnings ratio
3. Projected earnings growth
4. Stock price-to-sales ratio
5. Stock price compared to book price (P/B)
6. Dividend payout ratio
7. Dividend yield
8. Book value changes
9. Return on equity
10. Mergers and acquisition activity
11. Products—new or problems
12. Senior personnel changes
13. Insider buying or selling
14. Share price compared to that of other members of the sector

This is by no means a comprehensive list, but it gives you some insight into the type of data the fundamental trader looks for in general. Often the fundamentals that affect a specific stock, industry, or sector are more common than those affecting the overall economy.

Let's quickly look at an example from the pharmaceutical sector. What specific fundamentals and/or surprises might a trader be watching?

1. The sales of the company's basic lines of drugs
   a. Strength
   b. Profitability
   c. Contribution to overall company health
   d. Competition
   e. Time left on patents
   f. Plan to protect the market when patents expire

2. Drugs or products in the pipeline
3. Pending drugs or products
   a. USDA approval pending
   b. Field test results
   c. Competition
   d. Market situation—sales penetration and earnings potential

4. Distribution
5. Reputation
6. Legal problems, like lawsuits and so on

Here again, this list is not comprehensive and would vary with the size and type of company that is being evaluated and tracked. For example, an option trader may pay more attention to small, one-product pharmaceutical companies because these are higher-risk operations. Regular investors shy away from them because it is usually boom or bust. This also means that the daily trading volume of regular shares is low. Thin markets make for explosive opportunities, meaning that these types of stocks potentially make major moves on low trade volume. Visualize tossing a rock into a puddle and another into an ocean—the former will make a big splash, and the latter goes unnoticed. Option traders who play long shots bet on these types of stocks limiting risk to the premium they pay for the option. If they are not sure the drug company will be successful in getting its product approved, they can buy both puts and calls, thus playing both sides at the same time. If the company is successful, the price skyrockets and the calls leap into the money. If the opposite happens, the stock price crashes and the puts are the right prescription. This type of trade is known as a staddle.

As you can see, with fundamental analysis, you must be looking in all directions at the same time. I often thought that if fundamental analysts chose a god to make burnt offerings to, it would be Janus, the old Roman god of doorways, who had one head simultaneously looking in two directions. The analyst is looking one way to determine the size of the supply and the other way to gauge demand.

The strength of fundamental analysis is that it forces the trader to do a lot of research, so that he truly understands the entity he is trading. With a stock, the fundamental trader knows what the company makes or does, how it ranks among it peers, who the key managers are, its relationship with its customers and competitors, and the detailed financial history and outlook. The company is real to the trader, not just a stock symbol, as is often the case with technical traders. This in-depth knowledge and understanding can also be a liability. Some traders, and more often investors, fall in love with their asset. They become loyal to it. This sometimes prevents them from selling it when it becomes stodgy and uncompetitive. When you have spent a great deal of time studying, admiring, and owning a stock, it is often painful to cut it loose when it is has lost its usefulness. Maintaining your objectivity is a cornerstone of success.

A virtue of fundamental analysis is that it often signals a major move well in advance of other analytical systems, such as most technical approaches. This allows the trader or investor to gradually become more and more aggressive as the trade develops. For example, an industry or company may be fading slowly over a period of years, but prices do not reflect the problems until they become so obvious that they are on CNBC. The meticulous fundamental analyst is aware of these problems well in advance and can build a large position in an orderly fashion.

The negative side is that fundamental analysis is weak regarding the timing of trades. If the analyst acts too soon, the option expires before the move materializes. The trade must be rolled over into more distant months, at a cost of additional commissions. As you will see soon, technical analysis can help.

Here is an example. A fundamental analysis of a friend of mine, a few years ago, determined that the U.S. dollar was going to make a major correction to the downside. He studied the market and selected 10 major companies, mostly in the financial sector, that he felt were going to be affected if the dollar dropped by 20 percent or more. He began buying puts on these companies, 100 lots at a time for the next several months, until he had built a large position. It took several months for the dollar to fall because Japan and China defended it as they attempted to keep their exports flowing into the United States by keeping the dollar artificially high. They were buying dollars to keep the dollars higher than their currency and simultaneously dumping merchandise on the American market to keep their people working. Before the dollar collapsed, some of the puts approached expiration and were offset and replaced with new ones in a later month. The objective was to get the puts only a few dollars in-the-money and average $5 profit on each. On several thousand options, the risk-reward ratio was good, and the options were cheap.

Naturally, the risk was that after he had built up this huge position, the expected result, in this case the fall of the dollar, would not occur. It is always possible that all the options will expire worthless or have to be offset for less than the purchase price. And the trader must guard against two demons. First, the trader can fall in love with his or her brilliant analysis and not know when to cut the trade and salvage whatever is possible. Let's call that demon hubris. The other one is despair. It causes the trader to give up too easily or too soon. The strength of conducting all the detailed fundamental analysis is that it gives you enough of an understanding of the overall universe of the stock that you can hold the line against these two fiends. By now you should be starting to come to the conclusion that trading is as much a mental game as it is anything else. If so, you are exactly right!

One final virtue of fundamental analysis is that the study you do on your primary stock teaches you how the entire sector performs. This can lead to some dandy ancillary trades. These are sometimes referred to as *sympathy trades*. For example, your primary target is Intel. Some news hits the Street unexpectedly, and Intel pops. You missed that trade for some reason, but you know that the other stocks in the chip sector will move in sympathy. You immediately buy some in-the-money calls and profit from Intel's move, but with one of its sister tech stocks.

Because of trades like this and all the specialized information a fundamental trader must have at his or her fingertips, it is common for these traders to become what is known as shepherds. Shepherds are traders who closely follow a manageable number of stocks. Selecting just the right number of sheep takes experience and skill. The trader knows everything there is to know about the industry, the sector, all the stocks composing the sector, and the specific target stock.

Before moving on to technical analysis, let me leave you with a few words of caution. Avoid myopic fundamental analysis. You must totally understand and analyze your target stock, but you must not suffer from tunnel vision. Do an analysis of the overall economy as a major part of your specific analysis. For example, your data indicate that a certain stock is poised for a major bull move, but the S&P is down big and heading lower. Earnings reports are dismal. Interest rates are searching for new highs. Housing starts are down. Get the picture? There is a bear market in progress. That does not mean that your stock cannot move higher vigorously, but it does argue strongly for caution. Nothing trades in a vacuum. Always put your analysis into the perspective of the overall economy.

It is also critical that you put your facts into perspective. Let's think housing. You are convinced that many of the public homebuilders are about to make a serious move north. Then boom! You see a headline saying that housing starts are expected to be 10 percent lower. Should this stop you? Not necessarily if you are aware that even with a 10 percent drop, home starts will still be at near record highs. Just put every new fact that comes to your attention into perspective, and then, and only then, act.

When your analysis indicates a major bear move in your target stock, you hesitate because you think that there is only room for a small move downward, since the current price is almost equal to the book value. Your conclusion is that it cannot move below book value. My reply: "When pork bellies fly!" A famous trader and trading system developer named D. W. Gann once said, "Gentleman, it can always go to zero." A lot of stocks trade below book value or some other value that is supposed to be etched in stone. If your analysis says it is going lower, believe your analysis. Of course, you might want to trade lightly, use a tight stop, or enter a position gradually.

Always err on the side of caution, especially in the beginning, when you are attempting to understand and interpret the data accurately. Often the nuances of the data for certain industries are not well understood by the universe of traders. What may sound good at first may not be good in actuality. If your analysis depends on a weak jobs number and the month's report is flat compared to last month, the actual situation may be worse than it looks at first because of the number of people who dropped off because they quit looking for jobs. My point is that you need to understand the data completely and all the possible interpretations before reaching conclusions.

Always take seasonality into consideration. A key statistic may be lower or higher than you expected. But before you bet the farm, check out comparable figures for the same period in previous years. Some retailers, for example, make over 70 percent of their profit during the Christmas season. Also, if you are missing a key piece of information, do not jump the gun. Wait until you have all the facts. Remember, a bus leaves this corner every 15 minutes—good trades are always coming down the pike, and the patient trader wins.

Technical Analysis

Now for some real black magic—the alterative to fundamental analysis (FA) is technical analysis, or TA for short. It has a somewhat murkier past, and you will hear some traditional analysts compare it to alchemy (and many a tech trader does try to change base price charts into gold—some even succeed). The focus of TA is internal, rather than external like fundament analysis. Where a fundamental analyst studies all the external factors, like the overall economy and the vitality of a company, the technician attempts to conjure the future solely from the price history of the underlying entity. The technician studies historical prices and patterns to predict future trends, while the fundamentalist searches for causes that are harbingers of future effects.

In this discussion of technical analysis, I will be making reference to both stocks and futures contracts. Unlike fundamental analysis, the technician uses similar or generally the same technical tools no matter what entity is under analysis, including options. The skills and systems that you learn apply universally. The scope of TA is so large that there is no way I can provide anything more than an overview. The purpose is to introduce you to TA and give you a rudimentary understanding of the subject.

To anyone new to financial analysis, it is somewhat easy to understand why fundamental analysis works. If a company is making money, it is worth more. Higher earnings equals a higher stock price. It is also simple to understand the other fundamental factors contributing to higher earnings. The better product captures more market share. The better management team makes better decisions—and so on ad infinitum. The changes in causes and events are transparent. FA appears to be common sense to the skilled and the unskilled analyst.

When it comes to technical analysis, newbies often balk when they see an analyst look at a price chart and say with absolute confidence that the bull movement currently in progress will halt at a certain price. Or they see an analyst draw a few lines or make a few marks on the chart and say, "Looks like it's time to short."

Another thing that always blows new traders' minds is the incredible variety of different approaches (see Figure 8-1). As an illustration, I often show students James E. Schldgen's book, *Analytical Methods for Successful Speculation*. This 275-page paperback is a study of gold from 1975 to 1985 using fundamental and technical analysis. The pertinent part for those who are new to trading is all the different technical approaches illustrated. First Schldgen looks at correlation analysis. If oil or the dollar goes up, how does gold respond? Besides these two, Mr. Schidgen correlates gold with banking reserves, budget deficit, the Commodity Price Index, the Consumer/Producer Price Indexes, corporate profits, gold stocks, industrial production, world money inflation, the trade deficit, and a few more. He then analyzes gold using 36 separate TA tools. Here is a partial list:

- Accumulation/distribution price analysis
- Bar chart analysis
- Commodity Channel Index analysis
- Contrary opinion analysis
- Elliot Wave analysis
- Fan line analysis
- Fibonacci progression analysis
- Fifty percent retracement
- Gann, W. D., analysis
- Harahus pentagon analysis
- Moving-average analysis

Technical Analysis

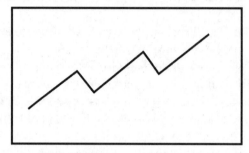

Price Charts and Patterns

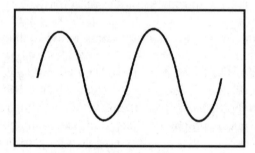

Cycles and Seasonal Patterns

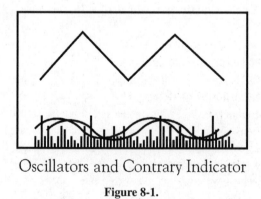

Oscillators and Contrary Indicator

Figure 8-1.

- Oscillator analysis
- Parabolic analysis
- Point-and-figure analysis
- Psychological crowd profile analysis
- Speed resistance line analysis
- Stochastic analysis
- Three- and four-dimensional chart analysis
- Volume and open interest analysis

If this isn't enough, there are dozens and dozens more—check out www.technicalanalysis.com for fun. The number and complexity of the TA studies and systems is simply mind-boggling. When you start out, you must do it in a controlled manner or you will become overwhelmed. Guard against jumping from one approach to another haphazardly.

I want to discuss a few of the most widely used forms of technical analysis to give you a feel for how and why they work. One of the most important issues is, why are there so many TA approaches? How does one select the one that is best suited for him or her? Which one or ones work? You must also keep in mind that there are individual studies that tell the technician a specific piece of information, such as that the price of a stock just dropped below an uptrend line. In addition, there are complete trading systems, often composed of several individual studies working in concert, that alert traders to opportunities and specify the prices at which to open a position, take profits, or cut losses. At times, it can be confusing which is which.

Technical analysis is so widely used that it often becomes a self-fulfilling prophecy. For example, up and down trendlines and moving averages are widely followed. An uptrend is a series of higher highs and higher lows in the price of a stock, option, or future. A downtrend is the opposite—a series of lower highs and lower low prices. When a trendline is broken by price movement, it is a sell signal if an uptrend is breached and a buy if a down trendline is broken. In other words, the trend has reversed.

A moving average is simply an average of a series of prices (5-day, 30-day, 100-day, 200-day) that is plotted on a graph. After each period (minute, hour, day, week, month, or some other period), the last number is dropped and the new one added, and the total is averaged. If a moving average that is trending up and is plotted on a price chart on which an uptrend line is drawn begins to fall, it eventually penetrates the uptrend line, signaling a sell or a shorting opportunity. The opposite is true—a down-trending moving average reversing and piercing a down trendline alerts traders to a buying opportunity. The 200-day moving average is particularly important for stock traders because it represents approximately a year of trading. You will even hear it mentioned on public forums, like CNBC. As a general rule of thumb, the longer a trend, the more reliable it is. So many traders follow the key TA signals that when they see one, they all act in concert, fulfilling its prophecy.

TA assumes that everything you need to know about a stock, option, or futures contract resides within its price history. By studying that history and converting it into various forms, the technician makes predictions as to what future prices or trends are going to be. To be able to accomplish this, there must be some repetitious patterns that can be discovered, as discussed at the opening of this chapter.

Cycles and Seasonal Patterns

Starting with one of the most basic observations of patterns in nature, every society, ancient and modern, recognizes some very obvious patterns that can be interpreted as technical analysis. The most obvious are the seasons of the year. Spring becomes summer, which leads to fall, followed by winter—simple and predictable. All agrarian societies understand the drought-flood and planting-harvesting cycles. Larger patterns were also known to the ancients, such as is written in the Old Testament of the Bible. In Genesis, Chapter 41, verse 30, Joseph tells Pharaoh Imhotep about the seven-year cycle of feast and famine. Or those who have studies the Mayan civilization are aware of the extensive work that civilization did in tracking economic cycles. They learned that by being aware of the cycles and embracing them—preparing for them rather than fighting them—they were able to mitigate the negative effects.

A relatively modern version of this is the work on cycles conducted by Nikolai Kondratieff (1892–1938). He studied the price behavior of wages, interest rates, commodities, foreign commerce, personal income, banking, and many other key economic factors. The result was the famous Kondratieff Wave or the Long Wave. It predicts a long economic cycle ranging from 50 to 54 years in length. Proponents believe that this cycle predicts major swings in the economy, which moves up for 25 to 30 years, then down for 25 to 30 years. The down cycle is deflation-contraction, and the up leg is inflation-expansion. It is tied to generations. One generation is financially fearless to the point of being reckless. This generation produces a crash, causing the next generation to grow up fearing debt and the economy contracts. The $64,000 question is: will the baby boomers, who have borrowed enough money personally and nationally to put the next generation in debt for the next 30 years, take the economy into massive recession? Time will tell if the Kondratieff Wave predicts the fate of the next generation.

A modern version of the cycle theory is the Elliot Wave theory, developed by R. N. Elliot in the 1920s and currently espoused by Robert Preacher (www. elliotwave.com). The theory states that markets move in a series of five waves. For a bull move, the first wave is up. That continues to a price at which traders consider the underlying entity to be overvalued. Wave 2 retraces the first move, but not to previous lows, as the longs from wave 1 take profits. Wave 3 takes the entity to new highs, above the high of wave 1. This is usually the longest and strongest wave. Wave 4 is again a correction as more profits are taken, but it is weak. Wave 5 completes the wave cycle. It goes up to a blow-off top, and this is, unfortunately, where the masses of uninformed investors get burned. Does anyone remember 2001? After a topping action, another wave formation exerts itself. A bearish wave pattern is also possible; it is basically the reverse of the bullish pattern. Futures traders might want to look at the work of Jake Bernstein. He is a psychologist, option trader, and fund manager whose extensive cycle studies on futures contracts warrant study.

The value of cycles for the option trader is that they help you understand where a market is psychologically. Are the majority of traders aggressive buyers? Are they at a point where they are considering taking profits? Is it time to stand aside or reverse positions? Cycles reflect the mood of the markets and specific stocks, options, or futures contracts. Some people trade them and others use them as a clue to understanding the sentiment of the market.

Another way to get this feel for the current market is through chart analysis. This is probably the most common type of TA. Charts reflect the conviction of everyone in the world who is buying or selling a specific stock, futures contract, or option at a given moment. Learning to read charts is a must for any option trader. Again, this is a complex subject that takes years to master. The following is only a brief introduction to the subject.

Bar Charting

I touched on this subject at the beginning of this section, but it deserves more attention. Price charts are a graphic presentation of price activity at a specific time. Think of them as a photograph of the price history of a specific stock, futures contract, or option. The time period covered can be from a few minutes to years. Charts are available in real time using the cutting-edge trading software platforms. If you do not have any sophisticated trading software, you can visit Web sites that will provide all the charts you want; try www.bigchart.com. All you do is fill in the required information, such as the symbol of the stock or futures contract and the time period. In a flash you have a price chart.

Just as a photographer takes pictures from many angles to capture the essence of his or her subject, the analyst often likes to start with a long-term chart, say a year's worth of data, and then zoom in, meaning the last 90, 30, 10, and 5 days. Finally, the analyst looks at yesterday's and the current trading session's prices, if live or real-time data are available. Real-time or live prices are the actual prices at which an entity is trading tick by tick. Real-time data are more expensive than historical data because the exchanges charge a fee for them. You will not get real-time data free on most Web sites, but you may get them from your broker, depending on the size of your account and your trading activity.

Bar Chart

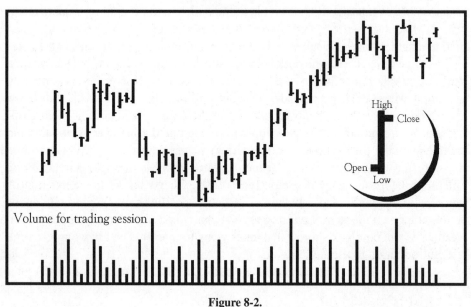

Figure 8-2.

The basic element of a price bar chart is the price tick (see Figure 8-2). The horizontal axis represents the time (minutes, hours, days, weeks, months, or some other period). For example, in a long-term chart showing several years, the price tick might represent the price range for a month. The vertical axis denotes price. For a real-time chart during a trading session, you would specify the time frame, such a five-minute tick or a one-minute tick. At the end of each interval, a tick would be recorded on your chart. The top of the tick is the high, and the bottom is the low. This gives the trading range for the period under study. For ticks covering one full trading session, like a day, the short horizontal lines on the left denote the opening prices and the ones on the right (as you face the illustration) are the close. Not all charts include opening price ticks, while most show closing ticks. Nontrading days, weekends, and holidays are skipped, so there is no break in the pattern.

Long-term charts of commodities, covering months and years of price activity, periodically show price distortions up or down. These long-range charts record only the prices of the nearby (contract closest to expiration) month. Careful analysis reveals gaps between prices when the contracts roll over from one contract month to the next. For example, the June silver contract expires and the chart service continues the chart using the December contract. In this case, there could be a price gap or distortion between the closing price of the expiring month and the opening price of the next contract month. The reason is simply that as the June silver contract approaches expiration or delivery, trading heats up, driving prices higher or lower. The farther-out contract month, December, trades with less volatility, and prices remain steadier. When a rollover from one contract to another occurs, there is often a gap between prices depending on the factors influencing the different delivery months. These longer-term charts are often referred to as "continuation" charts. This aberration is naturally not present on stock charts.

As a rule, the longer the term of the chart, the smoother the price pattern. This means that the price patterns on weekly charts are usually smoother than those on daily charts, and that monthly charts are smoother than weekly ones. Also, the longer the term of the chart, the more reliable the pattern is considered. For example, an area on a monthly chart that has given support to prices (I'll be discussing specific price patterns shortly) would be expected to be stronger (or more reliable) than the same formation on a weekly or daily chart. This is generally true for all formations or chart signals.

Across the bottom of the charts provided by most daily charting services, you will find a record of the trading volume for that day. Volume indicates the total number of shares traded. On commodity charts, you will find both volume and open interest, which measures the number of contracts held at the conclusion of a trading session. These are very important figures because they tell you the degree of traders' activity or the volatility of the market.

Chart Formations

You could stuff a wing of the Library of Congress with full-length tomes discussing interpretations of bar charts for stocks and commodities. Several of the better ones have been cited in Appendix 4. All I can do here is highlight some of the more common formations (see Figure 8-3) to give you an insight into how a trading system based on bar chart analysis might work.

One of the most common tools, as I touched on earlier, is the trendline. It denotes an uptrend or a downtrend in the price of the underlying entity. Trendlines must touch at least two price points to be reliable, and the more points they touch, the higher their dependability. Also, the closer the line is to a 45-degree angle, the higher its reliability. Uptrendlines are drawn below the price ticks, and downtrendlines above (see Figures 8-4 and 8-5). The steeper the trendlines, the likelier it is that they will be

Common Chart Formations

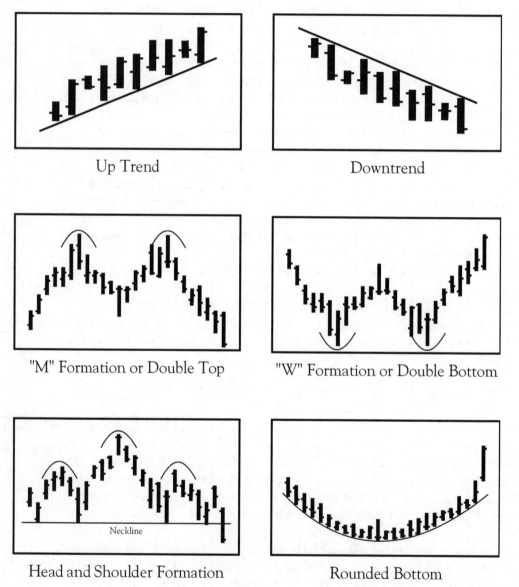

Up Trend

Downtrend

"M" Formation or Double Top

"W" Formation or Double Bottom

Neckline

Head and Shoulder Formation

Rounded Bottom

Figure 8-3.

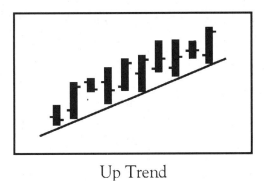

Up Trend

Figure 8-4.

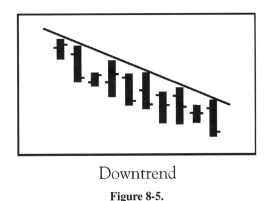

Downtrend

Figure 8-5.

broken and the trend will reverse. A line drawn parallel to the trendline (above for an uptrend and below for a downtrend) indicates a price channel or trading range.

All technical analysis accepts the premise that price history repeats itself. This is because it relies on human beings acting in a similar way when overwhelmed by fear and greed, the twin demons that are always prowling the trading pits. When a trendline is established, technical traders expect it to continue. When it gets too steep, they expect the trendline to break and reverse direction. This mindset is part of what makes technical analysis work—what makes it a self-fulfilling prophesy.

Think for a moment what is happening in the minds of the people who are actively trading a market. A stock or futures contract begins to rise in price. It goes from $20 to $20.25. Then up to $20.50. Before you know it, the price is $20.75. Trading volume is higher. Traders on the sidelines begin to notice the stock. They get greedy and want a part of the action.

This drives the price higher by a few dollars. The stock is suddenly up 20 percent. That is a big jump. Some of the early buyers think it is time to take profits, so they sell some shares. The price rise stalls. Others traders begin to fear that they are going to lose the profit they have in the stock if it tanks. These traders sell, and the price penetrates the uptrend. By golly, the stock begins to tank in earnest. Some other traders see the stock heading south and decide to short it. It is now in a downtrend. The stock drops $7, and the shorts take profits as some new traders see the lower price as a bargain and also begin to buy. The price stabilizes and a new uptrend starts. That is the anatomy of the bullish-bearish-bullish-bearish syndrome, which repeats and repeats and repeats. It is what goes on in the heads of active, aggressive traders.

A corollary to this scenario is the herd psychology that permeates trading floors all over the world. When a herd of traders see a lot of buying activity in a stock or futures contract, they trot over and buy some. When others start selling the stock, they start clawing their way to the head of the line of bears selling. This is instinctive behavior, not rational analysis. It reminds me of my first job on a fishing boat for tourists. Once at the fishing grounds, the weekend anglers spread out and dropped lines. The first time someone caught a fish, there was a mad rush to that side of the boat. If someone caught something on the other side, they stampeded back. Starboard to port . . . port to starboard . . . they almost capsized the damn boat. It makes no sense, but it is human nature and very characteristic of traders.

Part of the strange behavior of the amateur anglers and chartists has to do with the fact that no one knows the future. Therefore, traders who are risking their money on anticipating where prices will go next are uncertain and uncomfortable. The outcome is totally unknown. When people are uneasy, they like to stick together. They look to anyone who leads, which translated means anyone who makes the first move. Someone starts selling, and the traders in the herd conclude that that person knows something that they do not. This prompts them to follow blindly lest they be left behind and broke. Behavior like this evokes a basic human need and is responsible for history repeating itself. Just as in so much in life, none of the analysis is anywhere near 100 percent rational, but people follow technical signals because they are comfortable when there is nothing else to go on.

Another very reliable formation is support and resistance (see Figure 8-6), which has a more reasonable psychological explanation. There are certain price levels where downtrending markets come to rest repeatedly or uptrending markets tend to stall. For example, a market rallies and then falls back to a previous price level, from which a second rally is launched, only to decline back to the same price level again. This is a support area. The opposite, where a market rallies time and again, only to stall out at a certain price level, is a resistance area.

Areas of support and resistance are "zones of comfort," or neutral zones where traders agree, if only for a short time period, that the price is fair. Once a support area is penetrated, it becomes resistance when the stock returns to that level. This is because there are traders who bought at the support level thinking that the downtrend

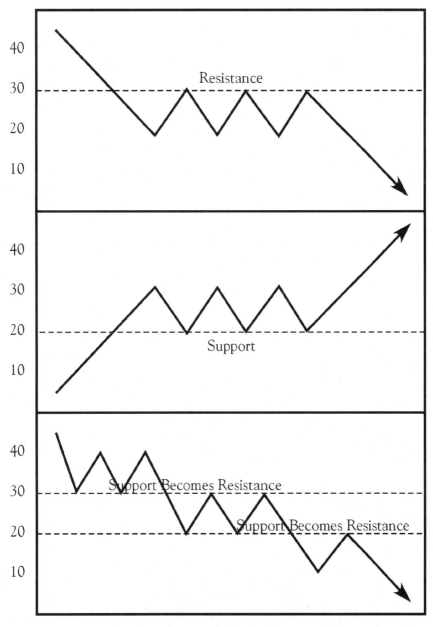

Figure 8-6.

was reversing, only to see the entity move lower. They now have losing positions, and they would be happy to get out of the trade at breakeven or the old support price. These traders offset (sell in this case) their losing positions, causing the uptrend to stall and making the old support level a resistance level. It works from the other direction as well. A resistance level penetrated by an uptrending move becomes a support level when the stock or other entity's price retraces. It is easy to understand why a trader holding a losing position for a while gives up on his or her original analysis and is happy as a bull in a pasture full of heifers to get out whole.

Closely related to support and resistance formations are multiple tops and bottoms. Take the double top as an example (see Figure 8-7). A market rallies, reaches an area of resistance, stalls, and begins to decline. After a short retracement, it rallies again, only to stall at the exact same resistance area. The chartist would call this a double top or "M" formation and consider it a sign of weakness. It would be a signal to buy puts. The risk, of course, is that a triple top could develop. The trader who shorted the double top would be whipsawed by the market. Whipsawing is

"M" Formation or Double Top

Figure 8-7.

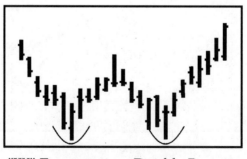

"W" Formation or Double Bottom

Figure 8-8.

what happens when you reverse your position, only to have the market turn against you. You lose twice, once on your original position and again on your reversal. Multiple bottoms are the opposite of multiple tops (see Figure 8-8).

A more complex version of the multiple top or bottom is the head-and-shoulders and inverted head-and-shoulders formation (see Figure 8-9). These formations resemble the silhouette of a person and are very important for several reasons.

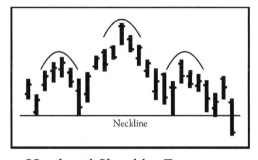

Head and Shoulder Formation

Figure 8-9.

First, they are generally considered very reliable by professional chartists for certain stocks and futures contracts. Furthermore, they foretell a major reversal in trend and can predict the length of the next move or the reversal.

A head-and-shoulders formation usually consists of the following four key phases:

1. Left shoulder
2. Head
3. Right shoulder
4. Neckline penetration

Prices often retrace and bounce off the neckline before heading toward the first price objective. This provides a second opportunity to short the stock or futures contract.

The first price objective is measured from the top of the head to the neckline and projected downward from the point at which the neck is broken. A second and even a third objective of the same distance can be projected, depending on the velocity of the market as it reaches the first objective. An inverted head-and-shoulders works in just the opposite way.

A formation I particularly find reliable is the rounded bottom (see Figure 8-10). These are long-drawn-out formations that can take months to mature. They are

134

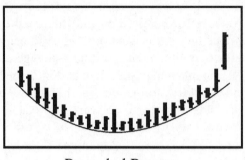

Rounded Bottom
Figure 8-10.

often called "saucer" bottoms because of their shape. When a saucer bottom matures, it signals a long-term uptrend. Remember back in the section of this chapter on fundamental analysis where I was describing the problem of determining, after a bottom was obviously in place, when to begin buying calls? If you bought too soon, the option would expire and you would have to roll over into the next option. A fundamental trader with some knowledge of TA would see the bottom as a rounded bottom. And when the price turned up and penetrated the rounded bottom, it would be time to begin putting on a call position. That is one of the ways that TA and FA can work together.

The reason a long-term uptrend follows a rounded bottom is that while the rounded bottom is maturing, the price of the stock or commodity is relatively low. It is at the bottom of its price range for a long time. While this is occurring, it is common for the company behind the stock to correct the problems that precipitated the decline or, in the case of a commodity, for new uses to be developed to increase demand. While corn was making a rounded bottom in 1986–87, new uses for it, as gasohol and corn sweeteners, were developed. When corn's price finally began to rise, it had a stronger demand base, and a long-term bull move developed. Also, at times of high inflation, a stock or commodity can look cheap after being in the cellar for a while.

There are hundreds of other bar chart patterns, such as triangles, boxes, key reversal days, and so on, but I cannot cover them all. If you are serious about trading, you need to spend some time studying all the formations—so that you will at least know what other traders are likely to do.

At the start of this section, I said there are two and one-half schools of thought on the best way to predict price trends. The two obviously are FA and TA. The half is the combination of the two. FA has one serious flaw: it does not have a good mechanism to tell you when to cut a losing trade loose. If a stock is a good buy at $10 per share or corn at $2.50 per bushel, according to FA, both must be even better buys at $5 or $1.25 if the fundamentals are right, except for the fact that you have lost half your money. TA, on the other hand, has self-correcting mechanisms. For example, if you are trading an uptrend and the price declines, penetrating the trendline, this is a clear signal to immediately exit the trade.

Another positive of TA is that it gives you signals of when to enter trades, as well as when to exit them. The rounded bottom is a good example, the way support and resistance tell the trader when a stock is over- or underpriced works. The price point at which the neck of a head and shoulders is broken is another reliable indicator for action. Many traders use fundamental analysis for their overall direction and technical analysis for timing. Together, they are stronger than either one alone.

This is where the art of trading blends with the science. As you will see as you get deeper into this book, trading is as much intuition as discipline and training. Intuition translates as education reinforced with experience. Intuition, discipline, and training are like the three legs of a milking stool, which tips over if any one is missing or weak.

One last thought: I've used the word *reliability* many times in this section regarding the use of fundamental and technical tools and signals. Burn the terms *reliable* and *reliability* into your mind. The basic principle underlying all analysis, whether fundamental or technical, is degrees of reliability. Thousands and thousands of studies have been done to find the most reliable indicators for the pricing of stocks, futures, and options. As you might guess, nothing has been found to be 100 percent reliable. If any does turn up perfect, someone will break the bank and close all the markets down. That will end the financial world as we know it, and we will all go home sad. Don't panic yet; I sure do not see it coming. Meanwhile, the operative words are "degrees of reliability," not fail-safe systems.

Quiz

1. Analysis of the option, stock, or futures market
   (a) is simple and reliable.
   (b) can only be done using fundamental analysis.
   (c) can only be done using technical analysis.
   (d) relies on human nature and its repetitious patterns.

2. Fundamental analysis uses the following to reach its conclusions.
   (a) Price chart formations
   (b) Economic data
   (c) Rumors
   (d) Econometric modeling

3. Describing the markets as random means what?
   (a) It is possible to analyze the market to predict price trends.
   (b) There are some price patterns that are more important than others.
   (c) Investors should be satisfied with index funds.
   (d) It is possible to get an edge on the market.

4. What does EMH mean?
   (a) Efficient market hypothesis.
   (b) Extra money helps.
   (c) The market knows more than any trader, and trying to beat it is foolhardy.
   (d) The keys to trading success are energy, money, and hope.

5. The seven cornerstones of Warren Buffett's successful investment philosophy are:
   (a) Easy-to-understand businesses
   (b) Low debt levels
   (c) Profitability and return on equity
   (d) Managerial expertise
   (e) Intrinsic value, margin of safety, and valuation
   (f) Economic moats
   (g) Free cash flow and owner's earnings
   (h) All of the above
   (i) None of the above

6. What does technical analysis have its roots in?
   (a) Black magic
   (b) People's attempts to measure and quantify the world around them
   (c) Attempting to find patterns where none exist
   (d) The work of Eugene Fama

7. A head-and-shoulder top forecasts
   (a) much higher markets.
   (b) increased volatility.
   (c) an opportunity to make some money buying puts.
   (d) that it is time to buy calls.

8. A trendline on which of the following charts would be considered most reliable?
   (a) 5-minute
   (b) 5-day

    (c) 5-week

    (d) 5-quarter

    (e) 5-year

9. Using technical analysis correctly helps you avoid which of the following?

    (a) A major gain

    (b) A small gain

    (c) A major loss

    (d) A small loss

10. Which came first?

    (a) Fundamental analysis

    (b) Technical analysis

Answers

1. d; 2. b and d; 3. c; 4. a and c; 5. h; 6. b; 7. c; 8. e; 9. c; 10. a.

CHAPTER 9

Just Trade It!

Buying Calls

Buying Puts

Spreads

Evaluations

Profits

Losses

Breakeven

Can you become a scratch golfer by reading books, reading magazines, watching webcasts, visiting the Golfer's Hall of Fame, or paying regular visits to a sports psychologist? Think about what it takes to become a professional golfer and pass Qualifying School. How many hours must one train and how many hundreds of practice and tournament rounds must a rookie play before winning his or her first pro tournament, not to mention a major?

Never forget that when you open a trading account and place your first order, you are matching your wits and experience against all the professional traders as well as all the amateurs trading that particular stock, futures contract, or option. It is somewhat like entering the U.S. Open. Anyone can enter; all you need to do is pay the fee. If you win locally, you move up to sectional and regional tournaments. And up and up until you qualify. Along the fairways to the Open, you must beat the very best amateurs, the top club pros, and all the local and regional champions. You are finally in the U.S. Open, after all that work and competition, and you are ranked dead last behind the big money winners who qualified by winning pro events. The odds makers give you a 1 in 1,000 chance of making the cut and 1 in 10,000 odds of winning the Open.

What does all this have to do with trading options? First, to learn how to trade, you have to trade, just as you must play golf to become a golfer. You won't become a competent trader by reading books or attending classes. These are very important for providing you with an overview. They help you learn what has worked for others and the mechanics of trading, but this is only the beginning. Second, you must practice all the shots required to become a competent trader and work hard on handling the unusual, the unexpected, and the pressure. For practice rounds, I recommend that you make simulated trades, or paper trade, using one of the free computer programs available. The day you place your first trade, you will probably be as bad, and as nervous, a trader as you will ever be. So be careful on day one, rookie.

The market puts you in as many unplayable lies and sand traps and on as many lightning-fast greens as a round at Augusta National. And never underestimate the competition. You are doing battle with institutional money managers with giant staffs of MBAs handling billions of dollars; professional traders like Victor Niederhoffer, who is a Harvard grad with a Ph.D. in finance from the University of Chicago; hundreds of market makers and specialists; trading firms with unlimited computer power; and individual professionals like Warren Buffett or George Soros, not to mention amateurs in the tens of thousands. It is heady competition, and you must be prepared to take on all comers. If all this were not tough enough, the securities industry does everything it can to rig the game in its favor. Never assume for a New York minute that you are playing on a level course.

Just for the record, some native talent and the right psychological disposition won't hurt. Just like golf, once you learn the basic strokes, it becomes a mental game. I delve more into the mental aspects of trading later; for now, I will discuss some strategies that you may want to begin using. This is by no means an exhaustive discussion. It is only a brief overview of some basic strategies to give you a feel for the sport and a place to tee off on your first round.

As mentioned earlier, the most basic option strategies are buying calls and buying puts. These strategies are good ones to begin trading because the reward can be substantial, while the risk is limited to the premium and transaction costs (commissions and fees). The negative side is that the vast majority of long options expire worthless because sellers are historically more attuned to the market than buyers are, and they are the ones that set the prices. They simply know how to price the options for what is anticipated, which of course does not always occur, meaning that hope springs eternal in the heart of every option trader.

If you are going to buy a call, how do you go about selecting one? Take a tip from a telephone broker who claims to never have had a loser? Burn some gray matter doing research before selecting your first trade? Step 1, as you learned in the last chapter, is to do some fundamental or technical analysis to find an underlying entity (stock or futures contract) that is poised for a decent move and is trending in the same direction as the overall market. If you need some assistance in stock picking, consider using one of the many fine screening software programs that are available. You might sort by stocks that have made new highs on strong volume that are 20 percent above their long-term averages with high volatility—hot stocks on the move.

Next, what are you looking for in a call? Should it be in-, at-, out-of-, or deep-out-of-the-money (two striking prices out-of-the-money)? Going long options is one of the most difficult option strategies to be consistently successful with because it requires both forecasting accuracy and market timing—accuracy in both the direction (bullish or bearish) and the distance (dollars and cents) of the projected move in the underlying entity, and timing in that the move must occur before the option expires. Nevertheless, it is still an attractive strategy because of the leverage. You may have only a few hundred dollars tied up in a call or put that returns thousands. Results of 200 to 500 percent or more are rare but happen. For a newbie, it gives you an opportunity to trade and to track the market with much greater intensity than if you were just hitting shag trades. It is like two people watching a football game, and one has a $100 riding on it and the other nothing. Who watches more intently? Who is more emotionally involved? Who won't leave the TV screen to get another cold one? Whose money is where his or her mouth is?

The next step is to consider the risk factors of the various options available compared to the confidence level you have in your price trend forecast for the underlying entity. Obviously an option that is already in-the-money has less chance of expiring worthless because it already has intrinsic value. The lower the risk, the higher the premium is the general rule. Even a small move could pay for the premium and the transaction cost. Keep in mind that someone, namely the seller, is betting that even a small move will not occur before expiration or that, if a move happens, it will be negative for the option's price. You are thinking bullish; the seller is counting on a retracement.

If your conviction is strong that the stock is poised for a substantial move higher, say a $10 or $20 move, study the pricing relationships of at- and just out-of-the-money options. Which is the best bargain? This is usually done via software programs, like OptionVue or Trade Station or one that your brokerage firm might provide, that evaluate the options as being either over- or undervalued. Basically these programs run an option-pricing program, like the Black-Scholes option-pricing model, to determine fair market price. If the CMV of the option is higher than the fair market price, consider the option overvalued. If the CMV is lower, rate it as undervalued. All other considerations being equal, the obvious choice is buying the undervalued option.

You should run some risk-reward ratios and see which option gives you the biggest bang for your buck. For example, you predict a $10 gain from the striking price of one of the undervalued options, which would cost you $500 in total (premium and transaction costs). A $10 move for 100 shares equals $1,000, or a 100 percent gain. An undervalued option at the next striking price might cost you $300, but you estimate only $500 profit on that option, which is less than a 100 percent gain. That makes the higher-priced choice more attractive. If the second option costs only $200, it would be a better selection because you would more than double your money ($500/$200 = 2½ times). If you are concerned about gross dollars in profit, you increase the size of your position. You buy a 5- or 10-lot (5 or 10 options) rather than a 1-lot. But don't do this on day one. Wait until your trading experience and confidence grow.

Another key factor to know before opening a position is your breakeven point (see Figure 9-1). Let's say you are thoroughly convinced that a retail stock, say

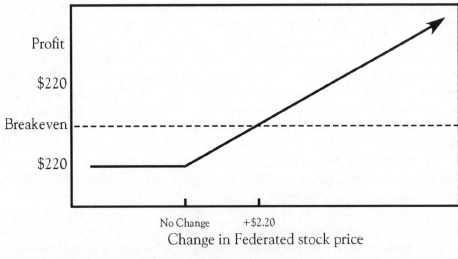

Figure 9-1.   Breakeven Analysis.

Federated Department Stores, is poised for a substantial move. You buy an at-the-money option for $220, or $2 per share plus $20 transaction costs. The next Friday unemployment figures come out lower than expected. Fewer jobs mean lower department store sales, and your confidence in your analysis weakens. At what price do you have to get out of the option in order to break even? You need to recoup $220, or a $2.20 move in the price of the stock for an at- or in-the-money option and more for an out-of-the-money option. If the stock is already there or nearby, do you bail out or do you stay the course? It is your decision based on how much conviction you have, the reason for your confidence (let's say you are positive that the company's earnings will still be substantially higher, driving the stock price up), and how much of a risk taker you are. But at least you always know where you stand when you know your breakeven point.

Another important consideration is the time decay of an option. The value of an option does not evaporate at a steady pace. The speed at which an option's price wastes away varies depending on the amount of time left to expiration. The nearer the option is to expiration, the faster the time value evaporates. Another way of saying this is that the rate of loss of time value for an option with three months left to expiration is faster than that of an option with six months remaining. Equally true, the rate for an option with six months to go is faster than that for an option with nine months. Why? Time is running out for the option to get in-the-money. The less time, the less value. The closer and closer options get to expiration, the less chance there is that it will happen, and there are generally fewer buyers and more sellers. Traders simply know more about what is likely to happen to a stock tomorrow than three months for now. More can happen to a stock in the next nine months than in the next three months, so traders will pay more for the time only if it equates to opportunity. In addition, most traders are reluctant to "pay up" for time value, as a rule of thumb.

Time value is easy to measure, but difficult to calculate. For example, if an option is in-the-money by $2 per share, or $200, and the price of the option is $300, the time value is $100. The formula is CMV − intrinsic value = time value. If the option in question has no intrinsic value, then whatever value it has is time value. Think of it as the cost of hoping that the option acquires some intrinsic value before expiring. This is why it is hard to get someone to pay up for it. Hope comes cheap.

Now, how do you tie the time value to the rate of decay of time value? If you are holding an option with no intrinsic value and it is approaching expiration, you know that the closer it gets to expiration, the faster it will lose time value. If you bought an option with six months to expiration and it cost you $200, what do you do when it reaches three, two, or one month to expiration? You see the value drop substantially from six to three months to expiration, say in half or more likely three-quarters. You know that by the time it approaches expiration, it will be worthless unless the market turns and it acquires some intrinsic value. At five, four, or three months, do you bail out to salvage some of your investment? The answer, of course, depends on your confidence in the analysis behind the purchase. What you need to do is to keep this kind of thinking uppermost in your mind as your options mature. An important characteristic of time value is that it is always highest when the stock price is at the striking price and always lowest when the option is deep-out-of-the-money. It is higher when volatility is high and the trend is in your favor. Time becomes very valuable when the option is gaining value, not when it is stuck out-of-the-money in limbo looking as if it won't be going anywhere soon.

You should also become familiar with the term *delta*. It describes the price relationship of the underlying entity to the option based on 1 point, or a dollar price move. If the underlying entity moves $1 higher and the option follows penny for penny, the option has a delta of 1, which is the case for an in-the-money-option option. If the option increases in value only 50 cents for each dollar gained by the underlying entity, the delta is 50 or 50 percent. Knowing the delta is another clue to selecting the right option to buy. The higher the delta, the faster the option will gain CMV as the underlying entity gains. The delta is calculated automatically when you run an option-pricing computer model.

Buying options with a high delta is particularly important if you are going to trade short-term, even day-trade options. The closer an option is to expiration, the more important and higher the delta normally is. Day traders trade options during the week prior to expiration because volume is normally highest at that time, as are delta and volatility—all ingredients needed for day trading. Day traders prefer to trade in-the-money options whose underlying security is moving in a profitable direction during the last days before expiration. They compete to squeeze the last penny of profit out of these options. As a trader's trading time horizon lengthens— moves from short-term (a few days to a week), to intermediate-term (weeks) or long-term (months)—the delta that is needed for a successful trade becomes lower.

As discussed earlier, the volatility of the underlying entity is the most critical factor. You will not get the price movement you need to push an out-of-the-money option into the winner's circle without an uptick in the stock's or futures contract's volatility. This, of course, is part of your screening process of trade selection.

After your research estimates the changes you expect in the variables affecting the price of the option under consideration, rerun the option-pricing model to determine what the price of the option should be when you plan to sell it if all the variables work in your favor. You do this by rerunning the option-modeling program with modified variables reflecting the after-trade situation. Determine whether this projected price is high enough for you to take the risk. You should expect a risk-reward ratio in the 1:2 or 1:3 range at a minimum. Keep in mind that your downside is zero if the option expires worthless, and these models are anything but perfect.

Later I will tell you how a couple of certified geniuses who won the Nobel Prize participated in taking down one of the hottest hedge funds by putting too much faith in their pricing models.

When should you take profits or cut losses? Do you have any choice? You buy a call, and it gains some value—what are your alternatives? The most obvious one is to hold the position as long as the stock is increasing in value, offsetting it on the last trading day, which is the third Friday of the expiration month. If you are a nervous Nellie, you could take your profits before expiration by offsetting the option whenever the spirit moves you. If your hope is that it will continue to gain value, you risk the possibility of a retracement to a price that would cost you your premium and transaction costs. You could consider using a stop-loss order to protect a certain profit level. This is an order to offset your position if it declines to a predetermined price. If you were very bullish on your position, your second alternative would be to exercise the option and hold the stock. Another choice if you were very bullish would be to roll up your position. Here you sell the in-the-money option and use the proceeds to buy additional calls that are slightly out-of-the-money, building the size of your position or pyramiding. Finally, you could create a bull spread by selling an out-of-the-money call against your profitable position, locking in a predetermined profit equal to the difference in the striking prices plus the premium you receive from the call sold.

An example may help clarify these five alternative courses of action. You bought a 30 April ABC call at-the-money for 3 points. The stock is now at 40, putting you 10 points in-the-money plus any time value. Alternative 1 is to hang tough and offset the option on the last day of trading. Alterative 2 is to offset it before expiration, taking the profits. This is a conservative strategy that makes a lot of sense if you become uncomfortable with how the market is performing.

Your third alternative is to place a stop-loss order to protect your gain. This is an order to offset your position if prices retrace a certain amount. Your option is $10 in-the-money or has $10 of intrinsic value. I will give it a dollar of time value and call the CMV $41, giving you a net gain of 8 points, or $800 per option, after paying the $3 premium per share for the 100-share option contract. You can calculate at what price to place the stop-loss order in a couple of ways. One way is to limit your loss to a certain percentage of the CMV, say 5 percent; another is to choose a specific dollar amount, like $1, and place an offsetting order at $2.05 cents (CMV = $41 × 5%), or a buck below the CMV. Another way is to look at the daily chart for the last few days and pick a spot below the trading range or slightly below a support level. If the CMV dips below the support price, your stop-loss order becomes a market order, and you are out. This strategy covers some of the risk by salvaging some profit, but you have no control over the price you get for your option once your stop order becomes a market order. The price could drop drastically before you get your fill.

Using stops should be a part of your overall trading plan from the beginning. You can use a stop to keep from losing the entire premium you paid for a call before your option is even in-the-money or once you have a $4, $5, or $6 profit that you don't want to give up. Using stops in the option markets is trickier than when trading in the stock or futures markets. The reason is that the daily volume of trades is often low. When you are trading a thin market like options, it is better to use a mental stop rather than actually placing a stop order in the market. A mental stop is a price at which you would offset the position if it were hit. The option in this example has gained $10. You might decide that if it retraces to a dollar or two, you will take profits. At this price, you enter a market order and offset. If you are using a full-service brokerage firm, you can give your broker instructions to exit positions at predetermined prices. In thick markets, or markets with high volume, like many of the futures markets, you can actually put the stop in the market. This is because the volume of trading around the CMV is plentiful and the underlying entity must trade down to the stop level to be hit. In thin markets, like those for most options, professional floor traders spot the stops and buy them. Almost immediately, prices return to where they were, and the pros take small, but risk-free, profits. It is not fair, but free markets never are.

Your next choice is to exercise the option and hold the shares of the stock for as long as you are bullish. Some investors buy calls as a way of entering a market. For example, they want to buy a stock once it trades above a certain price, say $50 per share. If they want 1,000 shares, they buy 10 calls at 50 or 55. When the stock trades in that range, they can decide to exercise the option immediately or wait a while to see how vigorously the move develops and exercise the options whenever they see fit before expiration. This is a cheaper way of entering a position if the move does not materialize or if the stock moves lower rather than higher. These traders see the 50 or 55 price as a resistance level. Once it is penetrated, the stock is a buy. Other traders may be looking for a fundamental reason that trips the buy switch at 50+. Buying options gives them some time for their analysis to pan out while avoiding the risk of a major loss. Remember the example of the small pharmaceutical company with a new product. If the FDA does not approve the product, the stock crashes and burns. Or the opposite happens if the company gets the green light from the FDA. The risk and reward of this strategy once the option is exercised are now the same as that of any shareholder—the stock theoretically goes to infinity or zero.

The next preference is a little more complex. Here you take your profits and roll them up. This means that you sell your current position and buy additional calls in a more distant month and at a price above CMV. For example, you sell your call for 11, less 3 for the premium, and end up with 8 points before commission and fees. You buy two 45 October calls at 2 points each. You now have doubled your position and pocketed some of your profits. You would do this only if you were still very bullish and the risk-reward ratio was still at an acceptable level.

Another idea was to create a bull call spread. With this strategy, you sell a call above the strike price of your long option. For example, you sell a 45 April call for $3. When you sell or write an option, you receive the premium. In this example, it is the same price at which you bought your original option. Now you are long and short the same option, which locks in a maximum profit of 15, the difference or spread between the two options. The proceeds from selling the second option cover the cost of the original option. You have zero at risk, except for commissions and fees. To achieve the maximum profit, the underlying entity must trade at $45 or higher. At this price, your short offsets your long if you sell it or if it is called away by the buyer of the call you sold. At any price below $45, your short is not exercised and expires worthless, meaning that you keep the $3 you sold it for. You offset your long position at CMV, which is your profit. If the stock crashes below $30, both options expire worthless and you break even. This strategy is the least risky, since breakeven is your worst downside, but the profit potential is limited.

This describes what happens when the market moves higher, but what can you do if your original option position, a 30 April ABC call, takes a tumble? First, of course, you can let it expire worthless. There is a strange truth that all options traders learn the hard way, and that is that there is always a seller when you want to buy an option, but there is not always a buyer when you want to sell. The reason is that the sellers are the ones who create the options and set the price. And they create them in their own likeness—likeness in the sense of creating a price that they believe will carry the option to its grave without being exercised, so they can live happy ever after. When you go to sell an option, there may or may not be any buyers. This occurs regularly with out-of-the-money options when the underlying entity is moving in the wrong direction, which is down for calls and up for puts. No one wants these orphans, and no one is required to make a market in them. So they pine away, like unwanted toys, until they expire worthless.

When this happens to you, there is a strategy that may allow you to mitigate some of your loss without increasing your risk. It is usually called rolling down, and it is somewhat similar to the rolling up strategy mentioned earlier. Instead of moving higher, your 30 April call loses half its original premium or value. Its CMV is $1\frac{1}{2}$, and ABC is trading in a 27 or 28 range instead of rallying to 40 as you expected. Your strategy now is to sell two 30 calls at $1\frac{1}{2}$ and buy one 25 call at 3. The key is that the cost of the option with the lower strike price must be the same as the amount that the options with the higher strike price are sold for to make this strategy work. What this spread does is lower your breakeven point by offsetting your initial option, since you now own a 25 call versus a 30. The negative aspect is that if the big rally that you originally expected does occur, you will not be able to take advantage of it because you are now long 25 and short 30. Your maximum profit is $200 ($500 − $300). This is a strategy for making the most of a bad situation.

Now, what can you do with a put? Where long calls give you the right but not the obligation to buy a long position from the seller, long put option contracts give you the right but not the obligation to buy a short position in an underlying market from the seller. The sellers of puts or calls must stand ready to deliver short or long positions, respectively, on demand. Sellers never know exactly if and when they will be exercised upon.

Besides the fact that long calls are bullish and long puts are bearish, they actually have a lot in common. First, for every stock with a call option, there is a put option as well. Also, the striking prices and expiration dates are the same. If they were not, it would not be easy to use the calls and puts in tandem as parts of a single strategy, such as the straddle strategy mentioned in the discussion of the pharmaceutical company that had a drug pending approval.

The basic trading strategy for puts, as I am sure you have picked up by now, is to profit when the underlying entity loses value. If your analysis indicates that the stock price of Dell Computer Corporation is going to tank, buy some puts. Be sure, as was discussed with calls, to calculate your breakeven price first and your risk-reward ratio. The cost of the premium and the transaction costs can easily be several hundred dollars. Therefore, Dell's stock price must decline enough to cover those costs and to make the risk worthwhile. In other words, most of what was discussed in the section on calls applies to puts except for the basic outlook, which was bullish for calls and is bearish for puts.

When trading puts, you must adjust to the fact that they are somewhat mirror images of calls. A put that is out-of-the-money is below the CMV of the underlying entity; an in-the-money put is above the CMV of the underlying entity. This is just the opposite of calls; however, at-the-money puts have approximately the same definition as at-the-money calls. The other basic terms and formulas—striking price, breakeven, premium, pricing models, delta, etcetera—are the same for both puts and calls.

The impact of dividends is another story. If dividends are paid at some point before expiration, this would be negative for the price of a call and positive for the price of a put. If you remember the discussion of pricing models, the Black-Scholes model, for example, one of the variables was the dividend. Think about it for a minute. What happens to the price of a stock when dividends are paid? Who receives the dividends? They are paid to the owners of record of the stock, not to the people who might have options on the stock. The date they are paid is called the ex-dividend date or the ex-date. When the dividends are paid, the price of the stock declines by the amount of the dividend, known as going ex-dividend or without dividend. Now if someone is short the stock when dividends are paid, the payments to the owners reduce the stock's price and increase the put's value. Remember that when someone shorts, he or she borrows the shares, usually from his or her brokerage firm. Therefore, when the short pays dividends, it reduces the price of the stock by the amount of the dividends. The larger the dividends, the lower the stock price goes and the more valuable the put becomes. For calls, it is the opposite. The stock price discounts the amount of the dividend, reducing the CMV of the call.

Almost everything you can do with a call, you can do in reverse with a put. For example, just as a trader would use a call to enter a long position, another trader would buy a put to get short. For example, a trader wants a stock to penetrate a resistance point that is $2 below the CMV before shorting the stock. He buys a put as close to that price point as possible and waits to exercise the put until the CMV reaches his entry point. When using this strategy, you cannot buy puts (or calls) at exact entry or exit points, since option prices are in intervals of $5 or $2.50.

There is one thing an investor can do with long puts that cannot be done with long calls, and that is hedging. The term comes from the practice of being on both sides of a market at the same time. You own 500 shares of IBM. It is a core position in your portfolio, meaning that you plan on holding it indefinitely. You have no plans for selling IBM every time it looks as if it is going to trade lower. You are sitting on these 500 shares, and your analysis indicates IBM is about to take a big dive. What do you do? You have already decided not to sell it and buy it back, because timing the market is a very risky strategy. If you feel certain about what is ahead, even if you are not sure of the timing, you can buy five at-the-money puts. If you were not as convinced that the stock was going south, you might buy five puts that were slightly out-of-the-money to reduce the cost of the hedge. Once these puts are in-the-money, their delta is 1—they gain in intrinsic value, dollar for dollar, as IBM descends. Granted, you would not make any money on this trade because your shares would be losing on a similar dollar-for-dollar basis, but the profit on the puts offsets your losses on the actual shares. In the end, you would be whole.

Some investors relate hedging to buying car or home insurance: it is a nuisance expense until one gets into an accident or the house burns down. Then it is the best investment they have ever made. If you were a gambling person, you could try to outsmart the market by selling the puts at a profit somewhere near where you think the bottom is or as the price of IBM stalls out and heads higher. Your expectation is for the stock to return to a price level at or above the price at which you entered the hedge. If you do this, you take the risk of being whipsawed. This happens if IBM reaches what appears to be a bottom and then begins to retrace higher. You cash in your puts, for a nice profit only to watch the price of IBM dive much lower. It is one of the most frustrating things to experience. You will swear that the market has personally singled you out for punishment the first time it happens to you. Please believe me, it is not personal. It is only the market telling you who is the boss.

Another variation of hedging with puts was popular when day-trading stocks was in its heyday, which it will be again. Some very active speculators limited their trading to a small number of very active stocks. The volatility of these stocks was off the charts, and swings of 10, 15, and even 25 points occurred almost daily. To make things even more interesting, these stocks moved up and down within these ranges on the same day. Amazon.com was famous for moves like these. To cover their derrieres, some of the more experienced day traders bought enough puts to protect themselves if they were trapped in a long position when the floor caved in on these stocks. It was just insurance, but every once in a while the stocks tanked when the traders were flat, delivering them an early Christmas present. As you will find, trading is one of the professions where it is sometimes better to be lucky than smart.

Now to trading strategies utilizing calls and put in combination, as in the bull call spread described earlier that was used to relieve some pressure on a long call when the bull move that had been anticipated did not materialize. In the call bull spread, you sell a call with a lower strike price and buy a call with a higher strike price. The mirror image of that trade is the bear put spread, in which a put with a lower strike price is sold and one with a higher strike price is bought. Where the call spread was a credit spread, the bear is a debit spread. This simply means that the options sold (the call with a lower strike price and the put with a higher strike price), are more valuable than the options bought (the call with a higher strike price and the put with a lower strike price). This is self-evident because the higher a call's strike price, the less valuable it will be. The reverse is true for puts—the lower a put's strike price is, the less valuable it will be.

As alluded to earlier, the attraction of spreads is that the risk is lower (a credit in a call spread and less than a full premium on the bear side) than buying a call or put outright. The flip side of the risk-reward coin is that the reward is fixed. The maximum profit potential is the difference between the strike prices less the transaction cost.

The more controlled environment of spreads is sometimes the reason that new option traders are attracted to them. If you decide to begin with spreads, it is critical that you work with an experienced broker. You want to avoid legging into a spread too slowly. Let me explain. Each side of a spread is called a leg. When you open a spread, it is necessary to place two orders—one to buy and one to sell the desired options—which are ideally executed simultaneously. If there is an appreciable time span between the establishment of these two positions, this is considered legging into a trade. The same thing can happen when closing a spread.

The problem is what can happen to the price of the options during this time lag. If your objective is to capture a 5-point spread and generate a maximum profit of $500 for each of the 10 spreads you are opening, and a delay in getting the two orders filled lowers the spread to 3 points because the options' prices moved closer together, you would be an unhappy camper. It could be even worse. For example, suppose you are closing a profitable spread, and you get one of the legs offset, but before you can exit the second leg, its price moves so far that you end up with a loss.

Some traders try to avoid this predicament by using a conditional order called a *limit order*. For example, suppose that a trader wants to open a bear put spread with the maximum of a 2-point spread. The order entered is, "Sell 1 June XXX 55 put and buy 1 June XXX 65 put at a spread of 2 or better." If the order cannot be filled at 2 or better, it is canceled. There are floor brokers who specialize in handling spreads. This is especially true in the futures market.

Pretrade Checklist

Option: *IBM July 85 Call*
Underlying entity trend: *↑*
Underlying entity volatility: *↑*
Historical option volatility: *35%*
Time to expiration: *45 days*
Interest rate: *3%*
Dividend *$0.75* Ex-date *May 30*
Stock CMV: *$79*
Option CMV: *$1.00*
Model Price: *$2.00*
Risk Reward: *1:2*

All I am trying to say is that you need to understand a lot about how the markets function before you begin to trade and use the more complex strategies. This will become even more apparent when you move beyond simple bull and bear spreads to butterfly, calendar, ratio, and index spreads, and then on to straddles, strangles, and condors. Option trading can be as simple and straightforward as you want, or as complex and esoteric. The choice is yours. The purpose of this text, as spelled out in the preface, is to provide you with a solid overview. With that in mind, I will move on to covered, uncovered, and LEAPS options.

Quiz

1. What is the maximum profit potential of a long call?
   (a) The difference in the strike prices
   (b) From the striking price to zero
   (c) Infinite
   (d) No more than $10 per share

2. What is the maximum profit potential of a long put?
   (a) Infinite
   (b) From the striking price to zero
   (c) The difference between the striking prices
   (d) Depends on when the trading curbs kick in

3. To offset a long call, what do you do?
   (a) Sell a put
   (b) Buy a put
   (c) Buy a call
   (d) Sell a call

4. When offsetting a long call position, make sure that which of the following match?
   (a) The quantity of calls offset
   (b) The strike price
   (c) The symbol
   (d) All of the above
   (e) Only a and b

5. Which of the following statement(s) about puts is/are true?
   (a) They are exactly the same as calls.
   (b) It is common to hedge with puts.
   (c) Puts lose value as the underlying entity gains.
   (d) Put are easier to make money with than calls.

6. Hedging is used
   (a) to keep pesky kids out of your yard.
   (b) to make extra profit in down markets.
   (c) to protect asset values in falling markets.
   (d) as a way of trading bull moves.

7. What is a spread trading strategy?
   (a) Long and short options of the same type on the same entity simultaneously

    (b) A butter substitute

    (c) Betting on the point difference between two options

    (d) Buying a call and a put on the same entity at the same time

8. Which strategy has the most risk?
    (a) Buying a call or put
    (b) Buying a stock or futures contract
    (c) Buying a bull spread
    (d) Buying a bear spread

9. What affect on price do dividends have when they are paid?
    (a) Increase the value of a put
    (b) Decrease the value of a call
    (c) Make the put option owner richer
    (d) Make the owner of the underlying entity richer
    (e) All of the above
    (f) None of the above

10. When should you consider putting on a straddle?
    (a) When you think volatility is going to spike higher or lower, but you are not sure which way
    (b) Just before a key jobs report is due, but no one knows how it will affect the market
    (c) When a company is in a very tight spot that will make or break its stock price
    (d) Just before an important announcement that could be positive or negative for the stock under study
    (e) All of the above
    (f) None of the above

Answers

1. c; 2. b; 3. d; 4. d; 5. b and c; 6. c; 7. a; 8. b; 9. e; 10. e.

CHAPTER 10

Some Advanced Concepts . . .

Covered Calls and Naked Options

LEAPS of Faith

FOREX Options

Philadelphia Options Market

In this chapter, I want to expose you to some of the more advanced uses of options and some special places to shop for options. It is critical that you understand my purpose is to do no more than familiarize you with the possibilities options offer. None of these strategies should be attempted until you have spent considerable time studying and paper trading and have developed a written option-trading plan, discussed in the final chapter.

In addition to buying calls or puts and some simple spreads, another conservative strategy for new option traders to experiment with is selling covered calls. There are two basic motivations for selling, writing, or granting covered calls. The first is income, and the second is the downside protection of existing assets. Like everything you do in the market, if the risk is controlled, so is the profit potential.

CHAPTER 10 Some Advanced Concepts . . .

Notice that I use three terms—sell, write, and grant—interchangeably. Options were once called *permissions*, as in one having the permission of the owner to assume the underlying entity at a predetermined price and time. Therefore, the person offering the entity granted the buyer the right—of course, for a price. Early options were over-the-counter; thus they were written by the party of the first part, which brought the phrase "to write an option" into the traders' lexicon. Since the person granting the option was the one in power, he or she did the writing. Last but not least, if someone bought an option, someone had to sell it. Thus the expression "selling an option" became commonplace, especially on exchange floors. All three terms mean the same thing, so they are used interchangeably.

Think for a moment about how stocks behave. They go up, down, or sideways. And, they do these three things vigorously or languorously. How do you determine if market conditions are right for writing covered calls? The answer, of course, is your old friends, volatility and price chart analysis. The first thing you do, as you consider the possibility of granting an option on a stock in your portfolio, is study the recent price activity and the volatility of the overall market, the stock's sector, and the volatility of the stock and the specific option under consideration. If your objective is increasing the income from a core asset in your account, meaning that you do not want the stock called away, you look for low volatility and mildly uptrending markets. If you are after ordinary income, you look for high volatility and strongly uptrending markets.

Why is this so? If you write or sell a call on a stock you own and you do not want that stock called away from you, a neutral trading climate is best. You will be long the stock (or other underlying entity) and short an option on that stock or hedged. The trading objective is to sell a call, collect the premium, and wait for the option to expire worthless. If you bought the stock for the sole purpose of writing calls against it, the more market volatility, the better, within reason. Your objective this time is to collect a high premium because volatility is high and to have the stock called away, which provides additional income as the stock gains value. As volatility increases, if prices move high enough, the owner of the option exercises the option and you deliver your stock. You receive both the option's premium and the gains on the stock as it moves from the CMV to the option's striking price. In both cases, you get some downside protection from falling prices. As the price of the stock declines, the short call protects you from loss up to the amount of the premium.

Regarding the call that you sell, why must the striking price be above the CMV of the underlying stock? Think about it. Why could the striking price not be below the CMV of the underlying security? If it were, the owner of the call would exercise it immediately, compelling you to deliver the stock. The only exception is if the stock is only slightly above the option's striking price, not enough above it to pay back the entire premium and the commissions to the owner of the option. Be

The Economics of Selling Covered Calls

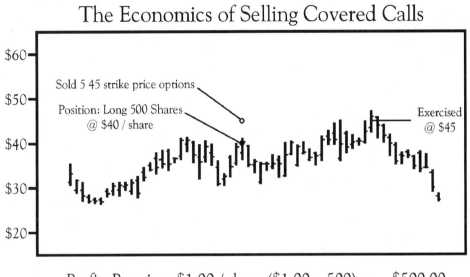

Sold 5 45 strike price options

Position: Long 500 Shares
@ $40 / share

Exercised
@ $45

Profit: Premium $1.00 / share ($1.00 x 500) = $500.00
Gain on Stock = $5.00 / share ($5.00 x 500) = $2,500.00
TOTAL = $3,000.00

aware that some clever floor trader who is paying pocket change per trade in commissions can call your option for a risk-free profit as quickly as an e-mail traverses the Internet.

There are two basic types of covered calls: at- or near at-the-money and out-of-the-money. Your outlook on the market and your intentions dictate the type you utilize. If you think there is a chance that the underlying security could move several points higher and you are using this strategy to generate income, you would select an out-of-the-money option to sell. This way, you get some income from the premium, and there is less chance that the stock will be called away than if you chose an option with a strike price close to the security's CMV. On the other hand, if your intentions are to extract a few extra points out of the market on the sale of your stock, you might sell an option that is almost in-the-money. This results in a higher premium to you because the options price is closer to the CMV, making it more desirable.

For example, suppose the CMV of your stock is $62 per share when you decide to sell a 65 call with three weeks to expiration and the volatility of the underlining security is above its six-month average. What are your intentions regarding the underlying stock? This call is near in-the-money, and therefore it would bring a decent premium. As a rule of thumb, the more out-of-the-money an option is, the lower the premium. Time value must also be considered. The longer the option has to exceed $65 per share, the more likely it is that your stock could be called away. As you learned earlier, traders rarely pay up for time value. "It is the volatility that counts!" It is normally best to sell covered options near expiration.

The objective is to make a few extra bucks when selling a position. Remember how to calculate breakeven for the owner of a long option: premium plus two commissions. In this case, call this amount $4.00. Your expectation is that the stock will shortly trade in the $67–$68 range. In other words, you hope to make another $2 or $3 per share plus the premium on the sale. If you do not, you either hold onto the stock or sell it at the market on the rally. If you really want to dump the stock, the risk is that the stock does not get called away and the CMV declines.

In this example, the CMV of the stock is $62 and a 65 call sells for 4 points. When the stock is called away, you get to keep the premium of $4 plus the $3 gain on the stock. The total return would be approximately $7 less the commission, or about 10 percent more than selling at-the-market. Not too shabby, unless the stock never stops climbing until it hits $80 per share. The risk in this strategy is lost opportunity if the analysis is incorrect. When this happens, just say to yourself, "Self, you will never go broke taking profits."

If you do not want to give up the stock, you would sell an option that is more out-of-the money. In this case, you would be looking for a time when volatility is low and the overall markets are calm. Many people do this with blue chip stocks traded on the New York Stock Exchange, relying on the specialist to keep trading under control. This has worked well in the past, but in recent times, even this staid old institution has become more volatile. In other words, take nothing for granted and do your homework.

What if you wanted to write a covered call on a stock you did not own? This is a common strategy. You would select a stock whose technical characteristics, such as volatility and recent trading strength, fit your trade criteria. Then you would study the options available to find one whose price matched your strategy. Now, do you buy the stock first or the option? Your trading technique here is the same as was discussed regarding spreads. The key is entering both positions, the stock and the option, at as close to the same time as possible. This is the only way to make sure you get the desired price relationship. You just add additional risk if it takes too long to leg into the positions. Even losing a small amount from the desired spread alters the outcome.

For example, in our earlier example, if you were opening the trade from scratch, you would be looking to make 10 percent on the trade. You are buying a stock at $62 per share and selling a 65 call for a $4 premium. You expect to pick up $3 on the stock price and $4 on for the option, for a total of $7 after transaction costs, on a net position of $58, or a gross profit of 12 percent. You would naturally settle for buying the stock at $62.10 and receiving a $4.10 premium because the net is the same. If you got the stock for $64 and sold the option for only $2, however, you would gain only $1 on the stock and $2 on the option, missing your profit objective. Buying and selling with precision is often the challenge. One answer is a brokerage firm or computerized trading platform that accepts conditional orders like: "Buy 100 shares of ABXC at 62 or better and sell one June ABXC 65 call at $4 or better." The problem is that these are "not held" orders, meaning that the brokerage firm does not guarantee to fill the orders. Not getting a fill is often better than getting a bad fill if it is not within an acceptable parameter. Some brokerage firms require a minimum size, say 500 shares and 5 option contracts, to do to this type of trade. Your second choice is to buy the stock first and then sell the option. Once you know the price of the stock, you can make an adjustment on the option side. The risk is being long a stock that is losing value and having the option you sell, because of the $5 increments, deliver minimal downside protection. Your response is to bail out and try again. Double-check your analytic tools for errors.

What about a covered put position? There is no covered put position comparable to covered call. If a covered call is being long a stock and short a call option, a covered put would be the opposite, that is, being short the stock and long a put option. When you short stock, you profit when the price of the stock declines, which is the same as with a long put. This would be a short-short position, not a hedged long-short position. The only other alternative would be to short the stock and sell a put. If you sell a put, you have the obligation to deliver a short position to the buyer. If you were short the stock, selling a put would give you no protection because you would be under an obligation to deliver a short position, which would double your liability, not cover or limit it. What is sometimes called a covered put is when someone buys a corresponding put with a strike price equal to or greater than the strike price of a put that person has already sold. In reality, this is a put spread, where one put is covering another.

The whole concept of shorting has never caught on with the investing public, even many professionals. It somehow goes against the grain, as if it is somehow unpatriotic to be bearish on the stock market. In addition, shorting is not well understood. Individual investors have problems intellectualizing the concept of selling something they do not own and buying it back at a lower price at a later date. The risk is also higher in that markets fall faster than they rise. This is because once the buying dries up, the stock has no place to go but down. Therefore, no one wants to buy the stock, and anyone who shorts it just drives it lower faster.

Upward or bullish movements are more methodical. Some buying starts. Then there is a pause, and investors think about where and how high a particular entity could or should go. Then another group of buyers joins the buying crowd. At some point, every pundit on the tube and the Internet is hawking the stock, and news of it reaches the public. The great unwashed are just in time for the blowoff top as the professionals sell into the public buying frenzy. Then slam, bam . . . it is over, and the stock crashes and burns! When you study call and put trading volume, you notice that there are usually more calls in play than puts, especially in the more distant trading months and even when the market is heading south.

Now to the most dangerous of options strategies—selling naked calls and puts. Naked options are pegged the most dangerous because, unlike buying an option, the risk is not limited to the premium and transaction costs. The price of the underlying entity can theoretically rise to an infinite level or plunge to zero. Additionally, the seller must deliver the underlying entity at the whim of the buyer. Since the seller of a naked option does not have the underlying entity in his or her possession, she or he will have to venture into the open market and acquire it at the CMV, which may be miles from the strike price at which he or she sold the option.

An example: You sell some 20 June calls on Intel when Intel is trading at 15. Right after you sell it, Intel announces a new, faster, smaller, more versatile chip— bingo! It is trading at 30, and those folks who bought calls from you at 20 want the stock. You have to come up with 100 shares for every option you sold. When the process of exercising begins, you have to deliver the stock. Do you get the luxury of placing some limit orders in the market and seeing if you can find fills at 28 or 29? No! You must deliver posthaste, which means using a market order, which fills at any price. Intel could be at 40 by the time you get your fills. (See Appendix 2 for an explanation of the different types of orders used in securities trading, if you are not familiar with them.) Your brokerage firm is responsible for delivering your positions in case you are late or default. It must deliver promptly, whether you have the stock or not. Your broker will be on you like red paint on a fire truck. You are forced to get the stock to replace what your brokerage firm delivered to the contra side of the option. If you do not, you face margin calls, and your broker will do everything possible to get its money back.

What is the problem with market orders? Most of them fill at or near the high of the trading range. With futures contracts, as you will read soon, it can be worse. In this example, the stock opened at 30 the day you received notice that your stock was being called away, but you do not get a 30 fill. Yours is in the 35 to 40 price range, or whatever the market wants to give you, depending on how fast it is moving or how strong volatility is. The fills are on the high side because the market is running away from your striking price. If your fill comes in at 35, you lose $15 per share, or the difference between the striking price and your fill price. That is $1,500 per contract less the premium; call it 3 points per share, or $300, netting out to $1,200 per option plus transaction fees. Your maximum reward, the premium less transaction costs, was approximately $300 per option, and you lost $1,200. That is what is meant by saying that this is the riskiest of strategies, a negative risk-reward ratio of 4:1. It could have been a lot worse. Intel could have gone up 50 or 100 points. There is no telling when a blowoff top occurs.

Are you up to that? On the other hand, you could have sold a put. Intel's arch competitor could have announced a new chip that was going to take most of Intel's business away. If Intel was trading at 15 at the time and you sold 12½ puts, you would at least have known that the lowest Intel could drop would be to zero. If Intel went out of business and the stock disappeared from the exchange, you would still settle with the trader who bought the puts in cash.

Moving on, many individual traders find LEAPS interesting. The acronym stands for long-term equity anticipation securities. LEAPS are listed options that are similar to the listed equity options discussed so far, but there are some important differences. The biggest is the term, that is, long-term means 2 to 2½ years compared to 9 months with regular options. Another difference is that LEAPS do not have standard strike prices, but the strike prices assigned conform to the intervals of regular options. For example, you may look at an option price array and see calls and puts as 55, 65, and 80, rather than the more orderly $5 intervals of regular options. Strike prices are added as needed, matching what the market is doing and traders are buying.

Conversely, many of the characteristics of LEAPS are the same as those of the standard equity options, and all of the basic option terminology applies. LEAPS come in two flavors and one size: puts and calls for 100 shares of stock. They are exercisable before expiration like any American-type option. Once a LEAPS has only nine months left to expiration, its symbol changes and it joins the class and series of the regular options to which it belongs. In other words, a LEAPS on ABC stock expires in 2½ years. Twenty-one months later, when it only has nine months left to expiration, it drops its LEAPS designation and melts into the group of regular ABC options. If you were an owner of this option, the only adjustment you would see is a change of symbol in your account. One day it would have a symbol designating it as a LEAPS and the next a symbol of a regular option.

One of the most common mistakes an option trader new to LEAPS makes is comparing the price of LEAPS to that of ordinary options, lets say one with three, four, five, or six months to expiration compared to the LEAPS with a year and a half to go. The LEAPS immediately looks cheap to those who are new to this type of trading. They buy so many that they need a wheelbarrow to haul them home. LEAPS may cost only three or four times more than a regular option but have six, seven, or even eight times more time left to expiration. Just looking at a LEAPS— a call with a striking price only $20 over CMV on a well-known blue chip stock that still has two years to expiration—it is hard to imagine it would not gain far more than the measly $20 per share needed before expiration. "What the hay? Inflation alone will make this LEAPS a winner," says the first-time trader. More often than not, the LEAPS expires worthless, like most long options.

The cardinal rule of LEAPS trading is, always price them using a reputable pricing model. As has been mentioned several times, time value is not as important in option trading as it is when you are waiting for your parachute to open on your first jump. This is true whether an option has two months or two years to expiration. The models are by no means perfect, but you ignore them at your own peril.

How can the average investor use LEAPS? If you have concluded that a particular company or stock sector has outstanding long-term prospects and you do not have the money to buy as much stock as you want, consider buying LEAPS calls. This is an efficient way of investing in the future. If your analysis is correct, the LEAPS gain value as the stock rises and you can always exercise your option for the shares. With this strategy, always buy calls with as low a strike price as you can.

There are LEAPS puts that you can use as a long-term hedge for an individual stock or a portfolio. I know some investors in this era of terrorism who buy them to protect against another unspeakable disaster, like the terrorist attack on the World Trade Center in New York back in 2001. Some LEAPS index options are available to provide broad coverage. Since indexes are futures contracts, see the next chapter. Always remind yourself that neither the most obvious nor the worse catastrophe seems to happen and consider these puts as you would an insurance policy on your home.

Another common use for LEAPS puts is in place of establishing a long-term short position. They are a lot less risky, can be held for a long period, and provide higher leveraging. What more could you want?

LEAPS, of course, can be a super speculative trading vehicle, particularly in very volatile times. When stocks are bouncing off the roof, only to crash through the floor, LEAPS give you the price punch of a regular option without worrying so much about timing and expiration. During the closing years of the last century, this approach to the market worked very well.

At that time, there was also a lot of stock-splitting activity, which is a great time to use LEAPS. Stock splits are as much a shareholder management tool as a public relations ploy. For instance, a stock's price increases quickly from $25 per share to $50. The company's board of directors decides to have a 2-for-1 split. For every share you have, you receive a second share and, simultaneously, the price is halved. One day you have 200 shares worth $50 each, and the next day you have 400 shares valued at $25 per share. Nothing has really changed, except now you have twice as many shares.

Companies do this to promote their stock. The board feels that more individuals will buy it at the lower price. They like to get their stock into the hands of as many individual owners as possible because individual owners are more loyal. Institutions, for example, will flip a stock out of their portfolio at the first sign of weakness. Individuals do not pay as close attention to their portfolio or are more forgiving. In addition, any stock that can climb from $25 to $50 in a reasonable time frame and do it over and over again is a fun stock to own. Cisco was just such a stock; check it out on some historical charts from 1995 to 2000. It shows the investor a robustness that is very appealing. If you own one of these stocks and it splits repeatedly, you feel you are getting free shares and getting rich quick.

Using LEAPS to trade these aggressive stocks gives the option traders the icing without having to buy the cake. In other words, they profit from the moves and the splits, since options split right alone with the stock, with less invested than the stockowners and less worry about timing or potential downdrafts.

As you will learn, one of the keys to becoming a successful trader is having a full bag of tricks to play at the right time. Putting the right strategy into play to match the market at the time you are trading pays big dividends. For this reason, I want to go over a few additional option opportunities. You just never know when one strategy will be the absolutely best way of trading a certain type of market. Learn to take what the market offers to maximize your opportunities. Become a Boy Scout or cowboy-type trader—always prepared and ready to graze on the greenest pasture, no matter what market that may be. Now here are a few more ideas.

What is the FOREX market? It is the international foreign exchange market, which means it is where one buys and sells money. It is a cash market, more like the stock market than the futures market. All the major currencies trade 24 hours a day. This market follows the sun from one country to another—Asia, Europe, and the United States. It opens 2:00 p.m. EST on Sunday and trades continuously until 4:00 p.m. Friday EST. On a daily basis, over $1.4 trillion changes hands, making FOREX the largest and most liquid market in the world.

The key to success depends on understanding what affects the value of one currency compared with another. For example, if country A pays substantially higher interest rates than country B, money flows from A to B (A is sold and B is bought), all else being equal. If B is an unstable country that does not protect outside investors, its interest rates reflect the higher risk. Another key factor is the balance of trade. A country that imports much more than it exports has an outflow of money entering the international market. When it gets to the point where too much of a certain country's currency begins to flood the international banks, bankers sell it, driving its value down. This is basic supply and demand at work. Knowing and being able to analyze all the possible fundamental events that could affect a country's currency is mind-boggling. You must juggle politics, wars, weather, international trade, tastes, and hundreds of other factors. This may be the reason that technical analysis is very popular and effective when making short-term trades in this market.

In addition to the cash market for currencies, FOREX offers two types of options. The first type is somewhat similar to the traditional options covered so far. There is a big difference, however: when you buy an option, you really are buying two options. It is more like a spread. That is because in the currency markets, when you buy one currency, you do so with another, which is the same as selling the first to buy the second. The relationship between the two currencies determines the value of both. As one loses, the other gains, and vice versa. If you were speculating on the value of the euro versus the U.S. dollar, you might buy a EUR/USD at 1.2000, which is a EUR call and a USD put. If the price stays below 1.2000, you lose the premium. If it increases to 1.3000, you win big! Close your position and pocket your profit. The euro contract is for 300,000 euro.

FOREX is an over-the-counter market, so you can choose the price and date on which the option is to be valid and then receive a quote on the premium. You can also select an American- or a European-style option. Because it is generally harder to create an OTC option, it is more common to use the second type of option, called the SPOT.

SPOT stands for single payment options trading. It is a lot like betting on a sporting event, where you give or take points. You create a scenario, "The EUR/USD will trade below 1.3000 in the next 10 days," and you request a bid on the premium. If you take it, you wait and see what happens. If the EUR/USD trades below 1.300, your position converts to cash and you win. Here are the standard scenarios:

- One-touch SPOT. You win if the price touches a specified price point.
- No-touch SPOT. You win if the price level is not touched.
- Digital SPOT. You win if the price goes above or below a certain level.
- Double one-touch SPOT. You win if the price touches one of two set price levels.
- Double no-touch SPOT. You win if the price does not touch either of two set levels.

It reminds one of working the spread on a college football game—you win if Ohio State beats Michigan State by 3 points. As with a bet on a sports team, you cannot offset the SPOT as you can a regular option. You buy it; you own it.

One good time to trade a SPOT is around the release of key government reports. For example, you feel strongly that the U.S. trade deficit with Japan is going to be huge—large enough to drive the yen higher and the U.S. dollar lower. You study the charts and buy a JPY/USD SPOT. If you are right, you buy dinner and some Grand Cru Classé wines tonight. If you are wrong, you try to learn something that will help you next time.

The next chapter covers the futures markets, where several of the best known index options trade. Before we go there, you need to know a little about the Philadelphia Stock Exchange (PHLX), because it is somewhere between the pure stock exchanges, the futures markets, and the FOREX. The index options that the PHLX offers go through stockbrokers, while the options on, say, the S&P trade on a futures exchange, utilizing futures brokers. A broker or a brokerage firm has the option of handling both, but not all are registered to do so. There are some clearing firms that deal with both, permitting customers to move funds easily from their stock to their futures account or vice versa. This is very handy if you plan to trade both.

Lastly, the PHLX makes an active market in options on currencies and is an aggressive innovator. For example, if you needed to hedge a portfolio of gold and silver stocks, you might consider its Gold/Silver Stock Sector Index (XAU). The PHLX's other sector indexes, such as Oil Service Sector (OSX), Semiconductor Index (SOX), Bank Index (BKX), and Utility Index (UTY), come in handy at other times. Its currency indexes and cross-currency indexes allow you to buy a spread with a single order and can be an alternative to FOREX. Being a full-fledged exchange, it trades approximately 2,000 stocks, of which 1,500 have options, making it fit in the middle of the cash, stock, and futures market spectrum.

Now, I will move on to futures markets and options on futures.

Quiz

1. What do the terms *write, sell*, and *grant* have in common?
   - (a) Nothing.
   - (b) The second two are the same.
   - (c) All mean the same thing.
   - (d) *Write* and *grant* are the same.

2. Which term was used at one time in place of option?
   - (a) Alternative
   - (b) Substitute
   - (c) Choice
   - (d) Permission

3. Which of the following do you want if you are selling covered calls for maximum income?
   - (a) High volatility
   - (b) Low volatility
   - (c) An upward price trend
   - (d) A gradual downward price trend

4. Which best suits a covered call strategy used to increase the sale price of a stock?
   - (a) Covered puts
   - (b) Deep-out-of-the-money calls
   - (c) Increasing volatility
   - (d) Medium volatility
   - (e) A rampant bear market

5. Which trading strategy works best under all market conditions?
   - (a) Covered calls
   - (b) Spreads
   - (c) Naked options
   - (d) Index trading
   - (e) Matching strategy to market conditions
   - (f) None of the above

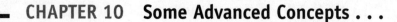

6. The FOREX is a
   (a) cash market.
   (b) futures market.
   (c) stock market.
   (d) options market.

7. LEAPS stands for?
   (a) Love, equality, appreciation, personality
   (b) Lost equity at PHLX
   (c) Long-term Equity Anticipation Securities
   (d) Let everyone arrive promptly

8. Which are uses for LEAPS?
   (a) Compensate for weak analysis
   (b) Hedge portfolios
   (c) Profit from very vibrant markets
   (d) Spread against regular options

9. Which market trades 24 hours a day?
   (a) NYSE
   (b) Midwest Stock Exchange
   (c) PHLX
   (d) FOREX

10. If you default on a trade, which entities are responsible for the loss?
    (a) Your brokerage firm
    (b) The firm clearing the trade
    (c) Your broker
    (d) The exchange on which the trade occurred
    (e) All of the above
    (f) None of the above

Answers

1. c.; 2. d; 3. a and c; 4. c; 5. e; 6. a; 7. c; 8. b and c; 9. d; 10. e.

11

The Mighty Futures Markets

What the world of finance calls the futures market is really two very distinct markets, one as old as the barter system and the second as young as the study of economics. Both are fair game for option traders, depending on your frame of reference, experience, and interest. If are you more comfortable trading something that you can feel and touch or that you have some experience with, such as a farmer trading grains and livestock or someone in the petroleum industry playing the crude oil or gas markets, you might want to start with the physical commodities. As you will learn shortly, the traditional commodities require a knowledge of how, where, when, and in what quantity they are produced. Conversely, someone who has traded stocks regularly and follows the financial markets might be more at home delving into financial futures, such as options on the S&P 500 or the Nasdaq

100 futures contract. Because these two types of futures contracts are so different, I tackle each separately.

The oldest segment of the futures market is more accurately labeled the commodity market. Commodities are real entities that you can eat, hoard, ply a reluctant lover with, use to improve your health, wire spaceships and houses, or just plain enjoy. I am referring to foodstuffs, like corn, wheat, barley, pork bellies (bacon, to those new to the futures game), live cattle, and so on. You can also trade gold, silver, palladium, and other precious metals. The third group includes cocoa, the base material for that large heart-shaped box of chocolates to win your sweetheart's favor. Fresh frozen orange juice does wonders for preventing winter colds, or at least that was my grandmother's prescription. Dr. Copper, the most intelligent of the commodities (I'll get back to this later), wires the houses of the world and can be found in just about every aircraft and spaceship. Last, but certainly not least, are coffee, shrimp, and sugar—where would you be without your double tall latte?

The commodity market was created to solve problems. As a cattleman or farmer, how do you get the things you need to survive and live comfortably that you cannot produce yourself? The answer, of course, is the creation of a local market where farmers bring excess produce to trade for the things they need, made by villagers who need to sell their production to buy the farmers' foodstuffs. The initial medium of transfer was barter, but eventually various forms of money evolved.

This worked fine for a few centuries. But as farmers became more and more productive, a new problem arose: they grew more feed than their livestock required and more food than could be sold locally. They did not have the capacity or financial resources to store all of it until the city folk needed it. Farm production has a funny way showing up at the same time, that is, harvest or calving time. These coincidences cause serious financial problems for both the producers and the users. At harvest, produce is plentiful and competition among the farmers is fierce. The villagers really enjoy the cutthroat struggle—until winter sets in and there is no fresh produce available, and what is available is priced so high that only the local princes can buy it with their tax money. If this is not enough, production swells one year because of excellent weather and shrinks to next to nothing when the rains fail to materialize.

Even the merchants are not very happy. They like the part about buying cheap at harvest, but they do not like running out of merchandise when it is most in demand. The answer to this feast or famine dilemma is to pay farmers in advance for grain and other produce if they store it on their farm and bring it to market in an orderly fashion. This became known as a "to-arrive" or forward contracting. The farmers receive enough money from their crops before harvest to pay their production costs and living expenses for the next year. They, in turn, store their produce and deliver it in an orderly fashion throughout the year. At least, that is how the forward contract system was designed.

The merchants who developed these contracts retained the right to sell or transfer them among themselves. Eventually, the merchants arranged to handle the storage in order to control quality, uniformity, and availability. When a crop appeared to be in trouble because of a drought, the prices of these contracts soared and trading was heavy, since every merchant knew that the crops in the fields were going to be more valuable as a result of lower supply and stronger demand. The next step was organizing the trading of these contracts. The Royal Exchange in London takes credit for being the first to officially trade these forward contracts on a formal exchange, although records indicate that such trading had been going on informally in England since the thirteenth century. It was a worldwide solution to this problem, as attested to by the Yodoya Rice Exchange in Osaka, Japan, which dates from at least 1650. As an aside, it was here and during this time that a very sophisticated form of technical analysis called Japanese candlesticks was perfected. It is still used widely by futures and stock technicians.

In the United States, the center of the commodities markets became Chicago, Illinois, because of the enormous amount of grain and livestock produced in the surrounding states combined with its access to excellent river systems and the Great Lakes. Grain could easily and inexpensively be shipped to New York City via the Erie Canal, which was completed in 1824, or to New Orleans via the Illinois and Mississippi Rivers. This area covered the majority of the U.S. population prior to the turn of the nineteenth century.

The first U.S. commodity exchange, the Chicago Board of Trade (the Board), opened in Chicago in 1847. By the end of the Civil War, contract specifications were standardized, and fungible contracts were being traded by Chicago's famous butter and egg (two popular commodity contracts at the time) men, as the rich commodity brokers became known when they visited the Big Apple for a good time. The Chicago Produce Exchange opened next in 1874. It became the Chicago Mercantile Exchange, or simply the "Merc," in 1919.

It was the Merc that fired the first shot in what became a war for the financial futures market. In 1972, it created the first currency contract. The Board returned a salvo when it created the first interest-rate contract. Bang went the Merc's heavy artillery when it introduced the T-bill contract. Bang the Board blasted right back with the T-bond contracts. While this was going on, the Chicago Board of Options Exchange (CBOE) came on the Chicago scene with futures and options on the S&P 500, S&P 100, DJIA, Nasdaq 100, Russell 2000, CBOE Volatility Index, and others. The Big Apple wasn't going to be left out. Its Commodity Exchange (Comex) captured the precious and base metals (gold, silver, platinum, copper, and so on) markets. Its Coffee, Sugar and Cocoa Exchange handles the softs, or breakfast commodities (coffee, sugar, cocoa, orange juice, and so on), and the New York Mercantile Exchange latched onto the petroleum markets (crude/heating oil and natural gas). Don't overlook the New York Cotton Exchange, New York

Futures Exchange, or the two regional exchanges, the Kansas City and Minneapolis Exchanges. For mini-contracts, there is the MidAmerican Exchange in Chicago. Europe wasn't retreating from these opportunities: several exchanges in England, France, and Germany made their cannons heard, as well as several Asiatic exchanges. Even Canada and Australia have very active markets. You can now open a contract on the London exchange and offset it in Chicago, virtually doubling the number of trading hours in a day. If that wasn't enough, GLOBEX introduced electronic, 24-hour trading for futures contracts. My point is simply that Marshall McCluhan's World Village described the futures and options markets long before the World Wide Web became a twinkle in Tim Berners-Lee's eye.

Enough history; let's get back to the commodities and financial futures markets. Analysis of the financial futures markets is very similar to what was discussed regarding the stock market because the financial futures and options markets derive their price trends from these underlying entities. For example, the futures options on the Dow Jones Industrial Average look to the DJIA for their value, which in turn gets its direction from the combined price trends of the 30 stocks making up the DJIA. Therefore, the key, as was described in Chapter 8, is income per share. The more profit a company generates, in general, the higher its stock price goes, which is then reflected in the appropriate financial futures contracts and the options on those contracts.

Some of the other financial futures, like interest rates, currencies, bonds, and bills, are influenced more by the overall economy of their country of origin. These factors, in turn, create the environment that encourages or discourages corporations in their pursuit of superior earnings and the flow of money from one country to another. Therefore, when you attempt to project price trends for financial futures options for American entities using fundamental analysis, you should track the three key economic indicators. Here they are with a breakdown of their components:

- Leading Indicator Index
  - Average workweek
  - Average weekly jobless claims
  - New orders for consumer goods
  - Vendor performance
  - Contracts and orders for new plants and new equipment
  - Building permits
  - Changes in unfilled durable goods orders
  - Sensitive material prices
  - Stock prices
  - Money supply (M2 in constant dollars)
  - Consumer expectations

- Coincidental Indicator Index
  - Employment on agricultural payroll
  - Industrial production
  - Personal income less transfer payments in constant dollars
  - Manufacturing and trade sales in constant dollars
- Lagging Indicator Index
  - Percent change in labor costs per unit of manufacturing output
  - Ratio of manufacturing and trade inventories to sales in constant dollars
  - Average duration of unemployment
  - Commercial and industrial loans outstanding in constant dollars
  - Ratio of consumer installment credit to personal income
  - Average prime rate change by ranks
  - Change in Consumer Price Index for services

As you can see from the composition of the indexes, the elements that you would expect to be affected first are included in the leading index. Once the economic machine is moving, the coincidental indicators reflect the second stage. By the time the lagging indicators begin to make a move, you should be preparing to take profits, as a possible slowdown or change of trend is beginning to occur. In addition to these markers, it is critical to follow worldwide political activities for clues to what surprises are ahead for the financial futures, particular the currencies, because they are strongly influenced by politics.

Commodities, meaning physical commodities, are as different from financial futures as T-bills are from timber. The key is not earnings with commodities because they don't earn anything. They just sit there waiting to be sold. Gold pays no dividend. Corn has no way of generating earnings per ear. Oil would just as soon stay hidden in the core of the earth as be cracked into gasoline. But let the market get too much or have too little of any of the physical commodities and all hell breaks loose. In other words, it is all supply and demand. This becomes completely clear when you realize that you can actually run out of a commodity. The world is now using more oil per day than it can pump out of the earth. It takes thousands of years for oil to be formed naturally. Guess what is going to happen some day? The world is going to use every drop of oil the earth has made over the last several million years. It will be all gone. Nada! Zero! Dry! The earth's gas gauge will be on empty. What will the price of oil be for the last 50 years? The last 25? The last 10? You would assume that the price will be astronomical, but you never know. That is the beauty and the most frustrating part of trading futures, and one of the best reasons for using options.

Obviously, as long as the world depends on oil and its derivatives, prices will trend higher. They will not decline unless more oil is discovered, a substitute is found, or usage diminishes. Will the substitute be electric cars? Will mass transportation push cars off the roads? Who knows? My guess is liquidation of coal, what's yours? But at some point all the oil in the world will be used up, except for a few jugs in the Smithsonian Institution. All along the route, there will be higher highs and higher lows, which describes a bull market trend. Prices will make major retracements along the way as new sources or substitutes become available, giving the world and traders hope. Eventually those discoveries will peter out and the prices will resume their climb. Then there will be a blowoff top, followed by a spectacular crash once traders accept the idea that oil is no longer a viable trading entity. This is the ultimate supply versus demand scenario.

Please don't confuse the supply and demand for an option with that for its underlying entity. Whenever an offer to buy an option enters the market, the seller writes a "new" option contract for the buyer. Sellers can create as many option contracts as they dare and regulate the demand by adjusting prices. Unfortunately, physical commodities are different:

- What can you do when the last bushel of corn in stock leaves the elevator?
- What can you do when the last ounce of gold comes out of the ground?
- What can you do when Starbucks perks the last coffee bean?
- What is for lunch when McDonald's flips the last piece of ground beef?

You can always get more of most commodities because they are renewable and theoretically an infinite amount is available, although others, like oil, will eventually vanish from the face of the earth. The question is one of timing: when will new supplies be available?

For example, the U.S. Department of Agriculture (USDA) keeps a running total of the worldwide supply of key agricultural commodities and publishes it regularly. You can find this information on the USDA Web site. It will tell you, for example, the number of days' supply of wheat that is available in the world. What happens when that figure drops below 90 days? Below 60 days? Below 30 days? The users, meaning just about every country in the world, get nervous. What do the five main grain dealers who control the world's supply do when they see supplies dropping? What do the wheat brokers of the world do? What do the producers of the world do? What do the major users do? What do governments do? What do commodity traders in the grain pits do?

The answer of course, is buy, buy, buy! Go long, long, long! They buy every futures and call option contract they can. Sure, more wheat will be produced somewhere in the near future, since the wheat harvest occurs almost monthly somewhere on the globe, unlike most other corps. Will it be enough? Can it be brought to market fast enough to replenish worldwide supplies? Does the country where the next harvest is taking place export it, or does it use all its production internally?

The answer to these questions tells you if wheat futures prices are soaring to $4, $6, or $8 a bushel. Naturally, the option traders of the world are buying calls until who laid the rail.

What is the formula that the USDA uses to predict supply? How does it know what demand will be? What can screw up both of these predictions?

Corn Supply

On-Farm Storage   +   Commercial Storage   +   Production   =   Supply

The formula is simple. Getting accurate numbers to use in it is nearly impossible. All one needs to do is determine how much of the previous production is still available, referred to as carryover from previous years or seasons. Then add that number to an estimate of production for the current or next time frame, referring to the next growing season for a crop or the annual production of a mine. Next, an estimate of usage or demand is made. A survey of all the possible users of the commodity is done to get a fix on next year's usage compared to that of the current year or past years. Will millers need more or less wheat? Will housing starts increase enough to accelerate demand for copper, lumber, and so on? If so, by how much? Then all the data are compiled, extrapolated, fudged, form-fitted to political agendas, and everything else Washington and other governments do before releasing the final price projections to the public.

This all seems pretty straightforward until you try to do it. What you find out is that everybody and his brother who is supplying information manipulates it before giving it to the collecting agency—even the American farmer. When I worked at Doane's Agricultural Report, its research department surveyed farmers regularly. One of the things it learned is that on some preliminary surveys, like planting intentions, farmers deliberately misled the surveyors. If they had a large amount of corn in on-farm storage, they would indicate that they intended to plant more soybean acreage than corn. They did this to artificially create a selling opportunity for themselves, meaning a bull move in the corn market when the survey became public. Seeing a large increase in soybean acreage and lower corn acreage would drive the corn market up and the soybean market down on the futures market. The farmers would empty their storage bins by selling on the futures market on the price bump, with the intention of delivering the corn at expiration of the futures contract, and then plant as many acres of corn as they wished that year. Midwestern farmers, in general, prefer growing corn to growing soybeans.

This illustrates several major differences between commodity futures, financial futures, and stock. First, all futures contracts expire, as do options on stocks or futures. Stocks do not, which reflects in financial futures. A stock theoretically continues forever. Now the big difference between options and commodities is delivery. Stock options expire, but you can exercise them to take possession of the stock itself, either long or short. If you exercise a futures option, you get a futures position, not the underlying entity itself. But once you have the futures contract, you can wait until expiration and take physical delivery of a commodity in the case of a long position or make delivery of the underlying commodity in the case of a short. Here I use the word *commodity* because if you had a position on a financial futures contract, it would be settled in cash. In the case of a T-bill future, you probably do not want to take delivery of $1,000,000 in T-Bills. Instead, before expiration you offset the position, and your futures account is credited or debited with the difference between what you bought the contract for and what you sold it for, or what you sold it for and bought it back for, in the case of short position.

The stock side of the business has two steps, stocks as the underlying entity and options on those stocks. The futures side has three levels, the underlying entity, futures contracts on the underlying entity, and options on the futures contracts.

Each futures contract has from four to twelve delivery or expiration months. For example:

Treasury bills: March, June, September, December
Wheat: March, May, July, September, December
CRB Index: March, May, July, September, December
Gold: February, April, June, August, October, December
Lean hogs: February, April, June, July, August, October, December
Silver: January, March, May, July, August, September, October, December
Crude oil: All months

For the agricultural commodities, the delivery months are related to the timing of planting and harvesting. With wheat, for example, there are two crops, spring wheat and winter wheat. The spring wheat is planted in the spring and harvested in September through December, depending on it geographical location. Winter wheat goes in the ground in late fall and is harvested in the spring and early summer. For other commodities, like oil and silver, the decisions on how many delivery months to offer were made on the basis of industry concerns and marketing conditions.

The fact that a commodity can actually be delivered has created the legend, which you may have heard, that a famous or infamous futures trading dentist in Peoria had 5,000 bushels of soybeans dumped on his lawn because he forgot to offset a long bean position. It is not true. Making or accepting delivery of a physical commodity takes place at special warehouses licensed by the exchanges to assure quality, quantity, and financial stability. If our dentist let his bean contract slip into delivery, he would get several notices and a second chance to sell it, called re-tendering. The negative side of doing so is that it would cost the dentist two additional commissions as the contract was bought and sold a second time, plus he would be at the mercy of the market as to price. If he decided to accept delivery, his futures account would be debited for the entire amount of the contract. One contract for 5,000 bushes would cost $30,000 (beans at $6 per bushel), compared to a maintenance margin of $500 or so. He would then begin receiving storage and insurance bills from the warehouse where the beans are stored, and he would eventually have to do something with them. If he did not have $30,000 in his account, he would get a margin call, and his broker would aggressively attempt to obtain whatever amount the dentist was deficient, since the broker or his or her firm would have settled with the clearinghouse.

There is a subgroup of futures traders, the commercial hedgers, who are very important. These individuals or entities, usually corporations, actually use (long side) or produce (short side) the commodities that they hedge. Major livestock producers hedge their feed usage by going long on the corn market and sell their meat production by selling live cattle futures contracts for delivery. Oil refineries go long crude oil to stabilize or average the price of oil and deliver against short gasoline and heating futures contracts, called the crack spread (as in cracking oil into gasoline). Any entity using copper (manufacturers), silver (jewelers), wheat (cereal makers), airlines (fuel) or any other commodity can lock in these costs to stabilize its business by using futures and options on futures. The positions of these large traders are tracked by the Commodity Futures Trading Commission (CFTC), which is to the futures industry what the SEC is to the securities business, in what is known as the Commitments of Traders (COT) in Options and Futures. There are two COT reports; one covers open interest, which is the net futures positions remaining open at the end of the week, and is released every Friday at 3:30 p.m. EST, and the second one details open options contracts.

It is important to study these reports because the holders of these contracts are mostly large corporations that need or produce the commodities. They have excellent intelligence and great trading experience. Therefore, if the consensus is pronouncedly bullish or bearish, it is a strong clue to where the market is headed. These types of traders are hedged; as you know, that means that they are on both sides of the market and are not affected, except for lost opportunity, if the market goes up or down. Additionally, they are well financed. This is what is meant when you hear an analysts say the commodity is held in strong hands.

Weak hands refer to average traders or speculators with naked or unhedged positions. They cannot hold a losing position for very long. As soon as their positions begin to lose money, most traders must dump them. On the other hand, hedgers hold large positions in adverse markets for months because they are price neutral and plan on taking delivery of the commodity.

Again, the COT report is just another piece in the price puzzle. Just because the big guys are bullish or bearish does not mean that they are right. For example, many of the major producers of gold hedged their production out several years in the beginning of this century, only to watch gold prices soar above $400 per ounce. Gold prices had been in the doldrums for a decade. It made sense to hedge at that time. For a producer, the idea is to know your production costs, build in an acceptable profit, and then sell your production on the futures market whenever the price of your commodity is above that price. This is how the producer locks in a profit. That works great until the commodity makes a major move in the wrong direction. Then producers deliver commodities at a price that is now below the market, and users accept deliver with the CMV above the locked-in futures price. When you hedge or even spread a market, you reduce your risk substantially and give up future opportunity.

Getting back to those farmers who fudge a few surveys now and then, this may not be a big deal, but some unethical countries do the same thing in spades. The best example is what came to be known as the Great Russian Grain Robbery of the early 1970s. Soviet grain futures traders working out of Switzerland knew that their grain crop was in huge trouble. They bought long futures and call option contracts heavily, very heavily, on the CBOT. The Soviet government did not release data regarding the crop's problems until the harvest began and it was obvious to observers on the ground, who had not been allowed into the country until then. Grain prices on the futures exchange blasted off like the rocket under Sputnik. The Soviet government, along with several of its traders who also traded secretly for their own accounts, reaped enormous profits.

The lesson is that corporations, producers, and governments cannot be trusted to supply reliable information to be used to build price forecasts. In underdeveloped countries, it is common for the officials not even to have usable numbers on production or usage. Many crops, like coffee and cocoa, are grown in remote areas. The governments just do not have the infrastructure in place to collect, clean, evaluate, and report information. Critical information like this is a political tool that can be used for good or evil, depending on the morality of the owner of the data. It is because of problems like these that the United States developed satellite surveillance of the world's major production areas. Satellite maps are available on USDA's Web site during critical periods of the growing seasons.

If all this is not discouraging enough, there are always unpredictable weather problems. Let's say you create a state-of-the-art econometric model to project supply and demand for a major commodity that is critical to your country's economy. Corn is a good example, since production takes place on all continents, the North and South Poles excluded. The key to the worldwide export price comes down to a few exporting countries, since most grains (like corn, rice, and wheat) are consumed in the countries in which they are grown. Only a few countries, like the United States, Australia, and South Africa, produce enough surplus corn to influence worldwide prices—thus creating raging bull markets for call buyers in times of scarcity and bear markets for put buyers when excesses swamp the market.

Your model projects that there will be an adequate supply worldwide and that prices will trade within a normal trading range. About the time you release your report, an El Niño is reported in the tropical Pacific. The Gulf Stream over parts of the United States shifts. Spring rains drench the midwestern section of the United States, forcing farmers to curtail planting corn and switch to soybeans. This happens because soybeans have a shorter growing season than corn and can still produce a decent yield if they are planted later. Corn prices skyrocket; soybean prices crash and burn.

Weather can disrupt more than just crops. Back in 2004, Florida was hit by four hurricanes. The oil rigs in the Gulf of Mexico were taken offline for much longer than expected and contributed to the price of oil surpassing $55 per barrel. With oil, the real price mover is demand, for the time being. For the first time in history, the world is using more oil per day than it is extracting. China's demand for oil matches the spectacular growth of its gross domestic product. The government is working to control the growth, but how successful will it be? Can it prevent repeated boom and bust cycles in its economy over the next few decades? Will China be reminiscent of the United States' boom and bust economy at the dawn of the Industrial Revolution? How do you program this kind of activity into an econometric model?

Given the fact that building an econometric model and having the infrastructure to gather and process all the information needed is beyond the ability of average traders, and that most of us cannot afford ($30,000+ per year) to subscribe to one, is fundamental analysis useless in projecting commodity prices? Certainly not; just as with stocks, fundamentals give you the long-term picture. If there is a shortage in supply or an insatiable demand for a commodity, it will be positive for prices, and even the average trader can take advantage of the situation. With commodities, you must know a lot more about them than just earnings per share. And the different commodities have different factors affecting their price, whereas the factors affecting stocks are more uniform. For example, corn is fed to cattle. If it gets too expensive, livestock producers will feed their cattle wheat if it is available. This is called substitution and when substitution is possible, the commodity's price is said to be elastic, meaning that it will stretch or retract depending on supply and demand.

Some commodities are more inelastic in price. Chocolate and oil are examples. It doesn't matter much what price cocoa hits because chocoholics will buy regardless. Demand for oil appears to be impervious to price hikes and will probably stay that way until a cheaper, safer substitute comes along. Inelastic or not, however, there is always a price so high that it breaks demand.

There are some quirks on the supply side of the equation as well. Certain commodities are by-products of another operation and continue to be produced even when supply is overabundant and prices are low. Silver is an example. It is a by-product of the production of copper, zinc, and lead. Inventories can build even as prices fall. Speaking of copper, old-time commodity traders will tell you that copper has a Ph.D. in economics because it is one of the best barometers of financial activity. As its price rises, so does the economy, and when its price retracts, so does the stock market. Why? Because it is used in large amounts in manufacturing so many products, from batteries to homes. You find it all over the place, making demand for it a harbinger of economic growth. It is equally true that lower copper prices warn of a recession ahead. Also keep in mind that copper is an international product, meaning that copper's price may be up on the futures market, but that does not mean that the economy of the United States is hot. Growth in Asia can also drive copper higher, for example. Nevertheless, some of the smartest minds in the futures business watch the bobbing and weaving of copper prices as an economic barometer.

What you need to take from this discussion is that there are a vast number of varying factors influencing the supply and demand sides of the basic price equation for physical commodities. Many of these are unpredictable, like weather and politics. Governments with private agendas conceal others. Despite these factors, it is as important to trading options on futures to have a solid grasp of the fundamentals as it is to understand the overall economic situation when trading stock options—even if you use technical analysis as your primary decision-making tool. You want to know whether the wind is at your back or in your face before you launch your trading kite.

What is the best way to do that? What I am about to describe works for me. If you do not do it this way, you still need to do something to avoid peeing into the wind, which translates to trying to force a bull move in a bear market or a bear move in a bull market. What I do when trading futures or options on futures is put myself in the place of an inventory manager for the commodity I plan to trade.

Think about it. What are the concerns of an inventory manager whose year-end bonus depends on providing her firm with a steady supply of the commodity needed in its production process at the lowest average price? She gets no bonus if there is a disruption in production because the company runs out of the commodity and no bonus if the average price paid for the commodity is above a certain dollar amount. The key is locking in a sufficient quantity of the commodity using futures or options when the price is below the target price.

What is the thought process of an inventory manager for a soybean processor? The company crushes soybeans into oil and meal, the Crush Spread. The oil has a million uses in everything from paint to yogurt. A standard bushel of soybeans weighs 60 pounds. When it is crushed, the result is 48 pounds of meal and 11 pounds of oil. One pound is lost in the process.

To qualify for the bonus, the inventory manager must keep the bean bins full at an average price of $5.50 per bushel or less; in addition, she cannot have more than 100,000 bushels in inventory at the end of the year, and the company's storage facilities can hold only 1,000,000 bushels, or one month's usage. She will receive $10,000 for each penny the average price is below the target price. If she can save the company a nickel on each of the hundreds of thousands of bushels it buys, she cashes a $50,000 bonus on New Year's Eve. That should get the little gray cells in her brain agitated.

To do this, the inventory manager moves between buying in the cash market and futures. Cash buying occurs when the price of beans is at or above the target price. This is called buying from hand to mouth. When the price drops below $5.50, she fills the storage bins and buys futures and options. It is a balancing act. When price are low, she wants to buy ahead, but she does not want to buy too much in case prices go even lower. A big buy when beans are only a few pennies below the target can cost her big bucks at the end of the year if they drop even lower. But if she doesn't buy and prices scoot higher, she is out of luck. If bean prices are low, she can buy some cash and short futures (puts), speculating that they will go lower and using cheap options to hedge against their going higher before she needs the physical commodity. The profit from the puts offsets the price of the beans if they move up.

Putting yourself inside the mind of someone who has a financial stake in buying the commodity you trade and continually thinking with that mindset keeps your analysis grounded in reality. As mentioned before, the purpose of the exercise is to help you feel the markets—to make them more real rather than taking a detached, intellectual approach. Successful trading is as much art as science, and this is part of the art.

What about technical analysis? It is used more by futures traders than by stock traders. The most important reason has to do with how complicated and whimsical fundamental factors can be. The average trader, even if well informed, realizes that the commercial interests have so much of a competitive advantage when it comes to the fundamentals that he just doesn't have a chance. For example, there are five major grain companies that control the world grain markets. I know for a fact that some of them have access to satellite photographs virtually in real time. Even if the USDA posted the same photos that these grain giants see as fast as it could, the traders for these firms would have moved the market before you had a chance to call your broker.

There is no such concept as insider information in the futures market, as there is in the securities industry. For example, if someone becomes aware of information that will affect the price of a company's stock before the public becomes aware of it, there is a prohibition against trading on that information. This is not the case in futures. If a major player, like one of the big grain companies, sees the satellite photos even a few minutes before they hit the Internet and trades on this "intel," triggering a limit move, you are flat out of luck. Trading is over for the day, and you have to come back tomorrow. The market might trade limit up for several days. I have watched hogs limit down for six trading sessions in a row with crocodile tears in my eyes. Limit up or down refers to the amount a futures contract can trade up or down during any trading session before trading is halted. The limit for corn, for example, is a dime a bushel or $500 per contract.

Since most traders cannot compete on fundamental analysis, they become technicians. This is why futures traders have developed so many technical trading tools and systems. The key factor in technical analysis of futures, stocks, and options is volume—it always tells the story first. A good technician and short-term trader sees a blip up in volume as corn gains a few pennies when the traders at the giant grain company begin building a position as soon as they get their hands on new satellite photos. He does one of two things, or even both, as volume begins to move higher: he buys long futures and/or call options on the nearby contract. The nearby is the month closest to expiration and has the most volatility and liquidity. After establishing his positions, he attempts to find out what is happening. Action first, discovery second—that is how the professional traders function. The amateurs do the reverse: they see an abnormal blip in volume and wait for confirmation before acting. By that time, the best part of the initial move is often over, and when the amateurs decide to buy, the pros are selling into this new volume, taking profits and holding the options for the longer term. Traders call it selling into dumb money.

Using options and futures in unison makes dollars and sense. For example, there is a trading system called scale trading that has worked exceedingly well for years. The only drawback is that it requires a lot of patience and funds. I am not recommending it to anyone who is new to futures, but it is an excellent example of how the two trading vehicles work in tandem.

You begin buying any physical commodity, like cocoa, corn, hogs, or soybeans, when it moves into the lower 25 percent of its 10-year trading range. That is right—buy, not sell, as the commodity descends into the great unknown. The theory is the commodity will move lower until it makes a bottom, which is a good place to build a large long position for the eventual recovery. There is an old saying in the futures industry, "Nothing cures low prices as well as low prices." Once a commodity becomes cheap, everybody finds a use for it. When corn became too cheap, all of a sudden there were corn sweeteners and gasohol.

The buying and selling of the commodity is done using a scale, thus the name scale trading. I will set the scale in this instance to buy every time corn falls 4 cents and sell whenever it rises 8 cents. If you do this methodically, you will make a 100 percent profit from each position, but it takes time, patience, and margin money. The use of a scale creates the discipline that is essential to trading.

The fear and risk are limit down days; as mentioned earlier, the limit is 10 cents. For example, you bought your first three or four positions, and then there is a series of limit down days. How do you make the margin calls? How can you protect yourself? The answer is to buy puts to cover (hedge) each futures position. You now have a hedged scale trading system. It is best to buy the puts first and in advance of putting on your long positions, since they can be incredibly cheap, only a few cents a bushel when they are out- and deep-out-of-the-money. As the market retreats, you are adding long positions that are losing money, but the puts are gaining value. The gain on the puts balances the losing futures positions. If a limit down day or days occur and you are hit with a world-class margin call, you have some valuable puts to sell.

That is the bird's-eye view of the strategy. There are some other challenges that can occur. For example, some of your futures or option contracts can expire before prices reach the level needed to close out the scale. You then have to roll these contracts to more distant months. But all this is manageable if you are methodical, patient, and not underfunded. The most trouble traders get into with scale trading is being caught in a severe downdraft and not being able to meet margin calls and not having any put hedges. If this happens, all the long positions are sold at losses and the margin bill looms over the trader's head, like guillotine's blade over Marie Antoinette.

This risk explains why buying puts became part of scale trading. The purist scale traders reject the concept of using puts, saying that it reduces the profit when the commodity begins its inevitable bull move. That is fine if you have a ton of greenbacks in reserve. To compensate, my traders were encouraged to sell calls above the exit price on the scale. This did two things. First, the income from selling the calls paid for the puts. It was a credit to the account versus a debit.

Second, it reinforced trading discipline. When the bull begins to rock 'n' roll, traders are tempted to let some of the long positions, which they held as the commodity sank all the way to the bottom of a bear market and then back up to breakeven, ride the bull. The rules of scale trading state that you buy and sell on a predetermined price scale, 4 cents down and 8 cents up in this example. The bull move stirs the blood of traders, who are tempted to let their positions run as high as they can. This destroys discipline. By selling calls, the traders have no choice but to sell and avoid the risk of being whipsawing.

Why have I harped so much on trading defensively and taking steps to manage the risk? It is for the same reason futures are considered substantially more risky and volatile than securities, and it can be summed up in a single word—leverage. In physics, it is the principle of multiplying one's force many times by the use of a lever. In finance, leverage allows the investor or trader to own or control an asset using funds that are less than the value of the asset. The Federal Reserve regulates leverage in the stock market, and it has been at 50 percent for decades. An investor can buy $1,000 of stock by depositing $500 and borrowing the rest from his or her broker. That is a 1:1 ratio. In the futures market, the ratio is more in the neighbor of 20:1 or 30:1. In our corn example, the initial margin on a 5,000-bushel contract would be $500 or less. The ratio varies as the price of the commodity changes. For example:

Corn Price	Leverage Ratio
$2.25	22½:1
$2.50	25:1
$3.00	30:1
$3.25	32:1

The math is simple: corn price × number of bushels in the contract ÷ margin. But the results can be spectacular or devastating. The higher the leverage, the more risk one takes because if the investment or trade goes sour, you must make the contra party whole. In other words, you must pay 100 percent, whereas you have put only a fraction down.

Leveraging using options is even greater. You could easily buy a corn call or put for a penny or two per bushel when corn is $3.00 per bushel. If you paid 2 cents, the ratio is 150:1. Since this is even higher leverage than option traders get in the security markets, new option traders are often attracted to futures. As an added bonus, futures are more volatile most of the time. As you must know by now, there is nothing like volatility to create opportunity. The flip side, that most options on futures expire worthless and limiting risk limits reward, is just as true for futures as for stocks. There are no free drinks served at Casino Securities!

So you want to become a millionaire trading options—how do you go about it? Do you have the right stuff? That is the province of the next chapter.

Quiz

1. Which of the following are part of the commodities market?
   (a) Gold
   (b) Interest rates
   (c) Oil
   (d) Corn
   (e) S&P

2. Which of the following are part of the financial futures market?
   (a) T-bills
   (b) Currencies
   (c) Sunflower seeds
   (d) Pocket change
   (e) Natural gas

3. Forward or to-arrive contacts trade on which exchange?
   (a) Merc
   (b) CBOT
   (c) NY Merc
   (d) CBOE
   (e) None of the above
   (f) All of the above

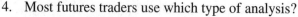

4. Most futures traders use which type of analysis?
   (a) Fundamental
   (b) Technical
   (c) Futures analysis
   (d) Econometric modeling
   (e) Supply-demand analysis

5. Which risk is unique to futures trading?
   (a) Loss of equity
   (b) Limit down or up days
   (c) Leveraging
   (d) Using faulty information

6. What are maintenance margin calls?
   (a) Demands for additional margin money
   (b) Those stupid calls you get during dinnertime
   (c) Nothing to worry about
   (d) A request to add money to an account so that trading can begin

7. What does increasing leveraging do for a trader?
   (a) Increases risk
   (b) Increases reward
   (c) Ensures margin calls
   (d) Reduces the volatility of a trade
   (e) All of the above
   (f) None of the above

8. Whipsawing is
   (a) a neck injury common in auto accidents.
   (b) a hunting device used by aborigines in Australia.
   (c) a raging bull move in key markets.
   (d) getting caught when a markets moves against your positions and then immediately reverses.

9. Why are new option traders attracted to the futures markets?
   (a) They are so easy to trade.
   (b) Almost everyone makes money in them.
   (c) All the fundamental information that one needs is immediately available on the Internet.
   (d) Volatility is often high.
   (e) Leveraging is extreme.
   (f) All of the above.
   (g) None of the above.

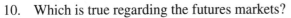

10. Which is true regarding the futures markets?
     (a) They are the easiest to understand.
     (b) There are always opportunities to make money in them.
     (c) There is little competition.
     (d) Brokers are always honest and willing to help.
     (e) All of the above.
     (f) None of the above.

Answers

1. a, c, d; 2. a and b; 3. e; 4. b; 5. b; 6. a; 7. a and b; 8. d; 9. d and e; 10. b.

12

Become the Bubble and Ride the Wind . . .

Your philosophy of life, whether it has been consciously formulated after years of study and thought or created by a series of random choices, governs every aspect of your life. All of us have one, and it dominates the style of option trader you will become because it controls how you interact with market stimuli, particularly fear and greed. Equally important, it defines your overall view of how the universe

functions—and, more critically in this context, how you perceive the markets and your ability to interact with them. How do you answer questions like these:

- Was the universe created by an accidental convergence of matter or in some orderly fashion or plan?
- Is there direction and meaning in your worldview, or do you lean toward the existential view of life?
- Is human existence governed by reason or by emotion?
- Do you believe in a mechanistic universe or the chaos theory to explain the interactions of people and the markets they create?

In short, what is your worldview?

Your philosophical approach to these questions defines your personality and your psychological makeup. Understanding yourself is the first critical step toward the development of a trading philosophy, which in turn determines how you can be most successful analyzing markets, picking trades, and taking profits. It even explains how you adjust to the demands and pressures of trading. Because trading is such an intense activity, it behooves you to do some soul searching before you leap into the unforgiving world of option trading.

What is your everyday life like? Is it organized, or do you like to just wing it and adjust to whatever is thrown at you? What things are most important to you? Wealth? Respect? Being loved? How do you react to uncertainty and unpredictability? Are order and regularity important in your daily life? Do you develop routines and patterns? Or do you resist regimentation? Are you a joiner or a loner? Where do money and wealth fit into your scheme of things? What would you be willing to do to make a half a million a year working part-time? Why did you buy this book in the first place, and what is your reaction after reading this far? The answers will define your trading approach as either discretionary or systematic. The former is more intuitive and adjusts positions as the market reveals itself. The latter has complete faith in a trading system and follows it to the letter, regardless of where the market goes. Make some notes before reading further.

The most critical question you must answer, if you are seriously considering trading options, is: Why do you want to trade options in the first place? What is your motivation? How strong or weak is your tolerance of risk? Even if you only buy calls and puts, and cheap ones at that, the odds are in favor of a lot of them expiring worthless. How will you deal with 10 or 20 or 30 losses in a row? Will you give up, or will it make you all the more determined to succeed?

Jeff Yass, a professional option trader, describes the option market as one big poker game. "The basic concept that applies to both poker and option trading is that the primary object is not winning the most hands, but rather maximizing your gains," as reported in the "Daily Reckoning." It is not like baseball, where hitters live and die based on how high their batting average is. It is closer to big game hunting, where only trophy-class kills count and are worthy of taking home for mounting. In the margin, write down your reaction to the statement by Mr. Yass. Positive? Negative? Do you agree with it, or does it upset you? You will use it later when I get to writing a trading plan.

An example here might help. If you are compulsive and require immediate results, you could have a problem. On the other hand, if you love assembling 5,000-piece puzzles on long winter days, there may be hope. It is also not uncommon for traders to have as much of a problem with success as with failure. If you start taking large profits out of the option market, will it rub your philosophical beliefs the wrong way? Would you care? Some traders feel guilty about taking home large sums of money because they are not working for it in the classical sense. They don't produce any products or services. They do not see any redeeming social value in trading. Their defenders say that traders are valuable because they facilitate the price discovery process and create liquidity for legitimate hedgers. But this is a somewhat weak argument because more often than not, traders distort pricing by running it higher or lower than the fundamentals dictate. At worst, they are just exchanging wealth with other traders and investors, not unlike the way gambling moves money from one player to another. Other traders have difficulty adjusting to working only when they feel like it and goofing off the rest of the time. Most traders rarely think about these concepts. For them, it is hard, stressful work. If you do not come to grips with your perception of what trading is, it can drag down your enthusiasm and affect your success. A bad attitude about trading inhibits rebounding from an equity drawdown, which is something that you must expect to happen. You begin to lose and do not have a clue as to what is happening. By the way, there is a Superdome full of shrinks serving the industry, like the sports psychologists or performance coaches that are so popular in society today. Some are helpful; others are quacks.

One of the first steps every option trader must take is committing to a concept of how the market works, so that she or he can find, develop, or borrow a trading system that matches her or his perception of the market, philosophy of the market, and psychological makeup. This was touched on in Chapter 8, but now I will revisit it from the standpoint of determining the type of trading system that best suits you. To say the least, markets are whimsical. One time you will follow all your trading rules to the letter and lose a fortune. The next time you will violate some of these rules and reap untold riches. (Excuse me if I sometimes resort to hyperbole.) This is a paradox that traders must embrace and not let interfere with their trading strategy.

The unpredictability of market behavior has confounded participants since the beginning of trading. Did you ever as a child while away a summer afternoon in your backyard with a bottle of Bubble Magic, watching the bubbles float erratically on the wind's currents? Many bubbles burst as soon as they are released; others float until they are out of sight. Think of your trades as bubbles; the soap is your capital, and the wind is the capricious trends of the market. When you wave or blow into the wand filled with soap, you initiate a trade bubble. The ones that burst as soon as they are released are your losers. Several float up; others down. You may or may not be on the right side of these trades. A precious few drift and drift and drift in the direction you intended all the bubbles to go; you win big. If you get excited and wave the wand too fast, you only waste your soap and go broke. Too slow a movement creates a bubble that is too heavy to be carried by the currents of air or greed. There is a perfect tempo and pace for every bubble maker, as there is for every trader. You must find one that matches your beliefs and temperament. As a Zen trader would say, you must become the bubble and ride the wind.

Become the bubble and ride the wind.

It is time to begin your trading plan—is the market efficient or unpredictable? Your answer must agree with your core beliefs. You can't accept capricious markets if you truly believe that there is order in the universe. Nor can you look for organization and patterns in the markets if you deny them in your life. Mixing and matching leads to indecision and lack of commitment when you need it most—like when one of your trades is sinking as fast as a Chicago mobster with cement shoes tossed into Lake Michigan. Reactions must be swift—there is no time for reflective thought. Flight or fight! Jump out of the way or get run over.

Developing a trading philosophy gets even tougher when you come to the realization that so much of what happens in the markets is mob rule. The great masses of people worldwide, all trying at the same time (during trading hours) to fix the price of a stock, option, or futures contract, often act like lemmings or stampeding cattle.

This is what causes prices to run to withering heights. Was Amazon ever worth 200 times nonexistent earnings? What about AOL, Lucent, JDS Uniphase, Redhat, or Qwest? If that does not convince you, explain Enron, Adelphi, and all the others. In other words, the price and thus the price-earnings ratio are often created by the mood of the crowd trading the stock, not by sound fundamental analysis of the company's earnings potential. Over the course of a year, the same stock with no change in earnings can be worth 10 or 100 times earnings depending on whatever traders feel as they bid for the stock.

Can a computer model be built that captures the patterns and predicts the next great move? Remember that in the early part of this book, I said I would tell you a story about how some super-smart Nobel Prize winners tried to break the bond bank but were instead hung out to dry? It is the tale of a hedge fund called Long-Term Capital Management (LTCM). One of the Nobel Prize winners was our friend Myron S. Scholes of Black-Scholes option-pricing model fame. The other was Robert C. Merton, a student of Paul Samuelson, the world-renowned economist and teacher. Scholes and Merton are giants in the option-modeling business. Overall, LTCM had 25 Ph.D.s crunching the numbers and several of the most successful bond traders ever to walk down Wall Street—the finest team of option and derivative traders ever assembled at a single trading desk.

The leader and organizer of LTCM was a world-class bond trader named John Meriwether, who had traded successfully for several large Wall Street houses like Salomon Brothers. The guiding canon of faith—and I really mean blind, unwavering belief—at LTCM was that prices traded within discoverable ranges and that whenever they moved outside of those ranges, risk-free trading opportunities presented themselves. Think back to the bell curves used to describe volatility. When price points occurred outside the widest bell curve, the people at LTCM believed that they could calculate the odds of those prices moving back inside and thus have sure winners. Ones they could bet the farm on.

Their faith rested on their past performances, reinforced by the overwhelming brainpower and trading expertise that the hedge fund could bring to bear on any trade. It had generated hundreds of millions of dollars in profits, a gain of over 400 percent in four years (1994–1998). What went wrong? LTCM accepted its models as failsafe and believed that market analysis is a pure science. Blind faith in the system led the firm to make some horrendous bets with 1,200:1 leveraging. Some positions had nominal values of as much as a trillion dollars. A $100 billion balance sheet evaporated in four months when prices of Russian bonds refused to return to the mean, a Black Swan event. A consortium of Wall Street bankers had to bail out the hedge fund.

I personally came to an understanding of how statistically improbable events can and do occur. I lived through two 100-year floods in two consecutive years in Iowa, events that had stupendous odds against ever happening. Even a peripheral study of the markets and nature reveals hundreds of events that any statistician worth his or her salt would swear are impossible. How many times have you read of lightning striking the same place or person twice? Keep this in mind when you uncover the perfect trade.

Nor do I believe that markets religiously adhere to the efficient market hypothesis. As you remember, this states that the markets are smarter than any investor and are always right. No matter how hard you try, you cannot beat them. The markets are the 3,000-pound hippopotamuses that go anywhere they damn well please. If you look closely, you will see egrets, small birds that live well by picking food right out of the hippo's mouths. This is the symbiotic relationship that traders have with the markets.

My understanding of the market's always being right (the title of one of my other books, so I had better explain it) is that at any given time, the price in the market is the only price for a stock, futures contract, or option, and this is what makes that price right, regardless of how it got there. In a larger context, the rationale or lack of rationality behind the pricing of a stock, option, futures contract, or an entire market is often wrong or out of line based on fundamental or technical analysis. It overacts and overreacts. If it did not, there would not be so many major and minor corrections taking place regularly. If it was right and efficient, it would run smoothly in response to the price-earnings ratio or supply and demand. Was the market right in 1929 or 2000? More specifically, it is the players who make the market that are wrong—the fishermen, for example, who stampede from one side of a boat to the other to try to catch up with the fastest-moving fish or who panic when their bait is stolen by the denizens of the deep.

Even with all this said, there definitely are discernible patterns that can be exploited for fun and profit. There are pricing and econometric models that are meaningful and that actually work. Their success has more to do with the amount of faith you place in them and how you use them. What you need to know and accept is that prices move in varied and unpredictable patterns that may or may not repeat themselves in a reasonable time period or act exactly the same each time they come by. This happens because these patterns reflect human beings trading, some rationally and others emotionally. I hope this doesn't come as a shock, but people are just not calm and consistent, particularly when their money is at risk. They desert a trade faster than a speeding bullet when it heads south and leap over high buildings to get back into it when it roars north a few minutes later. Moreover, being mere humans, they tend to repeat their behavior over and over and over again, but not always exactly the same way—thus you can take advantage of repetitive patterns once you learn to read people and price charts. You must be alert for familiar patterns reappearing with new wrinkles over varying time frames. Assume that the patterns and strategies you rely on will fail and build into your trading plan protection against catastrophic loss.

Part of human nature is contrariness, and there is even a trading school for those kinds of folks. If you are dreadfully independent and prefer to walk out of step with the rest of humanity, there is a place for you in the grand scheme of the world of options. Also, there are many trading systems, generally classified as character-of-the-market, that have been specifically created to measure the quality, rather than the quantity, of price movements and to anticipate reversals. The point is that no matter how you view the world and its markets, you can find a system or an approach that suits you individually.

Next question: are your financial muscles in shape for option trading? If they are not, your brokerage firm may sideline you to trading only long calls and puts, with a few covered calls tossed in for good measure. As was discussed previously, sellers must be able to buy the underlying entities at the market when it is running away from them and to deliver the securities to a buyer on demand. For the purposes of creating a sample plan, I will assume that you are eligible for any strategy.

After your self-analysis session, what type of option trader do you think you should become? Step 1 of your written trading plan describes your approach to the market and your overall strategy. Let me stress that the plan must be written. Writing stimulates thought. Once you commit a section of your plan to paper, your mind is freed up to move forward. You will also find that each statement you write cries out for refining and clarification. New thoughts, questions, and challenges are generated once you see your ideas staring back at you from your word processor. Resolution of all issues is critical before you are prepared to go face-to-face with the world's finest traders. Especially when you realize on day one of your trading career that you are the trader with the least amount of trading experience in the whole world.

Are there trading systems that can accommodate every personality type and worldview? Yes, and this is one of the least understood mysteries of trading. The reason goes back to the axioms that trading is as much an art as a science and that price discovery is a collective endeavor. The biggest mistake most people who are new to trading make is searching for the Holy Grail of trading, the perfect system.

You won't be any more successful at finding it than the Knights of the Round Table were in their quests. Just as in auto racing, it is the driver, not the car.

The most successful trading systems, especially for average traders, are ones borrowed from someone who is already trading. A system is attractive to a new trader because it seems familiar in the sense of having the same or a similar world-view as the trader, that is, it appears to be rational and orderly, chaotic, or contrarian, depending on how the individual trader filters reality through his or her mind. It also engenders confidence because it works, whether intuitively or methodologically, the way the trader interprets the markets. Each trader begins to trade and build experience. At some point, it is time for the trader to customize or personalize the approach, making it her or his own. Flourishing traders bend or shave the rules, using their intuition. This is the art side of the trading coin. Intuition gives traders the edge on the market needed to win. Intuition combines experience and knowledge, building confidence in the traders and making old systems new.

Therefore, the first section of your trading plan describes how you look at the markets, what general type of trading system you seek, and a description of your personality. Consider studying some of the classical personality typing systems and taking one or more of the personality tests available on the Internet. Do not try to do the analysis of yourself in a vacuum, since these descriptions are usually inaccurate. Look outside for an objective opinion. One personality typing system I occasionally use is the enneagram. It has been kicking around the globe for centuries and seems suited for traders. It may be able to give you an insight into what you look like to an impartial observer. There are nine core personality types:

1. *The Perfectionist.* Idealistic, controlled, righteous, orderly, efficient, opinionated, workaholic, inflexible, and compulsive. If these words describe you, use a technical trading system, but guard against following it to destruction. Avoid excess analysis and lack of spontaneity.
2. *The Mother Hen.* Caring, generous, giving to get, unselfish, gushy, self-important, domineering, coercive, saintly, overbearing, and patronizing. These folks need an intuitive system because they are feeling people. They often fail as traders because they are generous and concerned people in a very selfish business, but they make excellent mentors.
3. *The Pro Quarterback.* Arrogant, driving, competitive, status seeking, exploitative, pretentious, narcissistic, image-conscious, and calculating. If this type can learn to trade only for him- or herself and ignore the crowd, he or she can be an outstanding trader. However, if this type of person feels that he or she must show off, he or she loses site of the primary objective and can lose big time.
4. *The Artist.* Sensitive, temperamental, dramatic, artistic, creative, moody, melancholy, morbid, despairing, and decadent. Oddly enough, this type can be a great

trader if she or he has a healthy dose of self-awareness. The creative, especially musicians, see repeating patterns in the markets that most others overlook and with training can exploit this gift.

5. *The Professor.* Cerebral, intense, secretive, intellectual, paranoid, schizophrenic, and extremist. If people of this type can put a leash on theorizing and add some practicality to their approach to the markets, they do very well. The danger is developing theories that get more convoluted each day until their understanding of the markets is too complicated to trade.

"Sure your fear of success comes from your post-decline depression and the rough divorce from your last option, but I've got to ask you... How does your MOM trade?"

6. *The Enigma.* Loyal, suspicious, responsible, masochistic, trustworthy, engaging, anxious, and dutiful. An inferiority complex makes him or her paranoid, which is not necessarily a bad trait for this line of work. If people of this type can harness their feelings, they can work incredibly hard to overcome their inferiority complex.

7. *The Dilettante.* Vivacious, lively, fun-loving, versatile, acquisitive, addictive, compulsive, and hyperactive. He or she wants the best of everything and has an addiction to the things money can buy, often resulting in overtrading. Much self-control is required for success.

8. *The Politician.* Powerful, belligerent, megalomaniac, authoritative, self-willed, confrontational, and overconfident. The markets do not like this kind of person and consider themselves more powerful. Therefore, the eights must become more humble if they are to succeed.

9. *The Nice Guy.* Easygoing, agreeable, complacent, un-self-conscious, unreflective, unresponsive, passive, disengaged, and fatalistic. Mr. or Ms. Popularity likes trend-following systems, but people of this type must get a hold of themselves and become aggressive to some degree to make it as traders.

As I'm sure you've guessed, few people are perfectly one type or another. They are predominantly one type, but have characteristics of one or two of the others. Some types are more naturally traders than others, but winning option traders are found among all categories.

After completing your market philosophy and your self-description, run it by someone who knows you well and whom you trust, like your spouse or a friend who knows you well. Yes, your spouse! Your spouse must be at least accepting of your decision to trade or, better yet, supportive. If he or she is not, you may want to reconsider. Get your spouse's feedback. There is simply nothing more important to tradering than knowing yourself and taking steps in advance to protect yourself from your greatest enemy. As Pogo put it, "We have met the enemy and he is us!"

What is your level of skill and experience of options and how they trade? What more do you need to learn? The next step surveys your knowledge of option trading and develops plans to fill any gaps. The knowledge needed usually falls into the following categories:

- Learning to speak and understand optionese
- A general understanding of the mechanics of how options and their underlying entities work
- Specific comprehension of the options you actually plan to trade and their underlying entities
- The rules and regulations of the securities business and the exchanges on which your options trade
- An understanding of the trading platform, i.e. software or brokerage firm, you plan to use
- Technical and fundamental analysis and research techniques pertinent to your trading style
- The psychology of trading options in general and your own psychology in particular

- Reading account statements and tracking the progress of individual trades
- Developing trading rules to protect your equity
- Developing disciplinary rules specifically pertinent to trading options the way you are going to trade them
- Financial planning and money management
- Setting realistic goals and evaluation progress
- Ideas for managing adverse situations, such as recovery from unexpected setbacks or drawdowns of equity, rebounding from trading slumps, burnout, and so on
- Selection of a mentor and development of a strategy for working with that mentor

As you can see, the concept is to expect and prepare for the worst—so that you will never be disappointed or surprised. Here are quotes from two of the top traders in the world about the importance of losing and trading defensively:

"There are so many ways to lose, but so few ways to win. Perhaps the best way to achieve victory is to master all the rules for disaster and then concentrate on avoiding them." Victor Niederhoffer, *The Education of a Speculator*, p. 85. Mr. Niederhoffer traded successfully for George Soros, the world's most famous speculator, for 10 years. Mr. Soros refers to Mr. Niederhoffer as the trader he never had to fire.

"The most important rule of trading is to play a great defense, not a great offense." Paul Tutor Jones, a world-class trader featured in Jack Schwager's classic book *Market Wizard*.

There is an old proverb that you often hear traders repeat that is worth contemplating. "There are old traders and there are bold traders, but there are not any old, bold traders." If you read interviews with the most successful traders, they tell you that the key to success is taking only what the markets give you. When you try to force trades or push for extra profits, the result is often disastrous.

How are you going to educate and train yourself? There is almost too much information—too many books, too many perfect trading systems for sale, too many Web sites, too many newsletters, too many seminars, too many trade shows, too many schools, too much software, just too much of everything to sort through it all methodically. What is helpful and what resembles what you find on the ground behind a bull?

My advice is to start reading the list of books in Appendix 4 as you start writing your trading plan. Simultaneously, try to find a few option traders that you trust who will let you sit with them as they trade. You might try visiting public trading floors if there are any locally available. Look around the floor. Talk to traders on break. They are often helpful to new traders because it isn't the type of business or sport where there is only one winner on each trade. Lots of people win and lots lose every time prices change. Seek out someone who might become a mentor for you,

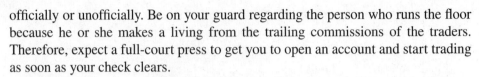

officially or unofficially. Be on your guard regarding the person who runs the floor because he or she makes a living from the trailing commissions of the traders. Therefore, expect a full-court press to get you to open an account and start trading as soon as your check clears.

What should you be looking for in a mentor? A mentor is a teacher and counselor. To teach, one must have experience in the subject, a willingness to share, and the patience to work at the pupil's pace. If you meet someone, say while visiting a trading floor, see if this person is the one other traders go to for help. Begin asking questions. Are the answers understandable and complete? Does this person show an interest in you? If so, ask if you can spend some time with him or her. Make your decision carefully, but look for someone who is obviously trading, appears to be competent, and knows a lot more than you do. If you want a lot of that person's time to review your written plan and sit beside you while you trade, you may have to compensate that person. No education is free, so this is not unreasonable.

Regarding the expansion of your basic understanding of options, consider all the sources that are available online and for free. Start with a through review of what is available from the Options Industry Council (www.888options.com). This is a nonprofit association sponsored by the American Stock Exchange, Boston Options Exchange, Chicago Board of Options Exchange, International Securities Exchange, Philadelphia Stock Exchange, and the Options Clearing Corporation. Granted, all these organizations have a vested interest in starting you on an option-trading career; nevertheless, the Options Industry Council has an enormous amount of information that you can access for free. For starters, there are several booklets worth reading on everything from trading strategies to taxes. You have access to three option-pricing models, the Black-Scholes & Merton (1973), the Cox-Ross-Rubenstein Binomial (1979), and the Barone-Adesi & Whaley (1987). The council recommends the last because it corrects some of the problems with the first two. You should also consider taking advantage of the council's free webinars (online seminars) and the classes they sponsor around the country. A schedule is on the Web site.

The OIC also provides an interactive CD to teach the various option-trading strategies. I would recommend it, plus there are several software training programs available from the options exchanges and brokerage firms. Utilize as many as you can. This falls into the area of paper trading, which, as was mentioned earlier, is a vital first step before actually trading. The interactive programs now available add much to the process by showing you schematics of the risk-reward ratio and suggesting strategies that you may not be aware of. It makes the training process more effective, realistic, and enjoyable.

Another somewhat neutral Web site to peruse is Investopedia (www.investopedia.com). It provides definitions of terms, articles, and a lot of free information. Also visit the Web sites of all the option exchanges, particularly the Chicago Board of Options Exchange and the Options Clearing Corporation. Then take a look at Schaefer Research. It has an interesting comparison of brokerage firms and commission rates, which could be a starting place for your search for a broker.

In your written plan, you need to state how you are going to execute trades. You have basically three choices. The first is the classic full-service brokerage firm, such as Merrill Lynch. It is the most expensive route to the exchanges, but it provides the most personal service. Let me caution you, as an ex-broker, that you do not always get all the help and education you might expect unless you are a large or active customer. Brokers, by the nature of their business, which is selling, have a built-in conflict of interest. They are generally paid based on the number of trades they sell their clients. It is also very important to find a broker who specializes in option trading. Most offices have such a person. If you currently have a good relationship with a firm, but the person handling your account is not the option specialist, ask the branch manager if the "option pro" can handle your option trades and let your regular broker deal with your other needs.

Your second choice is an online brokerage firm. This ranges from very low commissions–low frills shops to those that provide a substantial amount of research and help. Some, like Scottrade, are online but also maintain physical offices around the country. When you place an order online, you basically e-mail your order to the brokerage firm's back office, which relays it to the appropriate exchange. Some send the order first to broker's brokers, or wholesalers. They fill orders from inventory or match orders as they come in. If a firm uses this routing, it must tell you this in its disclosure document. It is more of a practice with stocks than with options. The negative aspects are the extra cost of the middle firm's commissions and slower fills.

Another brokerage concept is called direct access, such as Trade Station. Here the customer becomes his or her own order desk clerk and fires trades directly to the exchanges, bypassing the broker's back office. These systems provide streaming live price quotes, which accounts for their cost of up to several hundred dollars per month. If you execute a sufficient number of trades each month, the software is comped. Direct-access trading was developed for stock day traders, but now options and futures trade directly as well. You would need to be a very active trader to warrant the expense.

If you plan to do a lot of spread trading, look for a firm like Benjamin & Jerrold. It can handle spreads the way a broker should—that is, filling both sides simultaneously rather than legging into them—and can deal with conditional orders. I suggest you visit several Web sites of the different types of brokerage firms to understand all the alternatives available. Several of the direct-access providers offer free trials or have excellent interactive demonstrations to give you a feel for how their systems work.

What strategies do you plan to use when you start trading, and how are you going to find enough good trades to make some serious money trading options? Whatever strategy you select must reflect the risk tolerance level stated in your written trading plan. Let's assume there are three possible levels—low, medium and high. What strategies match up with these risk categories? I can cover only three of the most basic strategies. You know by now that buying a put or a call is relatively low risk—with the understanding that you can easily lose the entire premium and transaction costs. Spreads give you a fixed profit and a fixed loss parameter, but are a little more complex. Selling naked calls has the most risk, while the risk of selling naked puts depends on how close the striking price is to zero. Covered calls, on the other hand, are on the low-risk list, as long as you can live with occasionally delivering a favorite stock to a stranger. The next consideration is the number of options contracts you buy per trade. Naturally, a single contract is less risky than a 100-lot. I'd strongly recommend beginning modestly and increasing your lot size as your experience and success dictate.

What should your next step be? Before you jump headlong into the ocean, check the temperature and surf conditions. I am assuming that you believe there is some deliberateness to price movement and that from time to time the markets are inefficient or out of line, meaning that there are times when you can get an edge on the market by taking advantage of prices that are unbalanced. This is the position of most successful traders. They believe that if there were not times when they could get an edge, they would never win, let alone win consistently.

This is a very important crossroads. If you, in your heart, do not accept the premise of an inefficient market that you can take advantage of, do not trade. Do not open a trading account. Invest in mutual funds, buy real estate, start a business—but do not trade, especially if you are not certain that you can cautiously experiment and continue to study it. You should not risk your money on anything you do not believe in or understand. Use Warren Buffett, the second richest man in the United States and its finest investor, as your role model. He deliberately avoided investing in the technology industry when it set all-time growth records toward the end of the twentieth century because he did not sufficiently understand its economics. As it turned out, the dot-coms became dot-bombs because the economics were flawed. He might have missed an opportunity on the upside, but he entirely sidestepped the crash—a good defense is a good offense.

In line with accepting the idea of an inefficient market, professional traders also strongly believe that external events can disrupt the market, causing severe losses. They have learned to accept the fickleness of price discovery without abandoning hope of consistent success. This does not mean that you cannot succeed consistently or that the markets are totally random. It does mean that you must accept both the good and the bad. At times some totally unforeseen event—a terrorist attack or a soybean embargo—will occur that trashes the market you were trading.

There is always the clear and present danger of overlooking or missing a key fact when using fundamental analysis or picking the wrong starting point with a technical trading system.

If you plan to trade, you must do two things. First, you must accept the fact that there is considerable unpredictability in all markets, which offers you opportunity and risk. If there were a way or a system that could predict every conceivable event that might influence price, it would shut all the markets down. Second, you must play a strong defensive game. A market is made up of winners and losers and cannot survive without both—and you will be a loser from time to time just as certainly as God makes little green apples.

Trading is like a religion that requires new members to admit that they are sinners as the first step in conversion and acceptance of faith. Or like Alcoholics Anonymous, which requires new members to admit that they are drunks before they can get control of their problem. Just the fact that the vast majority of options expire worthless should attest to the fact that you will have losing trades. Every option that expires worthless was owned by a loser, and you will have your share. The objective of trading is not to have all winners, which is an unachievable goal. Therefore, one of the goals in your written plan should be to make more money from your winners than you lose on your losers and skip the part about shooting for the highest winning percentage on record.

How should you decide on which strategy to use? It is not your decision, but the market's decision. What does this mean? This is a key concept. Take a moment to think about it. Why is it not solely your decision?

The reason is the bubbles. No one is big enough to fight the market. If you have doubts, study the attempt of the Hunt brothers' consortium to corner the silver market. When they began in 1973, silver was $1.95 per ounce. They bought and bought and bought futures in silver and took delivery when the contracts expired. By 1980, the consortium had amassed millions of ounces of silver and it hit a peak of $54 an ounce. The Federal Reserve and COMEX busted the silver market to stop the squeeze, and prices fell to $10.80 on March 27, 1980, and went then lower. The Hunt family, once one of the richest, went bankrupt, losing billions.

The point is, you must take what the market gives you. Sometimes the market is outrageously bullish; other times it is bearish. It can even trade flat for short periods of time. Or it can be totally erratic, shooting up only to be shot down a day or two later. The patterns change, but the opportunities remain, if you select a strategy that is in sync with the current situation. Think of reading the market as you would check the weather before dressing for the day. If it is cold, dress warmly. If it is rainy, take an umbrella and raincoat. Shorts fit hot summer days. My point is simply that the character of the market determines the general strategy. You must then choose a specific strategy that fits within the criteria of the overall outlook and strategy.

For example, a bullish market indicates taking long positions. Should you buy some call options, consider bull spreads, or use some other bullish trading strategy? Next, does the complexion of the market suggest trading an overall index, a sectional index, or a specific stock or commodity? In your trading plan, take the time to spell out how you think you will deal with the various personalities of the market. This helps you understand which strategies you have confidence in using, and assists you in evaluating the risk-reward ratio of each trade.

You must look carefully at the maximum amount you will risk on each trade. For example, it is common for new traders to limit the risk on any one trade to no more than 10 percent of their trading equity. If there is $2,000 in the account, the limit is $200 per trade. This amount can take some trades off the table. It is also critical not to let this factor encourage you to buy options that are so cheap that they have no chance of being successful. You do not want to sell yourself a loser just because you cannot afford the right trade.

What should you do? First, you must always be ready to walk away from a trade. There is a bus every 15 minutes. You will not run out of opportunities. Another approach is to use a strategy that makes the trade affordable. For example, you are looking at a stock or a futures contract that is poised for a dramatic move higher but the calls that are at- or in-the-money are costly. You want to take the trade, but it violates your max dollar rule. Try putting on a spread. Sell a higher call and use the proceeds to help pay for the long call you really want. This lowers both your cost and your maximum profit potential because your long call will be offset when the stock reaches the striking price of your short call. This is a better way of trading than ignoring your rules or totally passing up a good trade. Patience wins the race.

You could just take a chance and buy the long position, disregarding your maximum trade limit rule. This would result in a larger profit if you are right or a larger loss if you are wrong. The worse part of doing this is that it weakens your discipline. My experience has been that traders without discipline are like sailors who can't swim—eventually they get into something deeper than they can get out of safely. Trading without discipline is gambling, which forces you to depend solely on luck. It is not a long-term plan for success. To paraphrase Warren Buffett, discipline is the first rule, and the second rule is to follow the first rule.

What safeguards are you going to write into your guiding plan to keep yourself on track? Along with setting a specific amount for the maximum dollars risked per trade, do the same for the maximum loss you will take. Remember the allusion to the professional gamblers? When they are playing a game like seven-card stud, they have a specific number of cards that they will look at before folding. For example, if they do not see a hand developing after the first two or three cards, they fold. Good traders have stop-loss points for every trade as well. The name of the game in both cases is preservation of capital. If you do not preserve your capital, you will not be around for the next hand, which may be the one you have been waiting for since puberty.

You must track every trade. Put them on a spreadsheet: opening price, closing price, and profit or loss. Review your trades regularly. Their frequency depends on how active you are. Calculate your winning-losing percentage, but, most importantly, also calculate your net gain or loss. Highlight any losses that exceed your maximum. These are the ones that will cause you the most problems in your trading career and that have the potential end it. The worst enemy of new traders is hope. They hold losing positions, hoping for a rebound, but these positions get worse more often than not. You must be realistic and disciplined to survive as an option trader.

If you have a mentor, a trading partner, or a knowledgeable friend, ask him or her to review your progress and trades compared to your plan. Get an objective viewpoint, which surprisingly often will differ from your own. Hold these sessions on a regular basis. It might be weekly, or if you are not yet a frequent trader, it could be after every 10 or 20 trades. All that matters is that periodically you evaluate your performance objectively and rationally and make any adjustments needed to stay or get back on track. This is also a good time to update your trading plan if it needs it. Plans always need updating and refining. Think of them as works in progress, not as commandments etched in stone.

Finally, you want to strive to become as good a trader as you possibly can be. The steps to reaching this objective are no different from those one takes to reach any worthwhile goal. You must be hard on yourself, push yourself, and not cut corners. Create a checklist that details the steps you need to take before entering a trade and use this checklist religiously before opening every trade. Critique all your trades. Periodically meet with a mentor or friend. Be brutally honest with yourself, and demand your best every day. Rely on hard work—not luck.

If you find that trading is not pleasurable, quit. Do not try to force yourself to like it for some reason, such as the profit potential or the laid-back lifestyle. In my experience, the only successful traders I have ever met trade because they love it. They would trade even if there were no chance of making a living at it. That is how you have to feel to make it your profession.

Good hunting!

Quiz

1. Your outlook on life has no bearing on your option trading.
    (a) True
    (b) False

2. How much tolerance for risk do you need to have to be an option trader?
   (a) High
   (b) Medium
   (c) Low
   (d) Depends on strategy

3. One of the keys to successful option trading is
   (a) a high per trade success rate.
   (b) picking only high-risk trades.
   (c) maximum leveraging.
   (d) patience.
   (e) all of the above.
   (f) none of the above.

4. Option-pricing computer models are
   (a) infallible.
   (b) correct most of the time.
   (c) never on target.
   (d) useful as a guide.

5. LTCM failed because
   (a) of intellectual hubris.
   (b) there were not enough Ph.D.s on staff.
   (c) its price models never worked.
   (d) it was undercapitalized.

6. What is cornering a market?
   (a) Buying too many long positions
   (b) Taking delivery of too many long positions
   (c) Controlling a commodity in order to manipulate its price
   (d) Buying more of a commodity than anyone else

7. What are the six basic option strategies?
   (a) Buy calls
   (b) Buy puts
   (c) Sell naked calls
   (d) Sell naked puts
   (e) Sell covered call
   (f) Sell covered puts
   (g) Combinations of puts and calls

8. Who collects the premium on a covered call?
   (a) The broker
   (b) The clearing firm

(c) The brokerage firm
(d) The NASD
(e) The seller

9. Which of the following is (are) conservative strategy(ies)?
(a) Selling naked puts
(b) Selling naked calls
(c) Buying puts
(d) Buying calls
(e) Selling covered calls
(f) Selling covered puts

10. What is the best reason to trade options?
(a) To make oneself wealthy
(b) The adrenalin rush that accompanies trading
(c) To prove you are smarter than the market
(d) For the sheer love of trading
(e) For the admiration ordinary people have for traders

Answers

1. b; 2. d; 3. d; 4. d; 5. a; 6. c; 7. a, b, c, d, e and g; 8. e; 9. c, d, and e; 10. d.

Final Exam

1. If you bought 5 WIX June puts at a CMV of $1, how much margin would be required?
   (a) 25 percent or $125
   (b) 50 percent or $250
   (c) 75 percent or $375
   (d) 100 percent or $500

2. You are selling 2 calls and 2 puts that you have held for several weeks. This transaction involves
   (a) spreading.
   (b) offsetting.
   (c) dropping out.
   (d) shorting.

3. As a writer of a call, what are your alternatives?
   (a) Exercise against the buyer
   (b) Wait patiently for expiration
   (c) Offset the position
   (d) Hedge your risk

4. Which of the following describes the 45 September WIX put in your trading portfolio when WIX is trading at 44?
   (a) A hot trade
   (b) A sure winner
   (c) In-the-money
   (d) Out-of-the-money

5. A stock you have an option on split 3:2. What happens to your option?
   (a) The price is adjusted.
   (b) All options are automatically exercised.
   (c) The shares are adjusted.
   (d) You are issued a new option reflecting the split.

6. You open a position by writing 2 December 70 puts for $2. Which statement(s) are correct?
   (a) Your account is credited with $400.
   (b) Your account is debited for $400.
   (c) You can exercise the option and go long 200 shares of WIX.
   (d) You can exercise the option and go short 200 shares of WIX.

7. The CMV of gold is $425 per ounce. Your analysis indicates that it is headed for $600. What can you do about this?
   (a) Load up on calls
   (b) Buy puts on gold stocks
   (c) Put on a bull spread
   (d) Become a gold scale trader

8. If you were short puts, you would be in which camp?
   (a) Summer
   (b) Bull
   (c) Bear
   (d) Trading

9. Which strategy has the most risk?
   (a) Shorting naked puts
   (b) Volatility spreads
   (c) Covered call writing
   (d) Naked call writing

10. How much risk is a naked put writer taking?
    (a) Unlimited risk
    (b) The risk of catching pneumonia

(c) The risk that the underlying entity goes to zero less the premium

(d) The risk that the buyer defaults

11. A stock has a CMV of 15. Which trader is better off?
    (a) Call writer with $12\frac{1}{2}$ strike
    (b) Put writer with $12\frac{1}{2}$ strike
    (c) Long call buyer with 10 strike
    (d) Long put buyer with 10 strike

12. You think your broker executed unauthorized trades in your futures account. To whom could you complain?
    (a) Your broker
    (b) Your broker's manager
    (c) The NASD
    (d) The NFA

13. You have 1,000 shares of IBM in your account. You think IBM is stalling out on its most recent bull move, but you think it will still go a few points higher. Which is the best strategy?
    (a) Protect profits with 10 puts
    (b) Sell at the market
    (c) Straddle the market
    (d) Sell 10 covered calls

14. You would face a theoretically unlimited risk situation if you did which of the following?
    (a) Wrote a call on a stock you own
    (b) Wrote a put on a stock you shorted
    (c) Wrote a naked call
    (d) Bought a naked call

15. Rate the relative risk of the following option strategies, from least risky to most risky:
    Buying 10 naked calls
    Selling 10 naked calls
    Buying 10 calls and selling 10 calls with a higher strike price
    Buying 5 naked calls
    Selling 5 naked puts and selling 5 naked calls at the same strike price
    (a) 1, 2, 3, 4, 5
    (b) 5, 4, 3, 2, 1
    (c) 3, 4, 2, 1, 5
    (d) 3, 4, 1, 5, 2

16. Which option player is the most consistent winner?
    (a) The buyer
    (b) The seller
    (c) The spreader
    (d) The broker
    (e) The regulator

17. Which entity actually matches the millions of option trades done each trading day?
    (a) Brokerage firms
    (b) SEC
    (c) NFA
    (d) Clearing firms

18. Which strategies are suitable for new option traders?
    (a) Covered calls
    (b) Buying puts
    (c) Buying calls
    (d) Simple spreads
    (e) All of the above
    (f) None of the above

19. A put and a call on the same underlying entity at the same strike price and with the same expiration date will have the same price.
    (a) True
    (b) False

20. When can European-style options be exercised?
    (a) Whenever it pleases the owner
    (b) At the same time as American-style options
    (c) Only calls can be exercised
    (d) At expiration

21. Which exchange(s) trade virtually 24 hours a day?
    (a) CBOE
    (b) GLOBEX
    (c) FOREX
    (d) Chicago Merc

22. All option contracts expire on the same day, except for LEAPS.
    (a) True
    (b) False

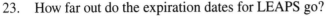
23. How far out do the expiration dates for LEAPS go?
    (a) 9 months maximum
    (b) 12 months maximum
    (c) 18 months maximum
    (d) Years

24. What is the best job on the NYSE?
    (a) Floor broker
    (b) Specialist
    (c) Runner
    (d) Janitor

25. Your 45 June TK call is 50 cents in-the-money. Will it automatically be exercised?
    (a) Yes
    (b) No
    (c) Depends on the rules of the exchange on which it trades

26. Your option is $5 in-the-money. When is the last time you can exercise it?
    (a) Monday of the week in which it expires
    (b) Friday of the third week of the month in which it expires
    (c) At expiration only
    (d) At noon on Saturday of the week of expiration

27. If you cannot find the price of your option in the *Wall Street Journal*, you can assume it did not trade during the last trading session.
    (a) True
    (b) False

28. All the symbols for LEAPS contracts for the same year start with the same letter.
    (a) True
    (b) False

29. When does a market-on-close order fill?
    (a) At the settlement price
    (b) During the last 15 minutes
    (c) As soon the order hits the floor
    (d) Right after the closing bell rings

30. A stock underlying an option that you own announces that it is doubling the dividend. What would you anticipate the impact on the options to be?

     (a) The price of calls decreases.
     (b) The price of puts decreases.
     (c) The price of calls increases.
     (d) The price of puts increases.

31.   How does a higher strike price affect the price of an option?
     (a) The price of calls decreases.
     (b) The price of puts decreases.
     (c) The price of calls increases.
     (d) The price of puts increases.

32.   The price of the underlying entity increases. What happens to the options?
     (a) The price of calls decreases.
     (b) The price of puts decreases.
     (c) The price of calls increases.
     (d) The price of puts increases.

33.   The volatility of the underlying entity spikes higher. What happens to the options?
     (a) The price of calls decreases.
     (b) The price of puts decreases.
     (c) The price of calls increases.
     (d) The price of puts increases.

34.   If interest rates increase, what happens to option prices?
     (a) The price of calls decreases.
     (b) The price of puts decreases.
     (c) The price of calls increases.
     (d) The price of puts increases.

35.   The more time there is to expiration, all other factors the same, what is the impact on option prices?
     (a) The price of calls decreases.
     (b) The price of puts decreases.
     (c) The price of calls increases.
     (d) The price of puts increases.

36.   If you traded options on a very short-term basis, when would you normally trade?
     (a) As soon as the option is available to trade
     (b) The last week before expiration
     (c) Right after the option made new price highs
     (d) Any time works

37. Most options
    (a) expire worthless.
    (b) are exercised.
    (c) are offset.
    (d) are rolled over.

38. Trading options is mostly a matter of luck, so it makes no sense to put much work into trade selection.
    (a) True
    (b) False

39. To trade consistently and successfully, you need
    (a) a system that provides discipline.
    (b) self-knowledge.
    (c) excess capital.
    (d) a method for estimating fair market value.
    (e) all of the above.
    (f) some of the above.
    (g) none of the above.

40. Many successful professional option traders believe which of the following is the most important aspect of trading?
    (a) A reliable trading model
    (b) Excess capital
    (c) A good source of tips
    (d) A strong defense

41. How long does it take to become a successful trader?
    (a) One year.
    (b) It depends on the aptitude of the trader.
    (c) Decades.
    (d) It can happen overnight.

42. What is the best reason to start an option-trading career?
    (a) To get rich quick
    (b) To enjoy the adrenalin rush
    (c) Out of the sheer love of doing it
    (d) To prove you can outsmart the market

43. How does the rate of deterioration of time value perform?
    (a) It increases the closer the option gets to expiration.
    (b) It is even over the life of the option.
    (c) It is highest in the first month.
    (d) It increases when volatility increases.

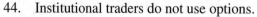

44. Institutional traders do not use options.
    (a) True
    (b) False

45. Which of the following are characteristics of successful traders?
    (a) Worry regularly
    (b) Read about and study the markets they trade
    (c) Prepare and update a written plan
    (d) Evaluate their performance periodically
    (e) All of the above
    (f) None of the above

46. Which of the following has a definite expiration date?
    (a) Stock
    (b) Bonds
    (c) Futures contracts
    (d) Options

47. What is the best method of analysis?
    (a) Fundamental analysis
    (b) Technical analysis
    (c) A combination of a and b
    (d) None of the above
    (e) It depends on the trader

48. When a trader takes a loss, who should be held responsible, under normal conditions?
    (a) The broker and his or her firm
    (b) The market—it just happens
    (c) The trading system or whoever suggested the trade
    (d) The trader

49. Working with a mentor is a waste of time.
    (a) True
    (b) False

50. If your son or daughter told you that he or she was going to begin trading options, which of the following would you tell him or her?
    (a) Do a lot of study and research first.
    (b) Observe others trading and pick their brains.
    (c) Develop a written plan.
    (d) Work at understanding yourself and find a trading method that suits your personality.
    (e) Paper-trade before risking money.

(f) Be sure not to risk any money you cannot afford to lose.

(g) Begin slowly and cautiously.

(h) Always be on the defensive and prepared to walk away whenever you become uncomfortable or do not understand what is going on.

Answers

1. d; 2. b; 3. b, c, or d; 4. c; 5. a and c; 6. a; 7. a and c; 8. c; 9. d; 10. c; 11. c; 12. a, b, and d; 13. a or d, depending on whether you wish to continue holding the stock; 14. c; 15. d; 16. d; 17. d; 18. e; 19. b; 20. d; 21. b and c; 22. b; 23. d; 24. b; 25. c; 26. b; 27. b; 28. b; 29. b; 30. a and d; 31. a and c; 32. b and c; 33. c and d; 34. b and d; 35. c and d; 36. b; 37. a; 38. b; 39. e; 40. d; 41. b; 42. c; 43. a; 44. b; 45. e; 46. b, c, and d; 47. e; 48. d; 49. b; 50. All of the above.

Option Symbols

The symbols used to designate stock options can be confusing, especially those for options on Nasdaq stocks. Basically, options symbols have three parts:

1. The first three characters of the base symbol represent the underlying security. It never exceeds three characters. This works fine for NYSE-listed stocks because they have three or fewer letters in them, but Nasdaq stocks have four or more letters. In this case, the OCC creates a symbol for the stock.
2. The next symbol is the month code. It is one character in length and designates the month of expiration. The months for calls are designated using the letters A through L; those for puts, using M through X. The letters Y and Z are not used.
3. The last character specifies the striking price. A represents 5, B 10, and so on through T representing 100. Then the sequence repeats, with the letter A equaling 105.

Here are two examples:

XOMFK = ExxonMobil June 55 call
CYPOD = Cisco March 20 put

APPENDIX 2

Types of Orders and Order Checklist

When you enter an order, either directly or via a broker, you have to decide whether you wish to attach any conditions on how the order is to be filled. There are two types of orders—unconditional and conditional. The basic unconditional order is the *market order*. When you place a market order, your instruction is to get the order filled as fast as possible, regardless of price.

"Buy 10 June 35 XYZ calls at the market!"

This order is filled immediately. You have no control over the price, and you might be filled away from the market when you initially entered the order. The purpose is to buy or sell something in a hurry. The primary virtues of a market order are that it is "held," meaning that you definitely are filled, and that it is executed ahead of conditional orders. Market orders take top priority.

Conditional orders add some restrictions to your orders. The restrictions may apply to time, price, or quantity. Since there are stipulations attached to these orders, they may not always be filled, depending on market conditions. They are "not held" orders. The brokerage firm is not held liable if they are not filled.

Time-Stipulated Orders

Day orders. These are good only for the trading session in which they are entered and are automatically canceled at the close of the trading session in which they are entered.

Good till . . . or good till canceled. These orders stay in the market for the specified time, such as good till May 1 or good till 1500 hours, or indefinitely, as in good till canceled.

Market on close or market on open. These orders must be filled at the period specified by the exchange as closing or opening, usually 15 minutes before closing or 15 minutes after opening.

Quantity-Stipulated Orders

All or none orders. This type of order stipulates that either the entire order or none at all be filled. The broker has the entire trading session to fill the order, unless it is canceled sooner.

Kill or fill. The entire order must be filled immediately, or it is canceled.

Price-Stipulated Orders

Limit orders. A price limit is established, and the order must be filled at that price or better.

Market if touched. A specific price must be touched; if it is, the order becomes a market order and is filled immediately.

Stop order. A stop price is designated. When that price is hit, the order becomes a market order and is filled immediately.

Stop limit order. A stop price and a limit price are designated. When the stop price is hit, the stop order becomes a limit order and must be filled at the limit price or better.

Administrative Orders

Cancel former order (CFO). A new order replaces an existing order. The old order is canceled, and the new order is entered in the market. This type of order is used to update limit order prices, for example.

Discretionary order. This is an order that you give to a broker along with some discretion as to when or at what price the order is to be entered. The owner of the account must decide which security to trade, whether to buy or sell, and the quantity. The broker can be given discretion as to time (when to execute the order) or price. For example, "If the market trades higher at the open, buy 5 December 45 T calls." No limited power of attorney is needed. It is also possible to give someone else discretion to trade your account. This requires executing a limit power of attorney.

Option Order Entry Checklist

1. State whether you are opening a new position or closing an existing position.
2. State the quantity of options in the transaction. Some new traders state the number of shares, rather than the number of options, and are unpleasantly surprised when they find that they have bought 100 call options when they wanted only 1 option for 100 shares.
3. Clearly state what you want to buy or sell. Do not worry about knowing the symbol; leave that up to your broker. If you enter orders by phone, I would recommend a simple recording device, available at Radio Shack for around $20, plus a tape recorder. After each call, play back your order. If it is wrong, call back immediately and make corrections. The order must include the type of option (call, put, spread, straddle, and so on), quantity, strike price, underlying entity, and expiration month. Your brokerage firm will also tape-record the order. If you have any questions later about the order, you can request that your broker play back his or her recording of the order to verify its correctness.
4. You may want to check the dividend, ex-dividend date, and current interest rate, if you did not include them when you ran a computer pricing model.
5. Order type—market, limit, discretionary, and so on.
6. After giving an order verbally to a broker, wait for him or her to repeat it back to you.

At the time of entering any order, you should have an exit strategy written in your trading or daily action plan. Plan for success in advance.

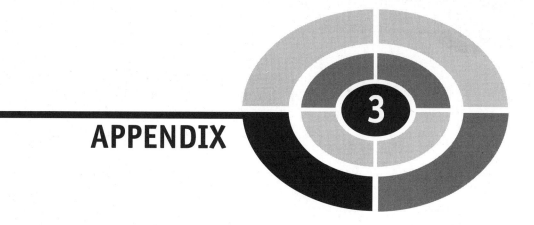

APPENDIX

3

Option Terminology

American-style option: An option that may be exercised at any time prior to expiration.

Arbitrage: The practice of buying and selling the same futures contract simultaneously on two different exchanges to profit from a price spread.

Arbitration: A forum for the fair and impartial settlement of disputes that the parties involved are unable to resolve between themselves. The NFA's arbitration program provides a forum for resolving futures-related disputes. The NASD handles stock-related complaints.

Assignment: Notice to an option writer that an option has been exercised by the option holder. This can happen at any time during the life of an option with American-style options and only at or near expiration for European-style options.

Associated person (AP or broker): An individual who solicits orders, customers, or customer funds on behalf of a futures commission merchant, an introducing broker, a commodity trading advisor, or a commodity pool operator and who is registered with the Commodity Futures Trading Commission (CFTC) or the National Futures Association (NFA).

At-the-money: An option whose strike price is equal to the market value of the underlying futures contract. Can also refer to an order to buy a futures contract at the current bid-ask price (*see* Market order).

Automatic exercise: The exercise by the clearinghouse of an in-the-money option at expiration, unless the holder of the option submits specific instructions to the contrary.

Back spread: A spread in which more options are purchased than sold, with all options having the same underlying entity and expiring at the same time. Back spreads are usually delta-neutral.

Balloon option: Most often found in foreign exchange markets, these options provide for greater leverage to the holder. This is because the notional payments increase significantly after a set threshold is penetrated.

Bear market (bear/bearish): A market in which prices are declining. A market participant who believes that prices will move lower is called a "bear." A news item is considered bearish if it is expected to produce lower prices.

Bear spread: Any spread in which a decline in the price of the underlying entity will increase the value of the spread.

Beta: A measure of how the options market correlates with the movement of the underlying market.

Bid: An offer to buy a specific quantity of a security or commodity at a stated price.

Board of trade (BOT): Any exchange or association of persons who are engaged in the business of buying or selling any commodity or receiving the same for sale on consignment. It usually means an exchange on which commodity futures and/or options are traded.

Box: A long call and a short put at one exercise price, and a short call and a long put at a different exercise price. All four options must have the same underlying entity and expire at the same time.

Broker (AP): A person who is paid a fee or commission for acting as an agent in making contracts or sales. In commodities futures trading, this is a floor broker, a person who actually executes orders on the trading floor of an exchange; in commission houses, it is account executive or associated person who deals with customers and their orders.

Brokerage: A fee charged by a broker for execution of a transaction, an amount per transaction or a percentage of the total value of the transaction; usually referred to as a commission fee.

Bull market (bull/bullish): A market in which prices are rising. A market participant who believes that prices will move higher is called a "bull." A news item is considered bullish if it is expected to lead to higher prices.

Bull spread: Any spread in which a rise in the price of the underlying entity will theoretically increase the value of the spread.

Butterfly: The sale (purchase) of two identical options, together with the purchase (sale) of one option with an immediately higher exercise price and one option with an immediately lower exercise price. All options must be of the same type, be for the same underlying entity, and expire at the same time.

Buyer: The purchaser of an option, either a call option or a put option. Also referred to as the option holder. An option purchase may be in connection with either an opening or a closing transaction.

Calendar spread: Another name for a time spread.

Call (option): An option whose buyer acquires the right but not the obligation to purchase a particular stock or futures contract at a stated price on or before a particular date. Buyers of call options generally hope to profit from an increase in the future price of the underlying security or commodity.

Carrying broker: A member of a commodities exchange, usually a clearinghouse member, through whom another broker or customer chooses to clear all or some trades.

Carryover: That part of the current supply of a commodity that consists of stocks from previous production/marketing seasons.

Cash commodity: Actual quantities of a commodity, as distinguished from futures contracts; goods available for immediate delivery or delivery within a specified period following sale; or a commodity bought or sold with an agreement for delivery at a specified future date.

Cash forward sale: The practice of paying commodity producers cash in advance of delivering the commodity to lock in the price.

Certificated stock: Amounts of a commodity that have been inspected and found to be of a quality deliverable against futures contracts, stored at the delivery points designated as regular or acceptable for delivery by the commodity exchange.

Charting: The use of graphs and charts in the technical analysis of markets to plot trends of price movements, average movements of price volume, and open interest.

Christmas tree: A type of ratio vertical spread in which options are sold at two or more different exercise prices.

Churning: Excessive trading of a customer's account by a broker who has control over the trading decisions for that account, to make more commissions while disregarding the best interests of the customer.

Class of options: All call options—or all put options—on the same underlying stock or futures contract.

Clearing: The procedure through which trades are checked for accuracy, after which the clearinghouse or association becomes the buyer to each seller of an option or futures contract, and the seller to each buyer.

Clearing member: A member of the clearinghouse or association. All trades of a non-clearing member must be registered and eventually settled through a clearing member.

Clearinghouse or clearing corporation: An agency connected with an exchange through which all futures and option contracts are made, offset, or fulfilled by delivery of the actual commodity, and through which financial settlement is made. Often, the clearinghouse is a fully chartered separate corporation rather than a division of the exchange proper. Once a trade has been cleared, the clearing corporation becomes the buyer to every seller and the seller to every buyer.

Clearing price: *See* Settlement price.

Close (the): The period at the end of the trading session, officially designated by the exchange, during which all transactions are considered to be made "at the close."

Closing range: A range of closely related prices at which transactions took place at the close of the market; buy and sell orders at the close might have been filled at any point within such a range.

Combination: A trading strategy. Combinations involve buying or selling both a put and a call on the same stock or futures. This is a position created either by purchasing both a put and a call or by writing both a put and a call on the same underlying entity.

Commodity: An entity of trade or commerce, services, or rights in which contracts for future delivery may be traded. Some of the contracts currently traded are wheat, corn, cotton, livestock, copper, gold, silver, oil, propane, plywood, currencies, and Treasury bills, bonds, and notes.

Commodity Exchange Act: The federal act that provides for federal regulation of futures trading.

Commodity Futures Trading Commission (CFTC): A commission set up by Congress to administer the Commodity Exchange Act, which regulates trading on commodity exchanges.

Condor: The sale (purchase) of two options with consecutive exercise prices, together with the purchase (sale) of one option with an immediately lower exercise price and one option with an immediately higher exercise price. All options must be of the same type, have the same underlying entity, and expire at the same time.

Confirmation statement: A statement sent by a commission house or broker/dealer to a customer when a futures, option, or stock position has been initiated or some other transaction has taken place. The statement shows the number of contracts (options, stock shares) bought or sold and the prices at which the contracts (options, shares) were bought or sold. It might also show any funds moved into or out of the account. Sometimes combined with a purchase and sale statement.

Contract month: The month in which delivery is to be made in accordance with a futures or option contract.

Covered option: An option that is written against an opposite position in the underlying stock, futures contract, or commodity at the time of execution or placement of the order.

Appendix 3

Covered writer: The seller of a covered option, put or call.

Credit: Money received from the sale of options.

Current delivery (month): The futures or option contract that will come to maturity and become deliverable during the current month; also called *spot month*.

Customer account: An account established by the clearing member solely for the purpose of clearing exchange transactions by the clearing member on behalf of its customers other than those transactions of a floor trader.

Dealer option: A put or call on a physical commodity, not originating on or subject to the rules of an exchange, written by a firm that deals in the underlying cash commodity.

Debit: Money paid for the purchase of options.

Debit balance: An accounting situation in which the trading losses in a customer's account exceed the amount of equity in that customer's account.

Deep-out-of-the-money options: Definitions vary by exchange. These are options with strike prices that are not close to the strike price nearest the current price of the underlying entity. A typical definition would be two strike prices, plus the number of calendar months remaining until the option expires, away from the strike price closest to the current value of the underlying stock issue or futures contract.

Delivery month: A calendar month during which a futures contract matures and becomes deliverable. Options are also assigned to delivery months.

Delivery notice: Notice from the clearinghouse of a seller's intention to deliver the physical commodity against a short futures position; it precedes and is distinct from the warehouse receipt or shipping certificate, which is the instrument of transfer of ownership.

Delta: The sensitivity of an option's theoretical value to a change in the price of the underlying entity.

Delta-neutral spread: A spread in which the total delta position on the long side and the total delta position on the short side add up to approximately zero.

Diagonal spread: A two-sided spread consisting of options at different exercise prices and with different expiration dates. All options must be of the same type and have the same underlying entity.

Discretionary account: An arrangement by which the holder of the account gives a written power of attorney to another, often a broker, to make buying and selling decisions without notification to the holder; often referred to as a *managed account* or *controlled account*.

European-style option: An option that may be exercised only on the expiration date.

Exercise: A decision by the holder elects to take the underlying stock or futures contract at the option's strike price.

Exercise price: The price at which the buyer of a call (put) option may choose to exercise his or her right to purchase (sell) the underlying stock or futures contract. Also called *strike price*.

Expiration date: Generally, the last date on which an option may be exercised.

Extrinsic value: The price of an option less its intrinsic value. The entire premium of an out-of-the-money option consists of extrinsic value. Also referred to as *time value*.

Fair value: Another name for theoretical value.

Fence: A long (short) underlying position, together with a long (short) out-of-the-money put and a short (long) out-of-the-money call. All options must expire at the same time. When the fence includes a long (short) underlying position, it is sometimes known as a *risk conversion (reversal)*.

Floor broker: An individual who executes orders for any other person on the trading floor of an exchange.

Floor trader: A member of an exchange who is personally present on the trading floor of the exchange to make trades for him- or herself and for customers. Sometimes called *scalpers* or *locals*.

Free trade: An option spread initiated by purchasing a close to in-the-money put or call and later completed by selling a further out-of-the-money put or call of the same expiration date at the same premium. When completed, it requires no margin or equity.

Front spread: Another name for a ratio vertical spread.

Gamma: The sensitivity of an option's delta to a change in the price of the underlying entity.

Grantor: A person who sells an option and assumes the obligation, but not the right, to sell (in the case of a call) or buy (in the case of a put) the underlying stock, futures contract, or commodity at the exercise price. Also referred to as the *writer*.

Hedging: The sale of futures contracts or options in anticipation of future sales of cash commodities as a protection against possible price declines, or the purchase of futures contracts or options in anticipation of future purchases of cash commodities or stocks as a protection against increasing costs.

Horizontal spread: Another name for a time spread.

Incentive stock option: An option qualifying for favorable tax treatment under Section 422 of the Internal Revenue Code granted to an employee to purchase company stock at a specific price over a specified period of time.

Intermarket spread: A spread consisting of opposing positions in instruments with two different underlying markets.

In-the-money: An option having intrinsic value. A call is in-the-money if its strike price is below the current price of the underlying stock or futures contract. A put is in-the-money if its strike price is above the current price of the underlying stock or futures contract.

Intrinsic value: The absolute value of the in-the-money amount; that is, the amount that would be realized if an in-the-money option were exercised.

Jelly roll long strategy: The sale and purchase of two call and two put positions, each with a different expiration date, in order to profit from a time-value spread.

Kappa: Another name for vega.

Limit move: A price that has advanced or declined by the maximum amount permitted during one trading session, as fixed by the rules of a contract market.

Limit order: An order in which the customer sets a limit on either price or time of execution, as contrasted with a market order, which implies that the order should be filled at the most favorable price as soon as possible.

Liquidation: Offsetting positions by acquiring exactly opposite positions.

Liquidity: The ability to buy and sell can be accomplished with small price changes. It simply means a lot of orders are being executed.

Liquid market: A broadly traded market in which selling and buying can be accomplished easily with small price changes and narrow bid and offer price spreads because of the presence of many interested buyers and sellers.

Long: One who has bought a cash commodity or stock or a commodity futures contract or option, in contrast to a short, who has sold a cash entity, stock, futures contract, or option.

Long hedge: Buying futures or option contracts to protect against possible increased prices of stocks or commodities. *See also* Hedging.

Margin: In the futures industry, an amount of money deposited by both buyers and sellers of futures contracts to ensure performance against the contract. It is not a down payment.

Margin call: A demand from a brokerage firm to a customer to bring margin deposits back up to the minimum levels required by exchange regulations; similarly, a request by the clearinghouse to a clearing member firm to make additional deposits to bring clearing margins back to the minimum levels required by clearinghouse rules.

Market order: An order to buy or sell a stock, futures contract, or option contract that is to be filled at the best possible price and as soon as possible, in contrast to a limit order, which may specify requirements for price or time of execution. *See also* Limit order.

Mark-to-the-market: Extending futures and option contracts in an account daily using the settlement price and calculating the profit or loss.

Naked writing: Writing a call or a put on a stock or futures contract in which the writer has no opposite cash or futures market position. This is also known as *uncovered writing*.

National Association of Securities Dealers (NASD): The industrywide self-regulatory organization of the securities industry.

Neutral spread: Another name for a delta-neutral spread. Spreads may also be lot-neutral, where the total number of long contracts and the total number of short contracts of the same type are approximately equal.

Nominal price: The declared price for a futures or options contract, sometimes used in place of a closing price when no recent trading has taken place in that particular delivery month; usually an average of the bid and asked prices.

Not held: A conditional order, which may or may not be filled depending on whether the conditions can be filled. If the order is not filled, the brokerage firm is not held responsible and the trader has no recourse.

Offer: An indication of willingness to sell at a given price; opposite of *bid*.

Offset: The liquidation of a position in the option or futures markets by taking an equal, but opposite position. All specifications must be the same.

Option class: All option contracts of the same type covering the same underlying futures contract, commodity, or security.

Option contract: A unilateral contract that gives the buyer the right, but not the obligation, to buy or sell a specified quantity of stock or futures contracts at a specific price within a specified period of time, regardless of the current market price. The seller of the option has the obligation to sell the stock or futures contract to or buy it from the option buyer at the exercise price if the option is exercised. *See also* Call (option) and Put (option).

Option premium: The money, securities, or property the buyer pays to the writer (grantor) for granting an option contract.

Option seller: *See* Grantor.

Order execution: Handling of a customer order by a broker; it includes receiving the order verbally or in writing from the customer, transmitting it to the trading floor of the exchange where the transaction takes place, and returning confirmation (fill price) of the completed order to the customer.

Out-of-the-money: A call option with a strike price higher than or a put option with a strike price lower than the current market value of the underlying asset.

Pit: A specially constructed arena on the trading floor of some exchanges where trading in stocks, futures, or options contracts is conducted by open outcry. On some exchanges, the term *ring* designates the trading area.

Put (option): An option that gives the option buyer the right, but not the obligation, to sell the underlying asset at a particular price on or before a particular date.

Appendix 3

Quotation: The actual price or the bid or ask price of either cash commodities or futures, stocks, or option contracts at a particular time. Often called *quote*.

Rally: An upward movement of prices.

Rally top: The point where a rally stalls. A bull move will usually make several rally tops over its life.

Range: The difference between the high and low prices of a commodity during a given period, usually a single trading session.

Ratio spread: Any spread in which the number of long market contracts and the number of short market contracts are unequal.

Ratio vertical spread: A spread in which more contracts are sold than are purchased, with all contracts having the same underlying entity and expiration date. Ratio vertical spreads are usually delta neutral.

Ratio writing: A strategy used by option writers. It involves writing both a covered call option and one or more uncovered call options. One of its objectives is to reduce some of the risk of writing uncovered call options, since the covered call provides some degree of protection.

Resistance: The price level at which a trend stalls. Opposite of a support level. Prices must build momentum to move through resistance.

Retender: The right of holders of futures contracts who have been tendered a delivery notice through the clearinghouse to offer the notice for sale on the open market, liquidating their obligation to take delivery under the contract; applicable only to certain commodities and only within a specified period of time.

Rho: The sensitivity of an option's theoretical value to a change in interest rates.

Scalper: A speculator on the trading floor of an exchange who buys and sells rapidly at small profits or losses, holding positions for only a short time during a trading session. Typically, a scalper will stand ready to buy at a fraction below the last transaction price and to sell at a fraction above, thus creating market liquidity.

Selling hedge: Selling futures or option contracts to protect against possible decreases in the prices of commodities or stocks that will be sold in the future. *See also* Hedging and/or Short hedge.

Serial expiration: Options on the same futures contract or stock that expire in more than one month.

Series: All options of the same class having the same exercise price and expiration date.

Settlement price: The closing price, or a price within the range of closing prices, that is used as the official price in determining net gains or losses at the close of each trading session.

Short: One who is expecting prices to decline. For example, a trader who has sold a cash commodity or a commodity futures contract or bought a put, in contrast to a long, who has bought a cash commodity or futures contract or a call.

Short hedge: Selling futures or options to protect against possible decreases in the prices of commodities or stocks. *See also* Hedging.

Spread (or straddle): The purchase of one futures or option delivery month against the sale of another. For example, the purchase of one delivery month of one option against the sale of the same delivery month of a different option. *See also* Arbitrage.

Statutory stock option: *See* Incentive stock option.

Straddle: A trading strategy. A straddle involves writing both a put and a call on the same stock or futures. Both options also carry the same strike price and the same expiration date.

Support: A price level at which a declining market has stopped falling. Opposite of resistance. Once this level is reached, the market usually trades sideways for a period of time.

Synthetic call: A long (short) underlying position together with a long (short) put.

Synthetic put: A short (long) underlying position together with a long (short) call.

Synthetic underlying: A long (short) call together with a short (long) put, where both options have the same underlying, exercise price, and expiration date.

Theoretical value: An option value generated by a mathematical model given certain prior assumptions about the terms of the option, the characteristics of the underlying entity, and prevailing interest rates. The most commonly used formula is known as Black-Scholes.

Theta: The sensitivity of an option's theoretical value to a change in the amount of time to expiration.

Time spread: The purchase and sale of options on the same stock or futures contract with the same exercise price, but with different expiration dates. Also known as a *calendar* or *horizontal spread.*

Time value: Any amount by which an option premium exceeds the option's intrinsic value. Sometimes called *extrinsic value* or *time premium.*

Trendline: A line that connects a series of highs or lows in a trend. The trendline can represent either support, as in an uptrendline, or resistance, as in a downtrendline. Consolidations are marked by horizontal trendlines.

Vega: The sensitivity of an option's theoretical value to a change in volatility.

Vertical spread: A spread in which one option is bought and another option is sold, where both options are of the same type, have the same underlying entity, and expire at the same time. The options differ only in their exercise prices.

Volatility: A measure of the tendency of the price of an asset (stock, option, or some other asset) to move up and down, based on its daily price history over a period of time.

Volume of trade: The number of contracts traded during a specified period of time.

Writer: *See* Grantor.

Writing: The sale of an option in an opening transaction.

Suggested Additional Study Material

Reading Suggestions

Lowenstein, Roger. *When Genius Failed: The Rise and Fall of Long-Term Capital Management*.

Mandelbrot, Benoit, and Richard Hudson. *The (Mis)behavior of Markets: A Fractal View of Risk, Ruin and Reward*.

McCafferty, Thomas. *All About Options, All About Futures, Understanding Hedged Scale Trading, Winning with Managed Futures*, and *The Market Is Always Right*.

McMillan, Lawrence G. *Options as a Strategic Investment*.

Natenberg, Sheldon. *Option Volatility and Pricing Strategies: Advanced Trading Techniques for Professionals*.

Niederhoffer, Victor. *The Education of a Speculator*.

Riso, Don Richard. *Personality Types*.

Schwager, Jack D. *Market Wizards* and *New Market Wizards*.

Taleb, Nassim Nicholas. *Fooled by Randomness: The Hidden Role of Chance in Life and in the Markets*.

Web Sites (WWW.) to Peruse

888options.com
Aiqsystems.com
Barchart.com
BigCharts.com
cboe.com
cbot.com
cme.com
coveredcalls.com
Futures.tradingcharts.com
investopedia.com
Options-all.com
Optionscentral.com
Option-max.com
Optionvue.com
Optionwizard.com
phlx.com
Pmpublishing.com
rickackerman.com
Schaeffersreach.com
Tfc-charts.w2d.com
wallstreetselect.com
ZeroDelta.com

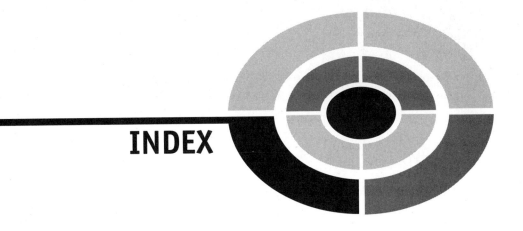

INDEX

Index

Index

Index

Index

Index

About the Author

Upon receiving an M.A. from St. Louis University, Thomas McCafferty began his writing career as a technical writer, eventually migrating to advertising, public relations, marketing, and professional books. He developed a specialty in direct mail and telemarketing while working at a variety of financial publications and firms, such as *Futures Magazine*, *Commodity Price Charts*, *Doane's Agricultural Report*, the Commodity Research Bureau, *Ragan Report*, Meredith Publishing, and the American Bankers Association. Coownership of a farm equipment manufacturer and a ready-mix concrete plant honed his business skills. During his career in the securities industry, he held posts as a broker, instructor, compliance officer, branch office manager, and CEO. His professional registrations included stock, options, and commodities principal and real estate and insurance broker. Additionally, Mr. McCafferty has written or ghostwritten 10 books to date and served his country as a Fleet Marine Force Corpsman with the 2nd Marine Division.